Search and Destroy, Second Edition

African-American Males in the Criminal Justice System

This tightly argued and methodologically sound volume addresses widespread social assumptions associating crime and African-American men. An exploration of the criminal justice system in America today and its impact on young African-American males, this book challenges the linking of crime and race and the conservative anti-welfare, hard-on-crime agenda. Jerome G. Miller has spent a lifetime studying and challenging our criminal justice system. He has worked to make it more progressive and more just. He has watched as it turned into a system of segregation and control for many Americans of color. That is the story told here in condemning, devastating detail.

Dr. Jerome G. Miller holds a Doctorate in Social Work from the Catholic University of America. In 1968, he became Associate Professor of Social Work at Ohio State University. He was subsequently appointed to the cabinet of Massachusetts Republican Governor Frank Sargent in 1969 to head the newly created Massachusetts Department of Youth Services and has also served on the gubernatorial staff of Milton Shapp, former governor of Pennsylvania. In 1977, he cofounded the National Center on Institutions and Alternatives (NCIA), a nonprofit organization to set up alternative plans for youth and adults otherwise institutionalized in reform schools, prisons, mental hospitals, and state institutions for the developmentally disabled. He has been consultant to the U.S. Justice Department, evaluating juvenile and adult institutions in more than thirty states, and has served as a special master for a number of federal judges. He has assisted in developing mitigative studies for individuals on death row in numerous states. He continues to see individuals clinically and is presently finishing a manuscript on the issue of sex offenders in our society and the "moral panic" in which modern industrial societies are caught up. His articles dealing with the topics of this book have appeared in the *Los Angeles Times*, *The New York Times*, and *The Washington Post*.

Search and Destroy
Second Edition

African-American Males in the Criminal Justice System

JEROME G. MILLER

National Center on Institutions and Alternatives

CAMBRIDGE
UNIVERSITY PRESS

CAMBRIDGE UNIVERSITY PRESS
Cambridge, New York, Melbourne, Madrid, Cape Town, Singapore,
São Paulo, Delhi, Dubai, Tokyo, Mexico City

Cambridge University Press
32 Avenue of the Americas, New York, NY 10013-2473, USA

www.cambridge.org
Information on this title: www.cambridge.org/9780521743815

Second Edition first published 2011

Printed in the United States of America

A catalog record for this publication is available from the British Library.

Library of Congress Cataloging in Publication data

Miller, Jerome G., 1931–
Search and destroy : African-American males in the criminal justice system /
Jerome Miller. – 2nd ed.
    p.   cm.
Includes bibliographical references and index.
ISBN 978-0-521-76779-8 (hardback) – ISBN 978-0-521-74381-5 (pbk.)
1. Discrimination in criminal justice administration – United
States.   2. Criminal justice, Administration of – United States.
3. African American criminals.   4. African American men.   I. Title.
HV9950.M55   2010
364.089'96073–dc22   2010038007

ISBN 978-0-521-76779-8 Hardback
ISBN 978-0-521-74381-5 Paperback

Contents

Prologue: From Which Aristocratic Colours Peep

The American "correctional" system is now defined by its grossly disproportionate numbers of black and brown men and boy inmates. More accurately, it has been refashioned to accommodate the feral racial phantasms that have haunted the nation since post–Civil War Reconstruction and been recently exacerbated with the election of an African-American president.

As the darkening of inmate populations intensified, the deep fissures so elegantly exposed by Alexis d'Tocqueville a century and a half earlier reappeared for all to see. The walls of our prisons and jails reverberated with a "goat-song" to racism.[1]

I originally wrote *Search and Destroy* to add my voice to a growing number of sociologists and criminologists then sounding the alarm over the troubling racial patterns showing up in our criminal justice system. I saw the still nascent crisis as portending problems well beyond those of crime and punishment.[2]

Frankly, none of this was news. For the better part of forty years, I had negotiated that labyrinth of dead ends we choose to limn American "corrections" – an excess of euphemisms covering a mélange of public and

The phrase in the title is from d'Tocqueville, Alexis, *Democracy in America 1831, Part I, Chap 2, "Origin of the Anglo-Americans."*

[1] Ancient Greek: "a goat-song" is a form of art based on human suffering that, paradoxically, offers its audience pleasure.

[2] Despite d'Tocqueville's generally positive impressions of American democracy, he saw the racial contradictions affecting black and brown persons in American courts and prisons as holding the seeds for the eventual undoing of the American experiment – constituting what the Swedish sociologist Gunnar Myrdahl would later refer to as the premier "American Dilemma."

private prisons, detention centers, training schools, reformatories, segregation units, holes, adjustment centers, protective custody units, holding chambers, boot camps, institutes for guidance, hot boxes, and supermax prisons – joined together only in their phenomenal success at warping their charges while nurturing the very behaviors and risky psychoses we had grown accustomed to seeing in their alumni.

The much-vaunted reforms that surfaced were vain efforts to vest nineteenth-century contrivances in post-modern attire. "New generation" jails and prisons abounded. Cells were contained in "pods"; "SWAT teams" wandered the corridors; "restraint chairs" displayed gagged men as struggling and helpless children; "spit masks" were locked over the heads of troubled youths dressed in paper gowns with hands cuffed behind their backs; "rubber rooms" were outfitted with "fireproof stuffing"; the dungeon-like chambers of sensory deprivation we call "supermax" prisons – designed to "break down" anyone who might be a bother (virtually unrelated to the reason for their original commitment) – were offered as a Hobson's "alternative" to torture or "rendition."[3]

Confirmed with "Good Housekeeping" seals of approval from in-house "experts" who duly certified whatever new atrocity might cross the radar screen, these devious goings-on were bolstered by a corps of professionals in good standing with the American Psychological Association and the American Psychiatric Association. It had been, in a very real sense, rehearsal for what we put in place during the later "war on terror."[4]

---

[3] An inordinately large percentage of those sent to supermax facilities are less likely to be there for having committed a particularly egregious crime than for having been a management problem in another facility.

[4] In "The Psychologists of Torture," in *In These Times*, April 2, 2009, Frederick Clarkson reported that medical professionals designed and helped implement Bush administration interrogation practices by devising, directing, and overseeing the torture of prisoners at Guantanamo Bay, Abu Ghraib, and Central Intelligence Agency (CIA) "black" sites. "Physicians for Human Rights detailed beatings, sexual and cultural humiliation, forced nakedness, exposure to extreme temperatures, exploitation of phobias, sleep deprivation, and sensory deprivation as among the tactics used. The Cambridge, Massachusetts–based organization that won a Nobel Peace Prize in 1997 said psychologists 'led the way' in legitimizing the use of these tactics. Eventually, Guantanamo Bay became known as a 'battle lab for new interrogation techniques,' which were later applied at military prisons in Iraq, Afghanistan, and at CIA detention centers."

The Senate report also confirmed the intimate involvement of health professionals in designing, supervising, and implementing "enhanced" interrogation programs – being present as "safety officers" during water-boarding and other interrogation sessions. "The monitoring of vital signs and giving instructions to interrogators to start and stop are some of the most severe abuses of the Hippocratic Oath and medical ethics imaginable,"

Hewing to the quaint pre–Hurricane Katrina belief that once public officials knew the dimensions of a tragedy in the making, they would seek ways to address it, I had reasoned (quite wrongly, as it turned out), "the truth would eventually out." Of course, nothing of the sort happened. I ignored one of the more obvious realities then taking shape in American culture.

As Pulitzer Prize–winning reporter Chris Hedges put it, "The Truth will no longer set you free," noting that when social and cultural assumptions break down in contemporary societies, they do so "at the speed of light" when exposed to the demands of "corporate totalitarianism."

Hedges cited media critic Stuart Ewen's belief that because "progressives have lost the gift of rhetoric, once a staple of a university education, they naively believe in the Enlightenment ideal that facts alone could move people toward justice. As a result, they remained largely helpless."[5] In today's world, *rhetoric* is as important as *fact*. Corporate and government propaganda aimed at swaying emotions rarely uses facts to sell their positions.[6]

The American criminal justice system – and its linchpin, the "correctional" system – is a case in point. In my experience, American correctional institutions and practices had always been something of which to be ashamed. In their post-modern version, however, they were as likely to provide grist for the musings of an Alexandre Dumas as to be subject to the turgid distinctions of a U.S. Justice Department lawyer.

The American prison system, in effect, had raced to the bottom in pursuit of the most fearsome "rogues gallery" it could muster to rationalize whatever brutal handling might yet be in the offing.

The possibilities were virtually limitless – demonstrating the perverse capacity of the human mind to craft punitive measures to the point of inducing organ failure when visited upon those held to be beyond civilized concern, an attitude with which the United States has recently demonstrated more than a little familiarity.

said Nathanial Raymond, of Physicians for Human Rights. "Strangely, the memos of former senior Bush administration officials use the presence of medical professionals in contravention of their professional ethics as a defense, when it is in fact, itself, a crime."

[5] Ewen holds that "effective communication requires not simply an understanding of the facts, but how those facts will take place in the public mind.... When Gustave Le Bon said it is not the facts in and of themselves which make a point but the way in which the facts take place, the way in which they come to attention."

[6] Ewen's books, *Advertising and the Social Roots of the Consumer Culture* and *PR: A Social History of Spin,* chronicled how corporate propaganda deformed American culture and pushed populism to the margins of American society.

How did this come to be? The distinguished American sociologist William Chambliss was among the first to recognize the reason. He saw it not so much attributable to any demonstrable surge in violent crime, but rather as being the result of a deliberately planned and artificially created phenomenon.

He asked, "How did we reach this point? . . . And how did we come to arrest and incarcerate such an incredibly disproportionate number of young men from minority groups? Quite simply, this state of affairs came about because political, law enforcement, and mass media interests coalesced . . . to create a 'moral panic' about crime . . . derived not from public opinion but from the manipulation of public opinion."[7]

As I penned this prologue, Irving Kristol, occasionally labeled the god-father of American neoconservatism, died. In a remembrance, *Weekly Standard* columnist Jonah Goldberg inadvertently put his finger on how the American criminal justice system came to enter the current period of full-throated neglect.

He recalled the late William F. Buckley's view that Kristol owed his influence over American conservatism to having introduced sociology into its lexicon. Until then, conservatism had been largely Aristotelian (questioning whether a government initiative violated the Constitution or some immutable moral law). As Goldberg put it, "Kristol's 'neos' were less abstract – asking instead, 'Will it work?'"[8]

In quest of the "practical," Kristol recruited what Goldberg termed "a cadre of America's finest social scientists" – including James Q. Wilson, Seymour Martin Lipset, Charles Murray, Thomas Sowell, and Stephan and Abigail Thernstrom, all of whom had *action*, not *theory* in mind. Goldberg saw no irony in his observation that their findings "usually confirmed that the Aristotelians were right all along."[9]

As this core of activists explored the dicey relationships of race to crime, their numbers were expanded to include then-Princeton political science professor John Dilulio, Harvard psychologist Richard Herrnstein, and social welfare expert at the Manhattan Institute George Kelling. Whether this stable of cosseted "hired hands" represented "America's finest social scientists" remained a matter of conjecture.

---

[7] Chambliss, William, "Moral Panics and Racial Oppression," in Hawkins, Darney (ed.), *Ethnicity, Race and Crime*, New York: SUNY Press, 1993.

[8] Goldberg, Jonah, *Los Angeles Times*, Opinion page, September 29, 2009.

[9] Ibid.

A tangle of like-minded ideologues freely commingling university research with ideological screeds delivered before carefully chosen audiences and potential funders, they bestowed new meaning on the heretofore traditional standard of "peer review."

Typically, their work surfaced in attenuated form in one or another of the "house organs" of a score of marketing outlets we had come, for some inexplicable reason, to call think tanks. It would develop that any major contributions to research were less likely to be found in compelling argument than in remarkable political successes at marketing.

Catchphrases were valued less for their persuasive content than their potential to generate high television ratings. Press releases masqueraded as research. Catered press conferences and awards dinners replaced reading. Slogans substituted for thought.

It all was in sharp contrast to the role criminologists, sociologists, social psychologists, or anthropologists had traditionally taken in crafting the nation's approaches to crime.

In my experience, politicians had never been much interested in best practice when it came to crime. Occasionally, an academic might get a hand into legislative sausage-making by placing a disconcerting fact or two before a committee, state commissioner, or federal official with the hope that it might give them pause.

George Herbert Mead offered a reason why: "The attitude of hostility toward the law-breaker," he wrote, "has the unique advantage of uniting all members of the community in the emotional solidarity of aggression. While the most admirable of humanitarian efforts are sure to run counter to the individual interests of very many in the community, or fail to touch the interest and imagination of the multitude and to leave the community divided or indifferent, *the cry of thief or murderer is attuned to profound complexes, lying below the surface of competing individual efforts, and citizens* who have [been] separated by divergent interests stand together against the common enemy" (emphasis added).[10]

Mead ruefully concluded, "There is nothing in the history of human society...which encourages us to look to the primal impulse of neighborliness for such cohesive power. The love of one's neighbor cannot be made into a common consuming passion."[11]

---

[10] Mead, George H., in his essay, "The Nature of the Past," originally published in 1929, reprinted in Rack, Andrew J. (ed.), *Selected Writings: George Herbert Mead*. Chicago and London: University of Chicago Press, 1981, p. 591.

[11] Ibid., pp. 359–62.

Recognizing the enormous potentials inherent in shilling quick fixes for crime control to those whose impulses might be attuned to "profound complexes, lying below the surface," the newly minted "neo" sociologists served up a smorgasbord of user-friendly rationales for wars on crime – indeed, for "wars" of all kinds.[12]

The packaging was greatly more important than the content. When it came to crime, it was nowhere more effective than when race was amalgamated with crime and genetics. It served as a clarion call to an assemblage of cheerleaders who felt, in their "gut," the "profound complexes that lay just below the surface."

It fell to Charles Murray to lay out the template in his proposal to the Manhattan Institute for what would be a highly successful book on welfare, *Losing Ground*. A consummate showman, Murray was accurately described by journalist Eric Alterman as having "an uncanny ability to offer what appeared to be a reasonable and scholarly-sounding voice to opinions and arguments that had hitherto been considered beyond the pale of respectability."

Murray asked his potential funders and advance men, "How can a publisher sell it?" He then answered his own question, "Because a huge number of well-meaning whites fear that they are closet racists and this book tells them they are not. It's going to make them feel better about things they already think but do not know how to say."[13]

---

[12] Down the hall from the pundits on crime, one could find the architects of the "preventive" war in Iraq, having taken refuge in this or that think tank until the wind blew over relative to whatever part they might have had in conceiving and cheering on wars in Iraq – largely based on false information and manufactured evidence.

[13] As the Institute for Public Accuracy noted, "Murray's denunciation of social programs for the poor – catapulted him to media stardom in 1984." More than a dozen years later, the *Philadelphia Inquirer* (10/13/97) recalled that Murray's book, *Losing Ground*, "provided much of the intellectual groundwork for welfare 'reform.'" As Murray wrote in the book's preface, the decision by Manhattan Institute officials to subsidize the book project was crucial: "Without them, the book would not have been written." Murray became a national figure only after joining the Manhattan Institute as a Bradley Fellow. In 1982, the think tank "offered the then-unknown Murray a position as a senior research fellow and the Institute's full financial backing to complete *Losing Ground*," authors Jean Stefancic and Richard Delgado recount in *No Mercy: How Conservative Think Tanks and Foundations Changed America's Social Agenda*. "The Institute raised $125,000 to promote Murray's book and pay him a $135,000 stipend, most coming from Scaife [Foundation], which gave $75,000, and Olin, $25,000. Upon publication, it sent 700 free copies to academics, journalists, and public officials worldwide, sponsored seminars on the book, and funded a nationwide speaking tour for Murray that was made possible by a $15,000 grant from the Liberty Fund."

The largesse from right-wing funders yielded big results. By early 1985, Murray's book had become a widely touted brief against spending tax dollars on low-income people. "This year's budget-cutters' bible seems to be *Losing Ground*," noted a *New York*

In a sentence, Murray summarized what would henceforth distinguish most of the social output underwritten by American neoconservative think tanks. The research would be attuned to those who felt, "in their gut," that certain others were marked with the sign of Cain but were ashamed to admit it.

It was a tectonic moment in the history of American sociology. Success was held to a new standard. It demanded skill in seizing politically advantageous moments and making them "work" while concealing whatever unintended consequences and serious ethical questions might be in store.

Social scientists were beckoned to hew to the principles likely to be held by their venture capitalist funders[14] – what Lewis Lapham limned "a small sewing circle of rich philanthropists."[15]

Times editorial (2/3/85). Among movers and shakers in the federal executive branch, the newspaper lamented, *Losing Ground* had quickly become holy writ: "In agency after agency, officials cite the Murray book as a philosophical base" for proposals to slash social expenditures.

    Media outlets marveled at the sudden importance of Charles Murray's work. *Losing Ground* "has been the subject of dozens of major editorials, columns, and reviews in publications such as *The New York Times*, *Newsweek*, the *Dallas Morning News*, and *The New Republic* – even the *Sunday Times* of London," wrote Chuck Lane in *The New Republic* (3/25/85). The book's success "is a case study in how conservative intellectuals have come to dominate the policy debates of recent years." That domination, Lane concluded, was being enhanced by the think tank behind *Losing Ground*. "The Manhattan Institute's canny innovation is to rely as little as possible on chance – and as much as possible on marketing. Of course, money helps, too."

[14] Recently, a former George Bush speechwriter, columnist for the *National Review*, and American Enterprise Institute "scholar" was suddenly dismissed for having the temerity to criticize what he saw as a potentially disastrous melding of the Republican Party with the so-called Tea Party movement and Rupert Murdoch's Fox News. As Christopher Buckley remarked, "It is not for the likes of me – non-intellectual, and post-partisan – to tell AEI how to handle its resident scholars. But the teapot having been heated, let me now drop in my leaves and say that it strikes me that AEI has not burnished its reputation as a center of right-intellectual thought... Another conservative banishee to hear the sound of accumulating oyster shells clacking around his feet was Bruce Bartlett. A comment of his goes, I think, to the heart of the whole mess. 'I have always,' he said, 'hoped that my experience was unique. But now I see that I was just the first to suffer from *a closing of the conservative mind*' (emphasis mine). As Dan Quayle once put it so well, 'What a terrible thing to have lost one's mind. Or not to have a mind at all. How true that is.' Indeed, how sad." (Christopher Buckley, "The Frum Flap," *The Daily Beast*, March 27, 2010.)

[15] Including, as Lapham put it, "Richard Mellon Scaife in Pittsburgh, Lynde and Harry Bradley in Milwaukee, John Olin in New York City, the Smith Richardson family in North Carolina, Joseph Coors in Denver, David and Charles Koch in Wichita, who entertained visions of an America restored to the safety of its mythological past – small towns like those seen in prints by Currier and Ives, cheerful factory workers whistling while they worked, politicians as wise as Abraham Lincoln and as brave as Teddy Roosevelt, benevolent millionaires presenting Christmas turkeys to deserving elevator operators, the sins of the flesh deported to Mexico or France. Suspicious of any fact

With massive financial resources at their disposal, the neos set about establishing the parameters of the debate on African-American males vis-à-vis crime, having claimed it as their turf early on.[16] They boldly connected the dots in a manner that would tell conservatives and liberals alike that their gut feelings had been right all along. Now, they could utter them aloud.

Those who knew better seemed unconcerned with the contrivances being put in place to marginalize legitimate objections – much of it from African-American academics who recognized the ill-omened precedents inherent in 200 years' experience of conflating crime, particularly violent crime, with race.

Upon its publication in 1997, the distinguished critic and writer Nicholas Lemann discussed *Search and Destroy* in the *New York Review of Books*. He limned it "a wail of outrage." As indeed, it was.

I mention this not to mount a tardy apologia, but because Lemann was prescient (however inadvertently) in charting the course the nation would subsequently take in addressing the thorny issues surrounding African-American males, violence, and crime.

Lemann's review reflected the fact that he had previously written a widely praised book on African-American males.[17] His comments were unusually sophisticated – citing a pantheon of sociologists, cultural anthropologists, social psychologists, and criminologists, most associated with the University of Chicago of the early to mid-twentieth century, out of which much of American criminology emerged.

However, after rendering his obligatory abeyance, Lemann saddled these early pioneers with the burden of having spawned a discipline – criminology – that was not only largely irrelevant today, but may have actually contributed to higher crime rates – particularly violent crime – with its preoccupation with putative social causes and correlates.

---

that they hadn't known before the age of six, the wealthy saviors of the Republic also possessed large reserves of paranoia, and if the world was going rapidly to rot (as any fool could plainly see) the fault was to be found in everything and anything tainted with a stamp of liberal origin – the news media and the universities, income taxes, Warren Beatty, transfer payments to the undeserving poor, restraints of trade, Jane Fonda, low interest rates, civil liberties for unappreciative minorities, movies made in Poland, public schools."

[16] Murray, in *Losing Ground* (1983), and Wilson, along with Herrstein, in *Crime and Human Nature* (1985).

[17] Lemann, Nicholas, The *Promised Land: The Great Black Migration and How It Changed America*, New York: Random House, 1992.

"Today," he wrote, "the liberal view that crime best be reduced by bettering the lot of the poor, and that many criminals can be reformed by supportive parole officers and social workers, has virtually no acceptance[18].... No Democratic politician would publicly express the view that greater social opportunity and rehabilitation reduces crime."

Lemann hailed the country's practical turn to the Right – citing a familiar roster of neoconservative experts who had staked out the criminological scene in the prerequisite stark black–white, either–or terms the times demanded.

Then, somewhat inexplicably, he chose to focus on the premise that had lain at the core of neoconservative thought on race and crime all along. Snatched from a Pandora's box of "southern strategies," it was a bric-a-brac reminder of harsher measures yet in store for African-American men and boys – albeit with a delay that vexed those who longed for the blessed closure it proffered.

"It is difficult," Lemann mused, "to estimate the effect of the idea that what (James Q.) Wilson and (Richard) Herrnstein call constitutional factors in people cause crime, because no politician or policymaker would dare voice it directly."

Hailing them for having breached the silence, Lemann was particularly taken with the fact that Wilson was "frequently consulted, and cited by Republican politicians, including Mayor Rudolph Giuliani of New York City" (with whom he presumably shared his views on genes, race, and crime "directly").

The neos had clearly tapped whatever "profound complexes" had theretofore lain silent among liberals, neoliberals, and conservatives alike.

In 1995, New York's former Democratic Mayor Ed Koch had written a glowing review of Herrnstein and Wilson's *Crime and Human Nature* for the Heritage Foundation's journal, *Policy Review*, titled, "The Mugger and His Genes."[19]

Richard Cohen, a generally liberal columnist for *The Washington Post*, had felt similar abdominal rumblings four years earlier. As he wrote in 1991, "Giuliani is a true Wilsonian – not as in Woodrow, but as in James

---

[18] A day that never existed, but if it had, had been pretty much replaced with what some now refer to as attack probation. In the case of social workers, I can think of no better appellation than that once applied to family child-protective service units by psychiatrist Salvador Minuchin as having become family dismemberment services.

[19] Koch, Ed, "The Mugger and His Genes," *Policy Review* Vol. 35, Winter, 1995, pp. 87–89.

Q., a social scientist at UCLA. Years ago, James Q. Wilson identified a phenomenon we all feel in our gut."[20]

By focusing the debate on putative genetic links between race and crime, Lemann hit upon the very reason nothing productive would occur in the near future. While he had prematurely outed those who harbored similar stirrings in their guts, he had also recognized the potential inherent in the phenomenon.

Conflating race with crime (cf. violent crime) has always been a white man's "demon rum" – holding out the false promise of freeing him from the troubling racial contradictions that lay at the heart of our democracy. It had the faux mystical quality of promising a "scientific"solution to citizens weighed down in racial ambiguity.

However, rather than forge ahead – a risky road at best – the nation chose to leave its despicable correctional system frozen in place to serve as a continuing "morality play" meant to justify what so many white citizens felt in their collective gut. "See how they act!" would be the mantra used to simultaneously stereotype, frighten, and allure.

It was a stratagem used with limited success in retrieving some of the political losses attendant to the Katrina fiasco. Rumors were circulated on Web sites and on cable television testifying to alleged incidents of jaw-dropping human disregard among black victims waiting in the football dome to which they'd been beckoned to find shelter and rest.[21] It was a pale attempt to redefine the disaster in a way that justified inaction.

It probably didn't help when the president's mother relieved herself of her views on the situation at a "back-up" dome in Houston.[22] Nevertheless, at some gut level, she was sharing "complexities" that lay below the surface in many Americans.

---

[20] As the liberal columnist for *The Washington Post*, Richard Cohen wrote, "If a neighborhood seems unsafe, it is unsafe. If petty crimes go unpunished, if vandalism and graffiti go unchecked, not only will criminals perceive a breakdown in authority, so will law-abiding residents." Op/Ed, *Washington Post*, July 7, 1994, p. A19.

[21] Rumors that were subsequently proven false. Indeed, as I write this, other rumors concerning police violence during the Katrina disaster largely overlooked by the media were being confirmed in indictments against police for murdering a number of African Americans making their way to the Superdome. Coincidentally, among those patrolling the streets of New Orleans during Katrina were employees of the "Blackwater" firm later to become well-known for alleged inappropriate violence on civilians in Iraq.

[22] As the president's mother told the Public Broadcasting Service, "So many of the people in the arena here, you know, were underprivileged anyway, so this is working very well." "Thanks Mom! Barbara Bush on Katrina's Victims," *The Guardian*, London, September 7, 2005.

However, it was different for African-American males who could be linked to crime. As they filled the prisons, media outlets competed with one another in crafting twentieth-century television shows to rival nineteenth-century entertainments with similar goals.

The British criminologist D. L. Howard described "the punitive English prison practices of the late 19th century" as fitting hand in glove with the neo-Darwinist views of the popular Italian criminologist Cesare Lombroso in identifying genetically formed criminals.

Howard saw the brutal DuCane system of managing British prisons as *directing*, rather than *following* public opinion. "Men and women went into prison as people. They came out as Lombrosian animals, shorn and cropped, hollow-cheeked, and frequently, as a result of dietary deficiencies and lack of sunlight, seriously ill with tuberculosis. They came out mentally numb and some of them insane; they became the creatures, ugly and brutish in appearance, stupid and resentful in behavior, unemployable and emotionally unstable, which the Victorian middle classes came to visualize whenever they thought of prisoners." Rather than portray inmates "as the commonplace, rather weak people the majority of them really were," DuCane's machine produced Lombroso's inbred criminal types.

In words that carry resonance today, Howard noted, "The theories of Lombroso and others on criminal types, and the Victorian stereotypes of the criminal were identical. Prison produced the criminal type, scientific theory identified him even to the pallor of his skin, and the public recognized him: The whole system was logical, watertight, and socially functional."[23]

He added that the change of prison conditions proceeded at a rapid enough rate "to satisfy the pressures of reformers, while continuing to produce the stereotyped 'old lag', the abnormal', the 'psychologically motivated', the 'inner-directed' delinquent whose maladjustment is 'deep-seated' and 'intransigent to treatment' and who, in his turn, becomes the scapegoat needed by society and the data required by the culture."[24]

It was all airtight and self-generating – embodying a theory of correctional management first advanced in the United States by neo pundit John Dilulio in a *Wall Street Journal* op-ed in 1994. The editors chose

---

[23] Chapman, Dennis, *Sociology and the Stereotype of the Criminal*, London: Tavistock Publications, 1968, p. 237.
[24] Ibid., p. 16.

to limn the piece, "Let 'em Rot."[25] It was similar in tone to other neo-conservative themes focused primarily on African-American citizens – for example, welfare and single-parent homes.

Just as the Victorian middle classes were afforded tours of English prisons and workhouses where they could observe men chained together in silent lockstep, or perhaps leer at gaunt youths trudging an endless stairway, hands cuffed to a treadmill[26] – so the American electronic media were flooded with "reality-based" visuals of prison inmates, executions, and interviews where the inmates could perform.[27]

For the Victorian middle class, it was all calibrated to embody then-emerging Darwinist imperatives that suggested the genetic sources of criminal behavior while ratifying the British meritocracy. Americans could sit on the couch and watch incredibly damaged individuals perform according to the intentions of their keepers.

Here's how a popular American television series, *Lockup*, was recently described on the Arts & Entertainment Web site: "At St. Louis County Jail, some of the inmates are on edge, and only one thing's for sure: Somebody's going to cross the line. Here, small-time offenders sleep next to career felons and collide with each other in open areas during the day. Tensions could erupt at any moment, but for each unit of 67 inmates, there's just one corrections officer – armed with nothing but a panic button and pepper spray – to keep all hell from breaking loose."[28]

A substantial majority of the nation now seems irretrievably won over to the "appropriateness" of variations on pain – from excruciating to occasionally fatal torture (predictably, limned enhanced interrogation) – having seen it "work" week after week in a fictionalized Fox TV spy drama.[29]

---

[25] Despite Dilulio's subsequent objections to the title given his piece by the *Journal*'s editors, it accurately reflected the tenor of his piece.

[26] University of Houston's Web site, "*Engines of Ingenuity*," "Treadmills came into English jails following a 1779 prison reform act. That act said that prisoners should be given '... labor of the hardest and most servile kind in which drudgery is chiefly required and where the work is little liable to be spoiled by ignorance, neglect, or obstinacy.'"

[27] A more recent example is one in which selected inmates displayed their eyes – in which they had tattooed the white of the eye dark blue.

[28] Arts & Entertainment network Web site, March 1, 2010.

[29] *The Nation*, January 15, 2000, p. 24: "Torture on TV: 24 is back on Fox TV. The hit show ... features at least one big torture scene in every episode – the kind of torture the Bush White House says is necessary to protect us from you-know-who. The show is much more successful than the White House at making the case for torture. Its ratings have gone steadily up over the last five years, while Bush's ratings have gone steadily down. Sunday night's two-hour premiere again argued not just that torture is necessary

Meanwhile, those who elicited this circus and wheedled the nation into its current racial dilemma now sit firmly in the "catbird seat," whence they prattle on in that state of "lucid inebriation" once associated with absinthe addicts. As a consequence, the country is now set on a path bound to realize its most dire predictions, having set the prerequisites in place.

The modern American criminal justice system now stands as an homage in concrete and steel to the Dred Scott decision[30] – quietly disenfranchising ever larger percentages of black males while assuring a continuing national ethic steeped in paranoia, neglect, and "watchful" waiting for whatever next explosion might confirm the ever-present gut test demanding more and longer imprisonment. It's an abiding threat that embodies what southern white men have (with good reason) feared since Nat Turner's slave rebellion.

The demons that always haunted captive–captor dyads were loosed with renewed vengeance. "Corrections," perpetually in a state of near-atrophy, hardened further. Policies and practices, in the past more likely to betray the lassitude of a warden or imperiousness of a probation/parole officer, now regularly spill out from the darker recesses of troubled minds, revealing obsessions that are quite something other than normal.

One could be forgiven for misconstruing many contemporary correctional practices as having been the issue of a sadomasochist's wet dream. Loosely grounded in self-hatred, trance, myth, and fearsome fantasies, the system has become quite loony – presided over by loonier overseers.

It is to our shame that a small band of primarily neoconservative "crime experts" have successfully contrived to establish an array of measures sufficient to the task of devaluing enough African-American men and boys for the nation to reach what British criminologist Andrew Rutherford has termed the eliminative ideal – not extermination, but an attempt to

---

but also that it works. And it's also really exciting to watch. The show as usual made the 'ticking time bomb' case for torture: we need to torture a suspect, or else thousands, or millions, will die in the next hour."

[30] *The American Prospect*, March 11, 2010: "Sen. Dick Durbin announced that he and Sen. Jeff Sessions had reached a 'compromise' in the Senate gym over Durbin's bill, which would have eliminated the 100 to 1 sentencing disparity for crack vs. powder cocaine. The compromise was that Durbin would accept Sessions' amendment to change the disparity from 100 to 1 to 20.... Instead of eliminating the crack/powder disparity, which practically everyone in the committee acknowledged disproportionately affects black Americans, the senators opted to make the law one-fifth as racist as it used to be. The senators on the committee spent the rest of the markup complimenting each other on all they had achieved with their bipartisanship."

solve problems by getting rid of troublesome or disagreeable people with methods that are made lawful and widely supported.[31]

Britain once led the way in this endeavor – eliminating the possibility of recurrent petty crime by physically transporting thousands of men, women, and children, first to America and then to Australia. Today, the method is exile via long-term imprisonment.

A familiar albatross has reappeared on the American horizon – stoking fears that the Civil War couldn't expunge and reminding citizens of an abiding disposition to compulsively toy with "solutions" that smack of another kind of "finality" – not as formal policy, but through the mundane practice of ensuring that our glut of life-consuming contraptions will devour ever larger chunks of the perpetual aliens in our midst – piece by piece, man by man, boy by boy, before they return the favor.

---

[31] Rutherford, A., "Criminal Policy and the Eliminative Ideal," *Social Policy and Administration*, 1997, pp. 116–35.

The Scope of the Problem

Amid two decades of economic growth and social neglect, the white majority in America presented its inner cities with an expensive gift – a new and improved criminal justice system. It would, the government promised, bring domestic tranquility, with particular relevance to African-Americans. No expense was spared in crafting and delivering it inside the city gates. It proved to be a Trojan horse.

While neoconservative commentators such as Charles Murray argued that welfare had undermined family stability and sabotaged work incentives,[1] the real value of Aid to Families with Dependent Children (AFDC) and food-stamp payments to the poor had steadily declined.[2] Not so with criminal justice.

[1] A 1993 University of Michigan Institute for Social Research study (Duncan, Greg J., Gustafsson, Björn, Hauser, Richard, Schmauss, Günther, Messinger, Hans, Muffels, Ruud, Nolan, Brian; Ray, Jean-Claude; (1993). "Poverty Dynamics in Eight Countries." *Journal of Population Economics,* Vol. 6, No. 3. August 1993) noted that among those who escaped poverty in the 1980s, the situation was decidedly worse than that of most of the industrialized world. Challenging the idea that welfare is a disincentive to escaping poverty, the researchers found that the chances of escaping poverty in those countries with more generous welfare benefits were much greater than in the United States. For example, when comparing the ability of poor families (those with a median income of less than 50 percent of the country's median income) to escape poverty, there were gross differences among countries. The highest rates of escape from poverty were shown in those countries with relatively liberal welfare benefits: Finland Sweden, France, Luxembourg, and West Germany. The lowest rate of escape from poverty registered was among U.S. blacks.

[2] Dionne, E. J., *Why Americans Hate Politics,* New York: Simon & Schuster, 1992, p. 96. As Dionne put it, "If Murray's argument were right, the trends he rightly deplores should have reversed themselves. 'When the relative advantage of work over welfare increased sharply.' They did not. In fact, the problems of youth unemployment and family breakdown grew worse in the 1970s and 1980s. That suggests that simply cutting

In a society obsessed with single mothers on welfare, more money ($31 billion) was being spent in 1993 at local, state, and federal levels on a failed drug war (mainly directed at African-American and Latino citizens) than on AFDC, that much vaunted symbol of liberal largesse ($25 billion).[3] Moreover, the politics of crime and welfare came with a decidedly racial cast.

As governmental investment in social and employment programs in the inner city was held stable or reduced, a surfeit of "wars" on crime and drugs were ratcheted up to fill the void. The rationale (and generally accepted view) was that the nation was caught in the throes of an exponential rise in violent crime – largely attributable to the arrival of "crack." Although reliable studies at the time found this premise highly questionable, it didn't matter. The country was being whipped into what the sociologists limn a moral panic.

So long as this public perception was carefully cultivated, the criminal justice system grew at an exponential rate: direct federal, state, and local expenditures for police increased 416 percent; for courts, 585 percent; for prosecution and legal services, 1,019 percent; for public defense, 1,255 percent; and for corrections, 990 percent. Federal spending on criminal justice grew 668 percent; county spending increased 711 percent; and state spending surged 848 percent. By 1990, the country was spending $75 billion a year to catch and lock up offenders.[4]

However, even these figures were grossly understated.[5] With the passage of "tough" federal crime legislation and the consequent pressure to enact similar measures at the state level, by the mid-1990s, the country was spending in excess of $200 billion annually on the crime-control industry.

In what fast emerged into a national malady, most of the anticrime initiatives of the 1960s, 1970s, and 1980s came wed to variants on themes of "war" – not against sovereign nations – but against conditions or perceived behaviors – wars on poverty, wars on cancer, wars on drugs,

welfare programs, though appealing from the point of view of conservative ideology, would do nothing to improve matters – and would very likely make things much worse." The average grant under "Aid to Families with Dependent Children" in 1992 was a painfully low $370 per month.

[3] Murphy, Patrick, "Keeping Score: The Frailties of the Federal Drug Budget," Rand Drug Policy Research Center: Issue Paper, January 1994, p. 5.

[4] U.S. Department of Justice, Bureau of Justice Statistics, *Justice Expenditure and Employment, 1990,* Bulletin NCLJ-135777, Washington, D.C., August 1992, p. 1.

[5] For example, a "Jail Expo" sponsored by the American Jail Association in the spring of 1994 announced that county and local jails alone represented a $58 billion "market" to prospective vendors and builders.

and on violent crime – culminating as an apotheosis in the history of shams – the war on terror – still some 30 years hence.[6]

All Our Young Enemies

What had been quietly happening to young African-American men and boys in our criminal justice system was a particularly noteworthy story in the 1980s and 1990s. However, it was thrust before the public in 1992. The televised brutal beating of a black man (Rodney King) during a traffic stop followed by the acquittal by an all-white jury of policemen involved spilled into the streets with general rioting in various parts of Los Angeles (L.A.).

As city prosecutors ran background checks on the first 1,000 arrestees charged with misdemeanors (most having to do with curfew violations), they discovered that 6 out of 10 had criminal records and nearly a third were on probation or parole. From this important bit of information, L.A. officials quickly drew the kind of flawed conclusion that had shaped justice policy in the inner city for most of the previous decade – and continues to provide the rationale for a series of "wars" on crime now, another decade and a half later. "This was not an instantaneous 'good guy rage' kind of thing," said deputy city attorney John Wilson. "This was a 'bad guy' taking advantage of a situation out of control."[7] Wilson's statement proved to be misinformed.

Indeed, a study of the Los Angeles County Adult Detention Center completed a year earlier revealed that one-third of all the black men between ages 20 and 29 living in Los Angeles County had been jailed at least once in that same year.[8] At this point, good guy versus bad guy

---

[6] The "War on Terrorism" was, in a sense, the logical next step in this trend of garnering support for a cause through marketing. A cynic might suggest that declaring "victory" in such wars is another marketing challenge – it is questionable whether one can successfully convey a conclusion that is not obviously or necessarily the outcome expected from a wide range of observers. The final analysis in such wars becomes a matter of who says so and whether they exercise sufficient power to ensure their declaration can be made to stick – again, essentially another challenge in marketing rather than an outcome dictated by the facts.

[7] Lieberman, Paul, "40% of Riot Suspects Found to Have Criminal Records," *Los Angeles Times*, Tuesday, May 19, 1992, p. B4. A later *L.A. Times* survey of 700 people convicted of riot-related felonies (more than 90 percent of "looting") found that 60 percent had been arrested previously (*Los Angeles Times*, Sunday May 2, 1993, p. A34).

[8] Austin, James and Donald Irie, "Los Angeles County Sheriff's Department Jail Population Analysis and Policy Simulations: Briefing Report," National Council on Crime and Delinquency, August 21, 1992.

comparisons begin to falter. Basically, this straightforward and largely ignored study revealed that something approaching the majority of young black males living in L.A. could expect to spend time in one or another of the county's jails, detention centers, camps, or prisons as they negotiated the years between adolescence and age 30. Virtually all would acquire a criminal record during this process and a not insignificant percentage would spend a significant amount of time in one or another correctional facility. Again, though largely ignored by law enforcement and the press, similar patterns were showing up in other large cities.

The L.A. city attorney seemed oblivious to the fact that had he stopped 1,000 individual African-American young men at random, whether rioting or simply going about their law-abiding daily business, about 600 would have had "criminal records." What he might have considered, however, was the kind of record it was. The L.A. deputy public defender cited the case of one of his clients, a 50-year-old man arrested during the riots. His criminal record consisted of a single drunk-driving arrest some 20 years earlier. However, it was, in fact, a criminal record.

The social disaster taking shape in L.A. had been brewing a long time. Nearly a quarter century earlier, in a 1967 article published in *The Annals of the American Academy of Political and Social Science*, the socioeconometrician Alfred Blumstein predicted that if then-current patterns continued, the chances of a black male city resident's being arrested at some time in his lifetime for a nontraffic offense was approaching 90 percent – and more than half of them would be charged with a felony.[9]

Blumstein's dire predictions didn't appear in the national press until nine months later, when he repeated them before an unlikely forum – the International Platform Association. A reporter happened to be covering

---

[9] Blumstein, Alfred, "Systems Analysis and the Criminal Justice System," *The Annals of The American Academy of Political and Social Science,* Vol. 374, November 1967, p. 99. As Blumstein put it, " ... one can approximate the probability of an American boy's being arrested. The Uniform Crime Reports reports 4,431,000 male arrests in its 1965 sample population, or an equivalent of 6,420,000 for the total United States; one-eighth of these, or about 800,000 would have been new arrestees. One can assume, for simplicity, that all first arrests occurred at a specific age, say, sixteen. Since there were about 1,710,000 sixteen-year-old boys in the United States in 1965, their arrest probability is thus calculated to be about 47 per cent, or conservatively, at least 40 per cent. More detailed calculations, correcting for race and residence (city, suburban, and rural), show that a city male's chances of being arrested for a nontraffic offense some time in his life are about 60 per cent, about 50 per cent for a United States male in general, and that they may be as high as 90 per cent for a Negro city male."

this public speaking event, and as a result, a brief, largely unnoticed or ignored Associated Press article appeared in *The New York Times*.[10]

At about the same time, in their classic 1970 "cohort analysis" of Philadelphia boys who had been born in 1945, University of Pennsylvania criminologists Marvin Wolfgang, Robert Figlio, and Thorsten Sellin noted that 52 percent of the nonwhite boys and 29 percent of the white boys had been arrested by age 18.[11]

In a later study (1981), Alfred Blumstein and Elizabeth Graddy examined 1968 through 1972 arrest statistics from the country's 56 largest cities.[12] Looking only at felony arrests, they found that one of every four males living in a large city could expect to be arrested for a felony at some point in his life. When broken down by race, however, they found that a nonwhite male was three and a half times more likely to have a felony arrest than a white male. Whereas 14 percent of white males would be arrested for a felony, 51 percent of nonwhite males could anticipate a felony arrest at some time during their lives.[13]

Misdemeanors (making up the largest share of the bookings into jails) weren't included in Blumstein and Graddy's calculations. Had they been, the percentage of nonwhite males arrested and jailed at least briefly would have fulfilled Blumstein's original "90 percent" prediction.

In 1987, Robert Tillman, a criminologist working in the California Attorney General's office, found a similar pattern among nonwhite males statewide, not over a lifetime but in the short 12-year span between ages 18 and 30. Drawing upon a 1974 "cohort" of 18-year-old males of all races, Tillman traced their arrest records between 1974 and 1986, when they turned 30. At least one out of three had been arrested. When he broke the percentages down by race, however, he discovered that two-thirds of the nonwhite adult males could expect to be arrested and jailed

[10] *The New York Times,* July 28, 1968.
[11] Wolfgang, Marvin, Robert Figlio, and Thomas Sellin, *Delinquency in a Birth Cohort,* Chicago: University of Chicago Press, 1972.
[12] Blumstein, Alfred and Elizabeth Graddy, "Prevalence and Recidivism in Index Arrests: A Feedback Model," *Law and Society Review,* Vol. 16, No. 2, 1981–82, pp. 265–90. (The cities surveyed were Birmingham, Phoenix, Tucson, Oakland, Long Beach, Los Angeles, Sacramento, San Diego, San Francisco, San Jose, Denver, Washington, D.C., Miami, Jacksonville, Tampa, Atlanta, Chicago, Indianapolis, Wichita, Louisville, New Orleans, Baltimore, Albuquerque, Buffalo, Rochester, New York, Charlotte, Cincinnati, Cleveland, Columbus, Toledo, Oklahoma City, Tulsa, Portland, Philadelphia, Pittsburgh, Memphis, Dallas, Houston, San Antonio, El Paso, Ft. Worth, Austin, Norfolk, Seattle, Milwaukee, and Honolulu.)
[13] Ibid. pp. 279–80.

before completing their 29th year (41 percent for a felony).[14] Tillman did not include juvenile arrests or later arrests (after age 30). Had he done so, the lifetime risk of arrest would have surpassed 85 percent.

Moreover, Tillman's cohort of 18-year-olds was drawn from across the whole state of California, including both rural and urban youth, not exclusively city populations. Had he confined his sample only to inner-city minority youth, the percentage arrested before completing their 29th year would have approached 80 percent.

A 1990 RAND Corporation study on the economics of the drug trade in the District of Columbia revealed a similar trend – with fully one-third of all the African-American males between the ages 18 and 21 living in the District of Columbia being arrested and charged with a criminal offense. Moreover, the fraction of one-third for black males aged 19 did not "decline noticeably over the age range of 20 to 29, as other studies of crime rates in the general population ha(d) suggested."[15]

Again, the RAND researchers did not include juvenile arrests. Had they done so, about half of the District of Columbia's young men would have been found to have been arrested and jailed or detained before reaching legal adulthood.[16]

In 1990, the Washington, D.C. – based "Sentencing Project" released a survey revealing that on an average day in the United States, one of every four African-American men ages 20 to 29 was either in prison or jail, or on probation or parole.[17] The study caused a brief flurry in the media, but the next logical question went unasked by the press. If one in four young African-American males was under correctional supervision on any one day, what percentage had been, or would be drawn into the justice system before age 30, or 40, or 50?

In 1992, the National Center on Institutions and Alternatives (NCIA) conducted another survey of young African-American males in Washington, D.C.'s justice system and found that on one day, 4 of every 10 African-American males (ages 18 to 35) residing in the District of

[14] Tillman, Robert, "The Size of the 'Criminal Population': The Prevalence and Incidence of Adult Arrests," *Criminology*, Vol. 25, No. 3, Fall 1987.

[15] Reuter, Peter; MacCoun, Robert; Murphy, Patrick; et al., *Money from Crime: A Study of the Economics of Drug Dealing in Washington, D.C.*, June 1990.

[16] Blumstein, A. and E. Graddy, op. cit. (Blumstein had discovered that a disproportionate percentage of arrests occurring in the lifetime of African-American males occur in the juvenile years [before age 18]).

[17] Mauer, Mark, *Young Black Men and the Criminal Justice System: A Growing National Problem*, Washington, D.C.: The Sentencing Project, 1990.

Columbia were either in jail or prison, on probation/parole, out on bond, or being sought on arrest warrants. This one-day count suggested that approximately three of every four young black male residents of the city would be arrested and jailed before reaching age 35. Again, the lifetime risk hovered somewhere between 80 percent and 90 percent.[18]

A few months later, NCIA replicated the study in Baltimore, Maryland – finding that of the 60,715 African-American males aged 18 to 35 then living in that city, 34,025 (56 percent) fell under the onus of criminal justice (that is, in prison, jail, on probation/parole, out on bail, or being sought on an outstanding arrest warrant).

Predictably, police and prosecutors attributed these daunting numbers to random violence arising out of the so-called war on drugs. The question as to which side instigated the violence remained – and still remains – trapped in the "chicken or egg" dilemma.

The drug war, from its inception, was concentrated virtually exclusively in the black community. It served as a kind of "show and tell" for the white community. Yet, a detailed look at arrests in Baltimore during this period revealed that fewer than 1 in 10 had to do with any violent crime. The bulk of young black men had been arrested for nonviolent felonies and misdemeanors often associated with drugs.

The racial disparities were most obvious when drug arrests were isolated. African-American males of all ages were being arrested for drug offenses at six times the rate of whites. More than 90 percent of arrests of African-American males were for possession. As for violence attributed to the drug war, there had been more murders in Baltimore 20 years earlier, in 1971 (323), long before the drug wars ramped up, than in 1991, the year of this survey (304).

Similar findings emerged from a 1993 study by the California State Assembly's "Commission on the Status of African American Males." It revealed that one-sixth (104,000) of California's 625,000 black men 16 and older were arrested *each year*, "creating police records and hindering later job prospects." Although 64 percent of the drug arrests of whites and 81 percent of the arrests of Latinos ultimately were not sustainable, 92 percent of the black men were released for lack of evidence.[19]

---

[18] *Hobbling a Generation: African American Males in the District of Columbia's Criminal Justice System,* Windsor Mills, Maryland: National Center on Institutions and Alternatives, March 1992.

[19] Nazario, Sonia, "Odds Grim for Black Men in California," *The Washington Post,* Dec. 12, 1993, p. A9,

Meanwhile, black men, who made up only 3 percent of California's male population, accounted for 40 percent of those sent into state prisons.

The Limits of "Them" versus "Us" Paradigms

In the end, the data challenged what Robert Tillman had called the "two (false) assumptions" underlying most popular discussions of crime:

1. The world is made up of two types of people: those who commit crimes and those who do not; and,
2. Criminals form a very small portion of the total population.

Tillman wryly noted that if being arrested and possessing a criminal record were the prime criteria for being classified a member of the so-called criminal population, "the number of criminals in our midst is much larger than we recognize." He concluded, "The fact that such large numbers of young men are being arrested is related less to criminal behavior than to 'social-structural' conditions, that is, political, economic, and social institutions that adversely affect large numbers of young adult males, particularly those within certain strata of society."

Unfortunately, Tillman's egalitarianism regarding "criminals" was anathema to both the ideologically driven mavens of the Right and the ostensibly more liberal legalists of the Left.

Concomitantly, academic sociologists and criminologists, who had hitherto been trusted to provide accurate empirical data and historical narrative concerning crime, were now portrayed by the mavens of the Right as impractical when dealing with crime, if not, indeed, part of the problem. Increasingly, they found themselves relegated to the very edges of the public policy debates on crime. The "stars" on Capitol Hill and in state legislatures came primarily from ideologically driven "think tanks" or congressionally invited individuals representing their political views – the early harbingers of what, in ensuing years, would become an ideologically driven Justice Department from top to bottom.

In the political fog that followed, the issue of a grossly disproportionate number of African-Americans being drawn into the criminal justice system was largely ignored (with the exception of a few members of the black caucus) by state and federal policymakers and lawmakers alike.

Sociologist Chambliss continued to ask the salient question aloud:

How did we arrive in the late 20th century to a world in which the United States incarcerates more of its population than any country in the world: including South Africa? And how did we come to arrest and incarcerate such an incredibly disproportionate number of young men from minority groups?

Sadly, two decades later, the same question was still being asked – and remained largely unanswered. Here's how the conservative scholar, Glenn Lourie, posed the dilemmas in 2008:

How did it come to this? One (argument) is that the massive increase in incarceration reflects the success of a rational public policy: faced with a compelling social problem, we responded by imprisoning people and succeeded in lowering crime rates. This argument is not entirely misguided. Increased incarceration does appear to have reduced crime somewhat. But by how much? Estimates of the share of the 1990s' reduction in violent crime that could be attributed to the prison boom ranged from five percent to 25 percent. Whatever the number, we long ago entered the zone of diminishing returns. Neoconservative John Dilulio who coined the term "super-predator" in the early 1990s, was by the end of that decade declaring in *The Wall Street Journal* that "Two Million Prisoners Are Enough." But there was no political movement for getting America out of the mass-incarceration business. The throttle was stuck.

A more convincing argument is that imprisonment rates have continued to rise while crime rates have fallen because we have become progressively more punitive: not because crime has continued to explode, not because we made a smart policy choice, but because we have made a collective decision to increase the rate of punishment.

The list of familiar rationalizations for the "wars," along with the incarceration of so many young African-American men and boys, proved to be just that – rationalizations.

The policies and practices that followed were either shaky to the point of disbelief, had minimal impact on crime, or were blatantly fraudulent. The list is familiar – from selective incapacitation to deterrence to the mother of all lies – the so-called broken window theory that ended in incarcerating minor offenders in previously unknown numbers.

It's now clear all this hullabaloo had little to do with rising violent crime. Indeed, a credible case can be made that we "came to this" through a highly successful campaign of deliberate misrepresentation designed to push the nation into what sociologists have called a moral panic. It resulted in an exponential growth in a crime-control industry that has come to resemble the military in its strategies, tactics, and near-romantic hold on the public's imagination.

One was reminded of Colin Powell's aside that armies are designed to kill people and break things. That has been precisely the legacy of our various "wars" on drugs, violent crime, and "uncivil" behavior – all demanding one wild charge after another up an unending series of virtual San Juan Hills.

In the process, the country has grown progressively less able to free itself from self-destructive "solutions" that have undermined our democracy at virtually every level while seeding neighborhoods with thousands of Stasi-like informers, instigating and feeding violent crime in the streets and ensuring a state of "moral panic" born of false premises and ill-borne rumors. The only constant in this admixture of faux patriotism and genuine racism is that it inexorably fell upon the black community.

The nation's tough on crime legacy is there for all to see – in the alienation, paranoia, family breakdown, fatherless children, and random violence – as ever-greater numbers of inmates return home or to the streets confirmed in the criminal roles crafted for them as they emerge from hothouses designed in every respect to nurture the very psychopathy the war's commanders pretended to address.

The rationale left to ponder is measured in the rotting detritus of an era of sloganeering by politicians, false claims trumpeted by faux experts, dishonest research churned out by ideologically driven think tanks, and policy papers published by kept house organs.

The "claims makers" have had an extremely successful run. Their dreams have been finally realized in the inner city as fit for the resigned rhetoric of Spanish citizens during the waning days of the Franco regime as "a country occupied by itself." More than two million American citizens are in prison or jail on any given day – about 90 percent of African-American men and boys now have to realistically expect (and plan to mitigate) a preordained stay in this or that jail or prison. It goes with being black in America.

The saddest commentary on this state of affairs – not unlike other contemporary "wars" conceived in deceit and waged under false premises – is that it leaves a democracy maimed. From some wounds, it's becoming well nigh impossible for some communities to fully recover.

2

Hyping Violence

How did violent crime become one of the premier social problems of our time – right up there with global warming, immigration, welfare, Islamo-Fascism, or terrorism? If anything is clear about this process, it's that social problems no longer can be accepted simply on their merits. They are "turf" to be fought over by interested parties. Consequently, they are better understood within the slippery rubrics of mass marketing – a largely political or ideologically driven exercise employed by a series of "claims makers" with grossly differential access to the financial or political resources necessary for effective marketing. Defining a problem such as violent crime as a social problem, for example, is highly subject to tampering.

During the late 1980s and early 1990s, violent crime was turned into a furtive street-corner game of "bait and switch" – largely the product of an aggressive law enforcement establishment at the time. The "bait" was the much advertised explosion of violent crime among inner-city youths. The "switch" occurred when police rolled out their armamentaria to confront this ostensible tide. The unmentionable reality was that few *violent* offenders could be rousted out from among the millions of citizens of color being arrested and jailed.

When the bulk of African-American males proved not to be so violent after all, the criteria were adjusted to widen the potential pool. Some were deemed potentially violent by administrative fiat that formalized theretofore randomly practiced police tactics; others, by enacting retroactively applicable new legislation that widened the definition of who would be considered violent.[1] The avowed purpose was to snatch up as many potential arrestees as possible, as often as possible. This became the most common way of bolstering the rationale for whatever "war" was being actively waged, or whatever criminal justice principals and planners might have in store.

The same self-aggrandizing dynamic had driven the Federal Bureau of Investigation's (FBI) "Uniform Crime Report" (UCR) from its beginnings. J. Edgar Hoover routinely inflated both the incidence and the seriousness of reported crimes while building a steady and largely unquestioned role for his agency. Whereas most European nations reported their crime statistics on the basis of *convictions*, the UCRs were (and still are) based on *complaints* or *arrests*.

Few citizens were aware that 43 of every 100 individuals arrested for a felony in the United States either weren't prosecuted or had their cases dismissed at their first hearing. There was not sufficient reason for prosecutors to proceed with the case.

Most felony arrestees were absolved of having committed a felony.[2] For example, of 399,277 arrests for aggravated assault reported by the FBI in 1990, only 13.4 percent (53,861) resulted in a felony conviction.[3] Though figures such as these are usually taken by conservative commentators to demonstrate the alleged permissiveness of the courts, quite something else was happening.

Police routinely inflated the realities of crime by charging arrestees with violent crimes that had not, in fact, occurred. The incidents usually involved fights and arguments between relatives and acquaintances – again, overstated by police. It became something of a tightrope for police departments under pressure to bring violent crime figures down. During these times, it was not uncommon to take questionable measures – as recently has been claimed in New York.[4]

---

[1] The most egregious recent example of this can be found in the plethora of sex offender laws enacted across the country to hold these offenders in prison. With the stroke of the governor's pen in Virginia, for example, the majority of state prison inmates listed as sex offenders were arbitrarily reclassified as violent statutorily.

[2] U.S. Department of Justice, Office of Justice Programs, *The Prosecution of Felony Arrests, 1987.*

[3] Langan, Patrick and John M. Dawson, *Felony Sentences in State Courts, 1990,* NCJ-140186, Washington, D.C.: U.S. Department of Justice, Bureau of Justice Statistics, March 1993, p. 5.

[4] Rashbaum, William R., "Retired Officers Raise Questions on Crime Data," *The New York Times,* February 6, 2010.

It's particularly crucial to the thesis of this book that arrests for index felonies be considered in individual detail. Too many ended up not being index *felonies* at all, but rather, index *arrests*.

Whereas a substantial percentage of one year's 3 million arrests for index felonies were bogus, the 11+ million arrests for "nonindex" crimes were more revealing, including everything from forgery (103,700) to public drunkenness (881,100); from curfew and loitering offenses (93,400) to runaways (177,300).

The category "other" made up fully 21 percent of the nonindex arrests in 1991. This was a true "catch-all" potpourri.[5]

Most might just as easily have been seen as collateral damage left for communities to clean up in the wake of this or that war on violent crime.

Race and Moral Panics

The hyping of violence – allegedly among African-American males – is precisely what I found when, from 1989 to 1994, I served as the federal "monitor" for the U.S. Court of the Middle District of Florida (Jacksonville) charged with overseeing the Court's orders relative to overcrowding in Duval County's jail system.

For example, only 20 percent of the single largest category of arrests for a violent crime – that is, aggravated assault – remained "aggravated" for more than a few hours. It constituted the difference between a violent felony and a simple or misdemeanor charge. Approximately 80 percent of the arrests for an ostensibly serious violent felony were downgraded to simple or misdemeanor assault.[6] The evidence didn't warrant the more serious charge and prosecutors opted not to proceed. This routine downgrading of charges occurred in a southern jurisdiction known for its punitive and harsh enforcement in prosecuting violent offenders.

More than a hundred retired New York Police Department captains and higher-ranking officers said in a survey that the intense pressure to produce annual crime reductions led some supervisors and precinct commanders to manipulate crime statistics, according to two criminologists studying the department.... But as the city annually reported reductions in crime, skepticism emerged in certain quarters – several police unions other than the one that assisted with this survey, elected officials, residents in some neighborhoods – about whether the department's books were being "cooked."

[5] U.S. Department of Justice, FBI, *Crime in the United States, 1991*, Washington, D.C.: U.S. Government Printing Office, 1992, p. 213.

[6] Miller, Jerome, *The Duval County Jail Report,* submitted to the Honorable Howell W. Melton, U.S. District Judge, Middle District of Florida, Jacksonville, June 1, 1993.

Nationally, a 1990 survey of "adjudication outcome" for felony defendants in the 75 largest counties in the country showed similar patterns. In fully half of the cases in which defendants were charged with an assault, the charges were dismissed outright and most of those remaining were reduced to a misdemeanor.[7]

Things were similar in the federal courts. In 1991, federal prosecutors declined to proceed in one in three (29.5 percent) cases of individuals brought to their attention as suspected of or under interrogation as likely perpetrators of a crime of violence, and in half (48.5 percent) of those cases of suspects charged with property crimes.[8] Again, nearly one in three (32.8 percent) of the cases alleging assault ended up being dismissed outright.

A 1993 study of California arrests revealed that 64 percent of the drug arrests of whites and 81 percent of those of Latinos were not sustainable. Moreover, 92 percent of the black men arrested by police on drug charges were subsequently released for lack of evidence or inadmissible evidence.[9]

These patterns were consistent with the observation that individuals routinely were being overcharged in racially biased ways. Paradoxically, very little of the intensive police activity had to do with serious or violent crime.

The prisons that were being built and staffed – often into perpetuity – would not be easily unwound. If past is prologue, inmates will be found and most of the prisons filled in a manner virtually unrelated to any putative increases or reductions in crime rates. A self-generating industry was put in place, aimed primarily at near-permanently exiling the underclass and minorities in the United States.[10]

---

[7] Smith, Pheny Z., *Felony Defendants in Large Urban Counties, 1990*, NCJ-1441872, Washington, D.C.: U.S. Dept. of Justice, Office of Justice Programs, Bureau of Justice Statistics, May 1993, p. 13.

[8] U.S. Department of Justice, Bureau of Justice Statistics, *Federal Criminal Case Processing, 1982–1991 with Preliminary Data for 1992*, NCJCJ-136945 Washington, D.C: U.S. Government Printing Office, November 1993, p 5.

[9] Nazario, Sonia, op. cit., p. A9.

[10] For awhile, it looked as though a near-vacant facility in rural Illinois would absorb the Guantanamo inmates. However, that prospect remains in limbo as the administration reconsiders an earlier proposal by the Attorney General, Eric Holder. As various political interests test the temperature of public opinion, we are now hearing that lo, it might be considered a good place for lesser, nondangerous offenders. This is the first time I've ever heard the Bureau of Prisons admit what, indeed, is the reality of most inmates in that system – the great majority are nondangerous and nonviolent. Among African-American males, that pattern is easily quadrupled.

There were an estimated 14,211,900 arrests in the United States in 1991.[11] Of these, 2,971,400 (20 percent) involved charges for "index," that is, more serious, crimes. However, a substantial percentage of these serious felony arrests didn't warrant an appearance beyond the initial "morning after" hearing.

An earlier (1987) study of 100 felony arrests brought by the police for prosecution revealed that 38 of the 100 would either be declined for prosecution or dismissed in court.[12] A survey by *The Washington Post* of arrest practices in the District of Columbia found that 5,444 (34 percent) of 16,013 felony arrests were either declined for prosecution or prosecuted on reduced charges. A similar study completed by the San Francisco Prosecutor's Office of arrests in that county revealed that the complaint was denied or no charges were filed in 41 percent of the felony arrests in 1990.[13]

In Duval County, Florida, a "profile-workload" report prepared by the state's attorney's office showed that of 11,542 noncapital felony cases brought by local prosecutors, 2,741 (24 percent) were reduced to misdemeanors; 2,360 (20 percent) were dismissed; and 524 (5 percent) were diverted by pretrial intervention. This meant that virtually half (49 percent) of the cases prosecuted were either dismissed or the felony charge was reduced to a misdemeanor. These figures did not include arrests in which the prosecutor declined to proceed – (ranging from 18 percent to 30 percent in most jurisdictions).[14]

The average person hearing these kinds of statistics usually attributes them to a permissive or neglectful justice system in which offenders are "getting off." My experience leads me to believe that is seldom the case in the real world of arresting millions of troublesome and troubled citizens.

The startling San Francisco figures, for example, reflect the now common police practice of arresting and overcharging individuals on evidence so flimsy that the prosecutor is usually unwilling to proceed with the case – *before going to court.* Even in those felony arrests in which the prosecutor elects to proceed, the complaint ends up as a misdemeanor in one

---

[11] *Crime in the United States, 1991,* op. cit., p. 213.
[12] U.S. Department of Justice, *The Prosecution of Felony Arrests, 1987,* Washington, D.C.: Office of Justice Programs, Bureau of Justice Statistics (1989).
[13] California State Attorney General's Statistical Report on Law Enforcement Practice, "Dispositions of Adult Felony Arrests, 1990: Type of Disposition by Race/Ethnic Group – San Francisco County," p. 45.
[14] Miller, Jerome, op. cit. p. 97.

of every three cases. The group most hard-hit by overcharging and most likely to garner a criminal record of felony arrest are African-American males. However, even in those cases, the complaint was denied 43 percent of the time.

Of the total arrests nationally each year, about 5 percent involve violent index offenses. However, even in those cases, the prosecutor declines to proceed about 20 percent of the time. Another 32 percent are dismissed by the courts.[15] This suggested that more than half of all arrests for violent index crimes didn't make it much past the first hearing. In Duval County, Florida, for example, fully half of the arrests for aggravated assault were lowered to simple assault or another misdemeanor before the prosecutor went to first hearing.

Measuring Crime Rates

For the past 40 years, officials have measured crime trends in two ways:

- FBI "Uniform Crime Reports" gathered from arrest statistics reported by state and local police departments;
- The "National Crime Survey" based on interviews with 100,000 people from scientifically selected samples of American households regarding crimes committed against members of their households.

The UCRs had always been subject to local police practices and policies and are prone to reflect the local politics of crime as much as actual reported crime. The UCR figures are derived not only from victim reports of crime but also from "officers who discover infractions" and the all-encompassing category entitled "other sources."[16]

Because police don't necessarily make arrests on the basis of citizen complaints, arrest patterns were highly susceptible to local police tactics and prosecutorial policies (for example, drug sweeps, sting operations, increased service of outstanding warrants, etc.).

The National Crime Surveys (NCS) established in 1972 were an attempt to mitigate these problems. It was believed that a large amount of crime – violent crime in particular – was not being reported to police and consequently not showing up in the UCR statistics. In addition, not

---

[15] U.S. Department of Justice, Bureau of Justice Statistics. *Tracking Offenders, 1988,* Bulletin NCJ-129861, Washington, D.C: June 1991, p. 2 Table 2.
[16] Federal Bureau of Investigation, *Crime in the U.S.: Uniform Crime Reports, 1989,* Washington, D.C.: U.S. Department of Justice, 1990, p. 2.

all reports to police were being recorded. Indeed, NCS data from 1973 to 1989 revealed that only half the robberies and aggravated assaults were appearing in UCR statistics.

For example, in 1973, only about one-half of the reports of aggravated assaults were recorded. By 1988, however, it was estimated that 97 percent of these reports were being recorded. In fact, by the early 1990s, police were recording rates for some kinds of offenses (for example, rape) that *exceeded* 100 percent.[17]

Though the NCS consistently recorded more crime than the UCRs, some argued that it still understated the number of incidents of serious crime because it ignored the transient, the homeless, and prisoner populations in conducting its surveys. It was precisely among these populations, said critics, that more crime was likely to occur.[18] In addition, it was hypothesized that many of the respondents in the NCS failed to report attempted crimes or minimized offenses committed by people they might happen to know.

Similar criticisms were leveled at the UCR statistics for masking the ubiquitous police practice of overcharging and omitting crucial narrative information such as arrest incident summaries, victim statements, and other observational indicators that placed the data within a discernible local context.[19]

My experience as federal monitor led me to believe that among the so-called index crime arrests, there was a swamping of *minor* offenses that masqueraded as *major* and were recorded as such. This was not

---

[17] Reiss, Albert J. and Jeffrey A. Roth (eds.), *Understanding and Preventing Violence,* Washington, D.C.: National Academy Press, 1993, pp. 413–14.

[18] Jencks, Christopher, "Is the Underclass Growing?" in Jencks, Christopher and P. Peterson (eds.), *The Urban Underclass.* Washington, D.C.: Brookings, 1991.

[19] For a discussion on the differences, validity, and reliability of the UCR vs. the NCS, the reader is referred to the following:

Blumstein, Alfred, Jacqueline Cohen, and Richard Rosenfeld, "Trend and Deviation in Crime Rates: A Comparison of UCR and NCS Data for Burglary and Robbery," *Criminology,* Vol. 29, 1991, pp. 237–63.

Menard, Scott, "Residual Gains, Reliability, and the UCR–NCS Relationship: A Comment on Blumstein, Cohen, and Rosenfeld," *Criminology,* Vol. 30, 1992, pp. 105–13.

MacDowall, David and Colin Loftin, "Comparing the UCR and NCS Over Time," *Criminology,* Vol. 30, 1992, pp. 125–32.

Blumstein, Alfred, Jacqueline Cohen, and Richard Rosenfeld, "The UCR–NCS Relationship Revisited: A Reply to Menard," *Criminology,* Vol. 30, 1992, pp. 115–24.

Boggess, Scott and John Bounds, *Comparison Study of UCR, NCS, and Imprisonment Rates,* Ann Arbor, Michigan: National Bureau of Economic Research, University of Michigan, 1993.

to suggest that there weren't proportionately more violent crimes committed in the inner city. Clearly, there were. However, they made up such a relatively small percentage (5 percent) of total arrests that they didn't properly reflect the massive exposure of minorities to various stages of the criminal justice system – most of which had nothing to do with serious or violent crime.

The Crime "Explosion"

Many knowledgeable criminologists saw little evidence of a burgeoning rate of serious crime over the past 30 years. A substantial part of the so-called explosion of crime between 1960 and 1972 is attributable to differences in police practices and reporting procedures, along with the so-called baby boom.

At the height of a putative 29 percent increase in arrests of juveniles between 1967 and 1972 as measured by UCR statistics (including a 326 percent increase in drug arrests), criminologists Martin Gold and David Reimer found no *actual* increase in criminal behavior among teenagers, notwithstanding the fact that offense rates surpassed UCR arrest figures by more than 15 times. Gold and Reimer also found that the *frequency* of delinquency among juveniles declined by 14 percent between 1967 and 1972, while the *seriousness* of the delinquent acts also declined by 14 percent.

The researchers asked the question, "What happened to the teenage crime wave?" and then answered it:

Journalistic accounts of the rise in youthful crime reflected official data such as the FBI Uniform Crime Reports and the records of metropolitan law enforcement agencies. Changes in rates might be accounted for by changes in record-keeping procedures, changes in definitions or policies relating to juvenile offenders, and other reasons, including even deliberate distortion of the data for political purposes. Official data on delinquency are tied so loosely to the actual behavior of youth that they are more sensitive to the changes in the measurement procedures than they are to the object of measurement.... It seems to us that the data we have reported here approximate as closely as any available the real levels and nature of delinquent behavior in the years under consideration. And they simply do not testify to rapidly rising rates of juvenile delinquency.[20]

This was hardly new. From their inception in 1972, "victimization surveys" had yielded results consistent with Gold and Reimer's contention.

[20] Gold, Martin and David J. Reimer, "Changing Patterns of Delinquent Behavior among Americans 13 through 16 Years Old: 1967–1972," *Crime and Delinquency Literature* Vol. 7, No. 4, December 1975, pp. 453–517.

Though the amount of crime was higher than the UCR statistics revealed, crime rates were more stable than the political rhetoric suggested. Overall, crime was declining.

The national perception of out-of-control crime rates was the result of a political process not unlike that described 30 years earlier by the respected symbolic interactionist sociologist Herbert Blumer. As a result, public expenditures had been transferred from other social problems into crime control.[21]

There was considerable evidence to support this conclusion. While the raw numbers generated by UCR reports and periodically released to the press by the FBI regularly suggested rises in both violent and nonviolent crime year to year, when these same reports were broken down by crimes per 100,000 population, and were age adjusted to take into account those in the age categories most at risk, serious crime was shown to have been stable or dropping.

University of Michigan researchers John Bounds and Scott Boggess reanalyzed national crime reports (both UCR and NCS), spanning the years 1979 through 1991, and concluded that the UCR reports demonstrated that, indeed, index crime had fallen 2 percent whereas the NCS simultaneously registered a 27 percent drop in crimes against persons and a 31 percent drop in property offenses during those years (see Fig. 2.1).

Summarizing their findings, they concluded, "(Despite) the widely held belief that there was a significant increase in the level of criminal activity during the 1980s, in general, we find that neither data source depicts increasing levels of crime over this period. The only exceptions seem to be murders among young adults and motor vehicle theft both of which exhibit significant upward trends in the mid to late 1980s."[22]

Even the increase in homicides (concomitant with the drug war), though lamentable, was not new. The record year for homicides in 1991 approximated the levels reached in 1981 and a decade earlier, in 1973, after which homicide rates tended to return to the relatively stable incidence of approximately 10 per 100,000 – the rate that obtained for the previous two decades.

In recent years, homicide rates declined to levels not seen since the rise in crime in the late 1960s (during the putative counterculture revolution). For example, the homicide rate nearly doubled from the mid-1960s to

[21] Chambliss, William J., "Moral Panics and Racial Oppression," in Darney Hawkins (ed.), *Ethnicity, Race and Crime,* SUNY Press, 1993, p. 36.
[22] Boggess, Scott and John Bounds, op. cit. (1993) p. 24.

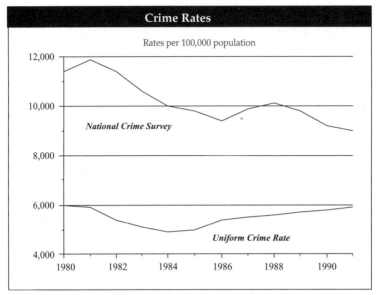

FIGURE 2.1. *Sources:* U.S. Department of Justice, *The Economist*, November 13, 1993.

the late 1970s, peaking at 10.2 per 100,000 population in 1980 and subsequently falling off to 7.9 per 100,000 in 1984. It rose again in the late 1980s and early 1990s and peaked again in 1991 at 9.8 per 100,000. From 1992 to 2000, the rate declined sharply. Since then, the rate has been relatively stable (see Fig. 2.2). The UCRs showed that after falling rapidly in the mid to late 1990s, the number of homicides began increasing in 1999 but remained at levels below those experienced in the early 1970s.

The Character of Violent Crime

In the media and in the public mind, the measure of violent crime too often is the arresting charge. Moreover, most people think that violent crimes involve a murder, a mugging, or a bloody assault resulting in serious injury to, or malicious wounding of, the victim. This is seldom the case.

Most "violence" consisted of a verbal threat or perceived threat. In approximately 68 percent of reported violent crimes, there is no physical injury of any kind to the victim. Of those one in three victims who sustain an injury, half require no formal medical attention of any kind. Most are

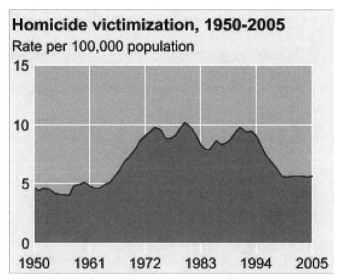

Homicide victimization, 1950-2005
Rate per 100,000 population

FIGURE 2.2. *Sources:* FBI Uniform Crime Reports 1950–2005.

treated on the spot by friends or neighbors and require no further care. About 8 percent of the victims of violent crime go to a hospital emergency room, are treated, and subsequently are released. Slightly more than 1 percent of all victims of violent crime require a hospital stay of one day or more.[23] Most injuries are listed as minor – for example, bruises, black eyes, cuts, scratches, and swelling.[24]

Similar studies on violent crime committed by juveniles suggest that actual physical violence is overstated in most instances. A survey of victims of juvenile offenders in 1981 indicated that there was no physical injury in 72 percent of the "violent" offenses. In 93 percent of those offenses in which an injury did occur, it wasn't serious enough to require formal medical attention.[25]

Ohio State University researchers Simon Dinitz, Donna Hamparian, et al. followed a cohort of more than 50,000 youth from birth to adulthood and identified 811 youths with a record of at least one violent crime. Of

[23] U.S. Department of Justice, Office of Justice Programs, Bureau of Justice Statistics, *Criminal Victimization in the United States, 1991*, National Crime Victimization Survey Report, NCJ-139563, Washington, D.C., December 1992, p. 91.

[24] Ibid.

[25] McDermott Michael J. and M. Joan Hindelang, *Juvenile Criminal Behavior in the United States*, Research monograph, Albany, New York: U.S. National Institute for Juvenile Justice and Delinquency Prevention, Criminal Justice Research Center, 1981, p. 27.

these, 73 percent had neither threatened nor inflicted significant physical harm during the commission of their offenses. Among the 811, a total of 21 youths committed two or more aggravated offenses in which physical harm was threatened or inflicted.[26] Little is new in this politically volatile arena. Witness the comments of a researcher on violent crime a quarter century earlier:

> In the course of this study I was impressed by the number of acts resulting in arrests of juveniles (even those labeled as violent) that do not seem to fit the usual conception of what constitutes a crime. Schoolyard fights, children striking adults who threaten them, minor acts of extortion: all appear with high frequency in police and court records, particularly, it seems, with regard to poor and minority juveniles.

The records may not present the whole picture, of course, but on the basis of the available evidence, I must agree with the conclusion of another study of assaultive boys. "The forbidding legal names of their offenses (Armed Robbery, Assault and Battery with a Dangerous Weapon, Homicide) both represent these boys at their worst and may even over-represent that worst... The minor-league quality of most of what pass[es] for 'assault' is the most striking finding from the general point of view."[27]

Russell and Harper's comments on aggravated assault were particularly on point. In at least 30 percent of the estimated 480,900 arrests for this offense in 1991, the prosecutor declined to proceed. An additional 25 percent to 30 percent were dismissed at the first hearing by the courts. Of the more than 480,000 arrests for aggravated assault, 280,000 went nowhere.[28]

---

[26] Hamparian, Donna, Richard Schuster, Simon Dinitz, et al., *The Violent Few, A Study of Dangerous Juvenile Offenders,* Lexington, MA: Lexington Books, 1978, p. 86.

[27] Strasburg, Paul A., *Violent Delinquents: A Report to the Ford Foundation from the Vera Institute of Justice.* New York: Monarch (Simon & Schuster Division of Gulf & Western Corp.), 1978.

[28] Boland, Barbara, Catherine Conly, Paul Mahanna, et al., *The Prosecution of Felony Arrests, 1987,* NCJ-124140, Cambridge, Massachusetts: Abt Associates, Inc., August 1990.

This study of the prosecution of felony arrests in 10 major U.S. cities revealed many interesting patterns. For example, in Manhattan, New York, 62 percent of arrests for aggravated assault were either declined for prosecution (1 percent) or dismissed outright by the courts (61 percent) in 1987. In San Diego, California, 32 percent of arrests were declined by prosecutors and another 16 percent dismissed. In Portland, Oregon, 32 percent were declined and 25 percent dismissed. In Washington, D.C., 31 percent were declined by prosecutors and 42 percent were dismissed by the courts.

Quite something else was happening. The alleged incidents were hyped from the moment the individual was seen as a potential arrestee and deemed a possibility for criminal justice handling. Indeed, as we made our way into the 1990s, the major actors in the criminal justice drama seemed unusually well rehearsed and ready to arrest as many as feasible on the highest charge possible, prosecute to the outer limits of the law, and seek the longest prison terms potentially available. The fact they couldn't always accomplish these goals was less a measure of permissiveness than a tacit admission that some vestiges of due process had survived the hysteria of the times.

By the early 1990s, it was routine for prosecutors (federal, state, and county) to seek indictments on the highest charge possible, knowing that it would be difficult to make the case. This was done not on the merits of the case, but rather for the potential it presented for using inflated charges as bargaining chips in later plea-bargain discussions.

Even neoconservative commentators had difficulty with the crime statistics being churned out by the Justice Department. As Charles Murray commented in a 1992 article, "Crime is an area where it is difficult to know what to make of the data. One of the most solid crime statistics is the number of homicides, and it shows that homicide victimization among blacks dropped in the '80s and the gap with whites closed modestly. On the other hand, arrests of blacks rose during the 80's after remaining flat during the '70s, and the public perception that crime has gotten worse seems universal."[29]

Murray's comments came on the heels of his compatriots, Wilson and Dilulio, who, in 1989, had concluded, "...most people believe crime has gone down. The Census Bureau's victimization surveys tell us that between 1980 and 1987 the burglary rate declined by 27 percent, the robbery rate by 21 percent. Despite what we hear, 3,000 fewer murders were committed in 1987 than in 1980. Even in some big cities that are in the news for the frequency with which their residents kill each other, the homicide rate has decreased. Take Los Angeles: despite freeway shootings and gang warfare, there were 261 fewer murders in 1987 than in 1980, a drop of more than 20 percent."[30]

One element at work regarding the false perception that crime was increasing probably had to do with changes in the race of the *victims* in

[29] Murray, Charles, "The Legacy of the '60s," *Commentary*, July 1992, p. 27.
[30] Wilson, James Q. and John Dilulio Jr., "Crackdown," *The New Republic*, July 10, 1989, p. 21.

some cities. A study by the respected Vera Foundation in New York City found that though crime overall had fallen in New York City in 1993, it did so in a selective fashion. Whereas crime dropped in those (black and Hispanic) sections of the city with previously high crime rates, it increased in some (predominantly white) areas of the city with traditionally lower crime rates. Though these neighborhood increases were not sufficient to erase the citywide drop in crime, more of the victims were probably white.[31]

The constant hyping of danger around every corner fed on itself. Despite legitimate concerns with violence in some urban schools, for example, the national problem never merited the kind of fear-mongering that came to characterize the issue in the late 1980s and early 1990s. For example, a national crime victimization survey of 10,000 youth who had attended school at any time from January through June of 1989 found that 9 percent of students ages 12 to 19 had been victims of crime in school. Seven percent reported experiencing a property crime of some sort, whereas 2 percent experienced a violent crime. This was a rather startling statistic. Indeed, were we talking about a violent crime as that image conjures up visions of murder, rape, robbery, and aggravated assault, 2 percent is a relatively high figure.

However, when the various crimes were specified, the situation was much less clear-cut. With reference to the violent crime, for example, we see this comment in the text of the report: "Violent crime is largely composed of *simple assaults*. These crimes involve attacks without weapons and may result in minor injury, such as cuts and bruises"[32] (emphasis added).

Another indication of what was actually happening was found in the finding that most of these violent incidents occurred between 13- and 14-year-olds. Older high school students (16- to 18-year-olds, who would be more likely to be involved in serious violence) were the *least likely* to engage in violent incidents.[33] One might conclude that the "violent"

---

[31] This perception also confirmed the comment of one of the leaders in the victims' movement in California to obtain a statewide referendum on a "three strikes and you're out" bill that would mandate life without parole for a third-time felony offender. As he put it, "When bad guys are killing bad guys, that's one thing. But when they start killing *regular people,* that's where you draw the line in the sand" (emphasis added). (Gross, Jane, "Drive to Keep Repeat Felons in Prison Gains in California, *The New York Times,* Sunday Dec. 26, 1993, pp. A1, A22.)

[32] U.S. Department of Justice, Office of Justice Programs, *School Crime: A National Crime Victimization Survey Report,* Washington, D.C.: U.S. Government Printing Office, 1992, p. 1.

[33] Ibid. p. 1.

incidents among the late elementary and junior high school students were, in fact, minor scuffles. The only thing the study proved was that with isolated exceptions, the level of teenaged pushings, shovings, and occasional fisticuffs resulting in "cuts and bruises" probably hadn't changed all that much over the years. Put another way, it's likely that considerably fewer than 1 percent of school students fell victim to bona fide violence in their school in 1989.

This is not to suggest that there was no increase of serious violence in some schools in certain cities or areas of the country. However, there was little indication these incidents were as pandemic as the public had been led to believe.

Most significantly, it did not rule out the possibility that there were enough special interests at work – beginning with the strong national education lobbies – that could conceivably derive some advantage in hyping the dangerousness of their jobs. However, school violence was not as widespread as some teachers suggested.[34] One wonders whether defining of the "crisis" of violence in the schools had not itself partaken of the mechanisms described by Blumer in his explication of how social problems are created.

Indeed, the records compiled by some individual schools seen as having an inordinate amount of violence were themselves more open to interpretation than the press generally granted.

For example, despite the headline in a *New York Times* article, "More Students Are Violent at Young Age: Rising Incidents Shown by Schools Report," the director of operations for a Queens school district recalled that in days gone by, teachers gave the best-behaved students a pocket knife at the end of the year. Now, that knife would be grounds for suspension or expulsion. The superintendent of a Bronx school attributed the alleged high number of violent incidents in his school to overzealous reporting during a period in which an interim principal was in charge.

A History of Violence

Violent crime in the United States comes with a long history, probably tied as much to regional differences as anything. The cultural historian David Hackett Fischer holds that there had always been more violent crime in the southern and southwestern states than in New England. He traced the sources of these regional differences to the markedly different

---

[34] *The New York Times*, December 4, 1993, p. 23.

"folkways" of the four large waves of English-speaking immigrants who settled in New England, Virginia, Appalachia, and the Delaware Valley between 1629 and 1775 – each of which came with distinctly different cultural traditions regarding violence.[35]

Fischer suggested that these early traditions persisted over the subsequent 300 years and are still roughly reflected in the regional differences in rates of violence. Fischer concluded that despite the changes in ethnic makeup that came with later waves of continental and Mediterranean immigrants to various parts of the country, contemporary regional differences in violent crime continued to "show remarkably strong linkages with the distant colonial past."

As he put it:

In 1982, the murder rate in the nation as a whole was 9.1 per 100,000. This level was four times higher than most western countries. But within the United States, the homicide rate differed very much from one region to another. The northern tier, from New England across the northern plains to the Pacific northwest, tended as always to have the lowest rates of homicide: 3.8 in Massachusetts, 2.1 in Maine, 3.1 in Wisconsin, 2.3 in Minnesota, 0.9 in North Dakota, 4.4 in the state of Washington. The middle states, on the other hand, had murder rates that were moderately higher, but below the national average: 5.7 in Pennsylvania, 7.2 in the middle-west, 5.7 in Kansas, 6.0 in Colorado. Homicide rates were much higher in the upper coastal south. The southern Atlantic states averaged 10.9 murders per 100,000 in 1982. The southern highlands and the southwestern states had extremely high murder rates – 14.7 in the west south-central states, and 16.1 in Texas. Homicide rates were also high in the northern cities with large populations of southern immigrants, both black and white. But southern neighborhoods occupied by migrants from the north tended to have low homicide rates. These patterns are highly complex; many ethnic and material factors clearly have an impact. But in ecological terms, homicide rates throughout the United States correlate more closely with cultural regions of origin than with urbanization, poverty, or any material factor.[36]

Fischer dismissed the comparative wealth of some New England states as the reason for the differences in homicide rates, noting, "many a hard-scrabble Yankee hill town is poor and orderly, and more than a few southwestern communities are rich and violent." He also rejected the hypothesis that southern violence is a legacy of racial diversity: " . . . some

---

[35] Fischer, David H., *Albion's Way: Four British Folkways in America*, Oxford: Oxford University Press, 1989. Fischer analyzed "folkways" of each of the four English-speaking waves of immigrants, teasing out empirical indicators for each group's specific ideas, practices, and rules regarding speech, building, family, marriage, gender, sex, naming, child-rearing, age, death, religion, magic, learning, literacy, food, dress, sport, work, time, wealth, inheritance, rank, association, order, power, and freedom.

[36] Ibid. p. 889.

of the most violent communities in the southern highlands have no black residents at all, and are in ethnic terms among the most homogeneous in the nation."[37]

Fischer concluded that from the beginning, the laws of New England gave little latitude to violence. Town schools taught children not to use violence to solve social problems. Town meetings condemned violence and town elites taught each other by example, violence wasn't an acceptable form of behavior. It simply "wasn't done." Fischer found that in the south and southwest, the tradition was precisely the opposite. He noted that the principle of "*lex talionis*" was still part of Texas law, placing few restraints on firearms, with Texas schools and schoolbooks glorifying violence, adding, "Texas elites still live by the rule of retaliation, and murder one another often enough to set an example. Texas is entertained by violence. Massachusetts is not amused . . . , violence simply *is* done in Texas and the southern highlands, and always has been . . . since before the Civil War and slavery and even the frontier – just as it had been done in the borderlands of North Britain before emigration."[38]

As the journalist Richard Harwood summarized the case for generally higher rates of violent crime in the South, "That is the way of the South. An eye for an eye, a tooth for a tooth. If you offend a man's sense of honor – 'dissing' is the street term – he responds with fists, guns or knives. A pickup truck with a rear-window gun rack is a mobile symbol of the male passage from adolescence. Lynching . . . was a regional sport for more than 50 years."[39]

But if regional patterns in violent crime hadn't changed, it was said that surely the incidence of crime, both violent and nonviolent, in our cities had changed in recent years. This wasn't true either. Indeed, there's always been a tendency for more violence in cities.[40] This was just as true when

---

[37] Ibid. p. 890.

[38] Ibid. p. 892.

[39] Harwood, Richard, "300 Years of Crime," *The Washington Post*, December 20, 1993, p. A15.

[40] Kett, Joseph E., *Rites of Passage: Adolescence in America 1790 to the Present*, New York: Basic Books, 1977. For example, Kett chronicled the violent riots among Irish immigrants in New York:

Violence was less quantified (than prostitution and gambling), but much more threatening to life and limb. New York City had eight major and ten minor riots between 1834 and 1871, the most famous and deadly being the Draft Riots of 1863, when mobs, mostly Irish, virtually seized control of the city for three days, terrorizing the police and yielding only before the massed artillery and bayonets of regular soldiers. So many people were caught up in the draft riots that organized gangs of toughs played a relatively minor role, minor at least in comparison to the riots between the Dead Rabbits and the

blacks were a small minority in some urban areas. It is in the cities that the dramas of social inequity are acted out. In 1851, for example, when San Francisco had only 30,000 citizens (few of them black), there were 100 murders. By comparison, there were 75 murders in San Francisco in 1984, when the city's population was 716,000.[41] Similarly, it is estimated that there were 1,300 murders in Los Angeles in 1842, when the city had between 20,000 and 30,000 inhabitants. The homicide rate for children in some cities is said to have been as much as 10 times greater a century ago than it is today. In the late eighteenth century, for example, more than 100 dead children were found annually on the streets or in shallow graves in Philadelphia.

A New Breed?

With rising concern over urban violence in the 1980s and 1990s came inevitable recycling of the familiar "new breed" theory of young offenders, with its implicit, if not blatant, focus upon youthful black male offenders. Indeed, it has become chic for politicians and human service professionals (psychiatrists, psychologists, social workers) to periodically call the public's attention to an ostensibly more unfeeling, cold, and dangerous young offender who stalks the streets. They are in pursuit of a monster – who appears at times to share the qualities of Dracula, perpetually rising from the grave – each time, attested to by a new raft of eyewitnesses willing to go to unusual lengths to provide expert testimony that they have seen him.

In December 1993, the *Los Angeles Times* interviewed Robert Dacy, an inmate serving a life term in the maximum security unit at the California state prison in Tehachapi. Dacy, described by the reporter as "a gaunt old man, dressed in faded blues, suffering from emphysema after decades of chain-smoking hand-rolled cigarettes in his cell," was introduced as

Bowery Boys at election time in 1856 and again in the celebration of July 4, 1858. Before that there had been anti-abolitionist riots in the mid-1830s, and casual street violence was rife at all times (p. 80).

Not insignificantly, the anger of the Irish mobs in the New York riots of 1863 was directed at such symbols as the "colored" childrens' orphanage, which was burned to the ground. The loss of life in these uprisings dwarfed the losses in the Watts and Los Angeles riots of 1992. One recoils from the prospect as to what governmental actions might have been taken and which policies instituted had those disturbances led to anything like the thousands of deaths and injuries that characterized the earlier white-instigated and led riots.

41 Figures obtained from Officer Robert Fitzer, San Francisco Police Department Historian.

an expert of sorts on the "new breed" of criminal walking contemporary streets and alleys. Dacy opined that "in the old days, the professional criminal had some kind of code. We would never consider pulling the trigger just for the hell of it." It was only parenthetically remarked that Dacy (presumably of an "older breed") had an arrest record dating back to 1947, having been sentenced to prison after kidnapping a 4-year-old boy for ransom. He was caught after leading police on a high-speed chase, along the way exchanging shots with the FBI and wounding an agent.

The new breed theory was routinely bolstered by human service professionals in their roles as spokespersons for law enforcement. Michael Zona, a psychiatrist with the Los Angeles Police Department, put it this way: "(W)hat psychiatrists call 'anti-social personality disorder' who 'basically has no feeling,' is more prevalent today than in the past."[42] Indeed, one could probably better make the case that the image of the criminal as portrayed in films and the media was about all that had changed. As one critic put it, "Today's screen murderers are young, sexy and not a bit sorry."[43] The implications of this statement were probably as frightening as the number of currently "not a bit sorry" delinquents on the streets.

One measure of the so-called new breed of young offender was contained in the supposed growth in stranger-on-stranger violent crime in the 1980s. However, this premise was highly questionable. A 1993 study of murder in the largest urban counties of the nation revealed that things hadn't changed as much as we had been led to believe. Approximately 80 percent of murder victims and their killers were acquainted with or related to each other. Fully half of all the murder victims had a social or romantic relationship with the murderer. *Among black victims, 87 percent were either acquainted with or related to the murderer.*[44]

Meanwhile, when it came to *interracial* homicide, data on incidents involving a lone victim and a lone offender revealed that almost 9 in 10 were murdered by someone of the same race.[45] Another study showed

[42] *Los Angeles Times,* Sunday, December 26, 1993 (reported in *The Washington Post,* December 26, 1993, p. A19).

[43] Weinraub, Bernard, "Despite Clinton, Hollywood Is Still Trading in Violence," *The New York Times,* December 28, 1993, p. A1.

[44] Dawson, John M., *Murder in Large Urban Counties, 1988,* NCJ-130614, Washington, D.C.: Bureau of Justice Statistics, U.S. Justice Department, May 1993, p. 4.

[45] Whitaker, Catherine J. and Lisa Bastian, *Teenage Victims: A National Crime Survey Report,* NCJ-128129, Washington, D.C.: Bureau of Justice Statistics, U.S. Department of Justice, May 1991, p. 11.

13 Known Homicides[46]			
Age	Nativity of Parents	Mentality	Circumstances
15	Irish	Febleminded	Street Hold-Up
15	U.S. (white-colored)	Normal	Burglary
17	Norway-Germany	Normal	Burlary
17	German	Normal	Robbery
18	Polish	Psychopathic	Robbery
18	German	Psychosis	Robbery
18	Finnish	Feebleminded	Burglary
18	Irish-German	Psychosis	Robbery
19	U.S.	Normal	Burglary
19	Polish	Normal	Burglary
20	German	Feebleminded	Jealousy
21	U.S.	Normal	Burglary
24	Italiand	Normal	Hold-Up

FIGURE 2.3. Chicago Series of Outcomes – Males

that 92 percent of the homicide victims of white juveniles were white, whereas 76 percent of the victims of black juveniles were black.[47]

Patterns of behavior among violent offenders hadn't changed much over the decades. In their influential study, *Delinquents and Criminals: Their Making and Unmaking,* William Healy and Augusta F. Bronner followed the criminal careers of 920 Chicago male delinquents from 1909 to 1914. From this group, they categorized 420 as "most serious" offenders. Thirteen (3 percent) of the 420 boys were subsequently convicted of murder. In the kind of analysis common today, the authors commented that, "the youthful age at which many of the homicides were committed is remarkable."[48]

Healy and Bronner diagnosed 7 of the 13 young murderers as "normal mentally," two as "psychotic, one "of psychopathic personality," and three as "mentally defective." More interesting for purposes here, was the ethnic background of these youthful murderers (see Fig. 2.3).

These early case studies were particularly pertinent in light of more recent studies regarding chronic or violent mostly black urban delinquents

---

[46] Ibid. p. 246.
[47] Fox, James Alan, "Teenage Males are Committing Murder at an Increasing Rate," prepared for the National Center for Juvenile Justice, Revised, April 18, 1993, p. 2.
[48] Healy, William M. D. and Augusta Bronner, *Delinquents and Criminals: Their Making and Unmaking, Studies of Two American Cities,* New York: MacMillan Co., 1926, p. 32.

who increasingly are characterized as a different kind of antisocial animal.

In their classic "cohort analysis" of 3,475 delinquent Philadelphia boys done in the late 1960s and early 1970s, Wolfgang, Figlio, and Sellin identified 627 "chronic offenders" who accounted for a disproportionate share of the serious offenses – much the same as the 420 "serious" youthful offenders identified in the Healy and Bronner study earlier in the century.

Among Wolfgang and Figlio's 627 serious and chronic urban youthful offenders, 10 (1.5 percent) were involved in homicide.[49] This was half the percentage of those identified in Healy and Bronner's smaller sample from the 1920s.

Similarly, a landmark series of studies on violent youthful offenders by researchers at The Ohio State University found that within their cohort of 985 "most violent" offenders, 15 had been arrested for murder.[50] This was precisely the same percentage found in the Wolfgang studies (1.5 percent), but half that found by Bronner and Healy in the 1920s (3 percent). One factor that affected the findings was the fact that by the time the Wolfgang–Figlio studies were completed, modern medical shock trauma procedures had significantly advanced, increasing the chances of survival by a victim of an attack or assault.

However, even this consideration couldn't wipe away the differences in murder rates between the 1920s and the 1970s – particularly in light of the research of William Doerner suggesting that response time for ambulances in minority communities is demonstrably longer than similar calls made for emergency assistance in white communities. As a result, more serious assaults end up as homicides among victims needing prompt medical attention.

In April of 1993, the U.S. Justice Department's Office of Juvenile Justice and Delinquency Prevention engaged the National Center for Juvenile Justice to analyze more than 1.4 million cases handled by the juvenile courts of 10 selected states from 1985 through 1989.[51] Although the study found that juveniles charged with violent offenses (that is, homicide, aggravated assault, violent sex offenses, and robbery) took up a

[49] Wolfgang, M, R. Figlio, and T. Sellin, op. cit.

[50] Hamparian, Donna et al., op. cit. p. 86.

[51] Butts, Jeffrey A. and D. J. Connors, "The Juvenile Court's Response to Violent Offenders: 1985–1989," *OJJDP Update on Statistics*, Washington, D.C.: U.S. Department of Justice, April 1993. (The states surveyed were AL, AZ, CA, MD, MS, NE, OH, PA, UT, and VA.)

disproportionate amount of time and effort of juvenile courts, those charged with violent offenses were a relatively small part (7 percent) of the average juvenile court caseload.

A significantly larger percentage of the violent charges against black youths were dismissed outright (31 percent) than among white youths (24 percent), again suggesting more overcharging of black juveniles at the time of arrest than of similarly situated white juveniles.[52] Cases dismissed this early in the process were more commonly thrown out when it became clear that the crime was overstated, with virtually no sustainable evidence warranting proceeding with the original charge. More than one in three (37 percent) of those *convicted* in juvenile courts of violent offenses were placed on probation – again suggesting that the alleged violence was not as serious as the formal charge implied.

Again, the popular response to this kind of statistic is to suggest that it only demonstrates the permissiveness of juvenile courts. However, that is not what the researchers found. As the summary note put it: "The NCCJ study... debunks a popular misconception that juvenile court sanctions for violent offenders are tantamount to a slap on the wrist. To the contrary, the record shows that juvenile courts respond severely to violent offenders, perhaps even more severely than do adult courts."[53]

Though a larger percentage of black youths (11 percent) were brought to juvenile court charged with violent offenses than white youths (5 percent) and youth of other races (7 percent), the fact remained that 9 of every 10 black juveniles appearing in juvenile courts were *not* charged with violent offenses.

Even among those (ostensibly more serious) delinquents committed to public juvenile correctional facilities, only 19 percent were committed for violent offenses.[54] More significantly, black youths were at double the risk of being waived to adult criminal court (4 percent) as were white youths (2 percent). Again, in almost one-third of the juvenile court cases (31 percent) involving black youths charged with violent crimes, the charges were dismissed – suggesting that arrest charges were routinely overstated.

The 1991 Annual Report of the Cuyahoga County, Ohio (Cleveland) Juvenile Court revealed that nearly one in three of its juvenile cases was

[52] Ibid. p. 6.
[53] Ibid. p. 1.
[54] Wilson, John J. and James C. Howell, *A Comprehensive Strategy for Serious, Violent, and Chronic Juvenile Offenders*, Washington, D.C.: Office of Juvenile Justice and Delinquency Prevention, U.S. Dept. of Justice, July 1, 1993, p. 3.

"resolved at intake," suggesting that they were not as serious as the original charge indicated. However, that overstated original charge is what went into the official record.[55]

The Black Criminal "Profile"

The largest group of African-Americans brought to the jail in Duval County, Florida, were arrested for "driving with a suspended license." This was particularly interesting in view of the fact that it is not a charge that is usually "reported" – that is, called in by a complainant. Rather, it tends to happen in the course of something else – for example, an individual stopped for some other reason and found to have an expired or suspended driver's license. In Florida, drivers' licenses were regularly suspended if the driver moved without informing the Department of Motor Vehicles of the change of address.

The common practice of stopping "suspicious" cars driven by black men who fit a profile accounted for a large number of these arrests.[56] It renewed a Southern tradition from a half-century earlier, when black men were regularly arrested and jailed for being "suspicious" – fitting a profile – but accused of no particular illegal action.[57]

It is a now a routine technique of law enforcement in the "war on drugs" to approach "targeted" individuals in buses, trains, stations, and

[55] *Juvenile Court of Cuyahoga County, Ohio: Annual Report 1991*, p. 13.

[56] In February 1993, the American Civil Liberties Union of Maryland filed a federal lawsuit challenging the practice of stopping motorists on the basis of a profile. The suit charged that state troopers target black men driving expensive cars. The profile was described as focusing on a young black man or men wearing expensive jewelry, driving expensive cars such as sports cars, wearing beepers, and carrying lists of telephone numbers. The lead plaintiff in the suit was Robert L. Wilkins, a 29-year-old Harvard Law School graduate who worked as a public defender in Washington, D.C., who was stopped for speeding. As *The Baltimore Sun* summarized the incident, "It was about 6 a.m., and Mr. Wilkins' aunt and uncle were asleep in the back seat of the car, a rental Cadillac.... The trooper went back to his cruiser, and returned to the vehicle to ask (the driver) to sign a release form consenting to a search. Mr. Wilkins identified himself as a lawyer, who had a case in a Washington court that day, and told (the trooper) that he had no right to search the car unless he was arresting (the driver). The trooper asked if they had 'nothing to hide, then what was the problem?'

Another trooper arrived and detained the car for a half hour while a narcotics-sniffing German shepherd was brought to the scene by an Allegany sheriff's deputy.... The plaintiffs were ordered out of the car. They refused at first, noting that it was raining, but got out because they were afraid of being attacked by the dog. The dog sniffed the car without visible reaction. The episode lasted about 45 minutes." (*The Baltimore Sun*, February 13, 1993, p. 1)

[57] Donaldson, H., "The Negro Migration of 1916–18," *The Journal of Negro History*, Vol. 383, 1921, pp. 415–16.

airline terminals and request that they present identification and tickets, explain the purpose of their travels, and finally, at times, to con-
sent to a luggage search. The person is targeted by police on the basis
of being a suspicious person. With the introduction of the PATRIOT
Act,[58] these activities have widened and intensified. There is also every
indication that racial profiling has increased, not decreased, in recent
years.

The profiles targeting primarily black and Hispanic males reiterated a
very old and familiar tradition mentioned by Schoenberg and Evans.[59] In
many parts of colonial America, blacks were required to carry "passes"
and after the Civil War were barred from entering certain states.

It is no surprise that when African-Americans are involved, civil liberties have always played second fiddle to whatever the immediate needs
of law enforcement might be. In September 1992, it was discovered that
the police department in Oneonta, New York, had compiled what came
to be referred to as "the black list." The list consisted of all the black
and Hispanic males registered at the State University of New York at
Oneonta. It had been made available to the local police by school administrators following an attack on a local elderly woman who told police
she thought she might have cut the intruder on the arm with a knife,
and she believed her attacker was black. The list was used to track down
black and Hispanic students in dorms, on their jobs, even in the shower –
taking them to the local police department for questioning. The police
demanded that each student account for his whereabouts at the time of the
attack and bare his arms. As one of the school's instructors commented,
"The only probable cause they had was, 'You're black!' – 'You're a
suspect.'"[60]

A similar example came to light in November of 1993 when it
was revealed that the Denver police department had compiled a list of

[58] 107th Congress HR 3162 in the Senate of The United States, October 24, 2001.
[59] Schoenberg, Peter and Risa Evans, "Unspeakable Suspicions: The Racist Consensual
Encounter," *The Champion* (National Association of Criminal Defense Lawyers),
November 1993, pp. 4–8.

   The authors point out that, "Today is not the first time in history that blacks have
been subjected to this dual deprivation. In many parts of colonial America, blacks were
required to carry 'passes.' Both before and after the Civil War, blacks were barred from
entering certain states." (Tracey Maclin, "The Decline of the Right to Locomotion: The
Fourth Amendment on the Streets," *Cornell Law Review*, Vol. 75, No. 1258, 1260 at
n.4, 1990.)

[60] Schemo, Diana Jean, "Anger over List Divides Blacks and College Town," *The New
York Times*, Sunday, September 27, 1992, p. 40.

6,500 names of "suspected" gang members. The list was put together on the basis of the following; people who

- Flash gang signals,
- Dress in the colors of a gang,
- Have been arrested in the company of gang members or are known to associate with gang members, as well as,
- Other information provided by informants.[61]

Though blacks represented fewer than 5 percent of Denver's population, they accounted for 57 percent (3,691) of those on the list. Hispanics made up another third, whereas whites, who represented 80 percent of Denver's population, accounted for fewer than 7 percent of those on the list of suspects. Significantly, the 3,691 blacks listed meant that *well over two-thirds of all the black youths and young men between ages 12 and 24 living in the Denver had been profiled as suspects.*

As Rev. Oscar Tillman, a senior official of the National Association for the Advancement of Colored People in Denver, commented, "This is not a crackdown on gangs; it's a crackdown on blacks." He accused the police department of "peddling a fear of blacks" to quell demands for public safety. Said Rev. Tillman, "My own son, who is now in the Army, was targeted many times... The police would stop him in front of our house and want to know, 'Where did you get that expensive watch?' He got it as a graduation present from us."

Ignored by the press was the fact that similar lists were kept in most large cities of the United States. They were not public, but used by police in targeting young men for harsher handling in the criminal justice system should there be an opportunity for arrest.

In the 1980s, the U.S. Justice Department assisted localities in developing computerized lists of juveniles labeled by the police as "shodi" youths, that is, "serious and habitual offenders." These lists were universally disproportionately black or Hispanic and were as likely to reflect police arrest activity as to demonstrate any pattern of violent behavior on the part of the young persons labeled.

In Duval County, Florida, the Sheriff's department kept such a list that was as racially skewed as the one in Denver, with well over 80 percent of the youngsters listed on it being black. It came within a local "social context" in Duval County wherein one of every four African-American

---

[61] Johnson, Dirk, "2 out of 3 Young Black Men in Denver Are on Police List of Gang Suspects," *The New York Times*, December 10, 1993.

juveniles between the ages 15 through 17 had been arrested during the last four months of 1991 alone.[62]

Casting the Net of Social Control

I soon discovered that although African-American males made up only slightly more than 12 percent of the county's population, more than half of those being brought to the jail each day were African-American. Moreover, because they were less likely to make even the most modest of bail bonds, they tended to be kept in the jail longer (often for want of $200 and a bondsman), thereby accounting for 65 percent to 70 percent of the jail's daily population.

The criminal justice system had penetrated the African-American community of this predominantly white county deeply and widely. A review of first-time admissions revealed that one in four of all the young African-American males (ages 18 to 34) living in the county were being jailed at least once each year.[63] Indeed, between 75 percent and 80 percent of all 18-year-old black youths living in the county could look forward to being jailed at least once before reaching his 35th birthday.

Among juveniles, the figures were even more depressing. This adult jail regularly held upward of 150 teenagers, 85 percent of them African-American.

When juvenile arrests were factored in with the adult figures, the risk to an African-American male of being jailed in this county again approached the 90th percentile – just as Blumstein had predicted some 30 years earlier.[64]

I thought that these figures would shock local authorities. Few seemed concerned. Far from being an embarrassment, the depressing numbers were taken as a badge of honor, demonstrating the fortitude of local law enforcement authorities in getting tough on crime. The disproportionate racial figures were quoted in a letter the State's Attorney circulated to be read in all the county's secondary schools, threatening adult handling.

---

[62] Jacksonville Community Council, Inc., "Young Black Males Study: A Report to the Citizens of Jacksonville," Summer, 1992.

[63] Miller, Jerome, *Duval County Jail Report,* submitted to The Honorable Howell W. Melton, U.S. District Judge, Middle District of Florida, Jacksonville, June 1, 1993, pp. 82–83.

[64] Blumstein, Alfred, op. cit. (1967) p. 99.

The presumption was that African-American youths and young adults were being dragged off to jail in such large numbers because, as one judge commented to me, "they're the ones committing the violent crimes." In the wake of this kind of analysis, the county invested approximately $100 million in building new jail complexes and was quite willing to spend approximately $150,000 to $200,000 per day to operate them.

It turned out, however, that something was very wrong with the premise meant to rationalize all the *sturm und drang* over violent black offenders. Relatively few could be found. Though African-American males committed a disproportionate share of violent crimes, particularly homicide and robbery, there were not so many of these crimes to explain the thousands being brought into the criminal justice system. A relatively small percentage of the routine arrests, trials, and jailing of blacks had to do with violent crime. However, most were stashed in jail for "public order" offenses, misdemeanors, and lesser felonies (see Fig. 2.4).

At times, it appeared that much of the frenetic criminal justice activity in Duval County was treasured less for its crime-fighting potential than to make some vague point like "upholding the integrity of the system," a phrase I heard repeatedly from the local State's Attorney to explain the large numbers of individuals brought to the jail on warrants for such things as missing court dates, driving with suspended licenses, and being in "technical" violation of conditions of misdemeanor probation.

The fact that there were a host of alternative strategies and tactics immediately at hand, short of arrest, by which defendants could be encouraged to fulfill these legal obligations seemed not to matter – particularly as one moved down the socioeconomic ladder. It was an early harbinger of what later came to be known as broken window theory – as the Right honed its marketing skills, to the detriment of all concerned.

As federal court monitor, I had unusual access to the police summaries of each arrest as well as the individual criminal histories of those being jailed. Counting heads, reading files, and interviewing those who sat in jail, I heard the stories that challenged the stereotypes. In its worst light, the criminal justice system seemed to be concentrating its considerable power disproportionately and discriminatorily upon African-Americans. In the "best" light, it was being inappropriately employed to deal with a wide range of serious personal and social problems that tend to afflict the cantankerous poor and minorities. It carried a resonance with sociologist John Irwin's unhappy characterization of jails as places for "rabble management."

Offense	Number
Homicide – Murder	23
Homicide – Justified	0
Negligent Manslaughter	4
Kidnapping	16
Forcible Rape	118
Forcible Sodomy	6
Forcible Molesting	65
Robbery	153
Robbery (outdoors)	64
Assault – Aggravated	*680*
Assault – Simple	*670*
Assault – Intimidation	3
Arson	19
Extortion/Blackmail	3
Burglary – Residence	*328*
Burglary – Non-residential	200
Theft (petit) – Pickpocket	20
Theft (petit) – Purse Snatching	4
Theft (petit) – e.g., shoplifting	*1,266*
Theft (petit) – Building	12
Theft (petit – Coin Device	3
Theft (petit) from Motor Vehicle	71
Theft (petit) – Any Other	139
Theft (grand) – Pickpocket	4
Theft (grand) – Purse Snatching	2
Theft (grand) – Shoplifting	79
Theft (grand) – Building	19
Theft (grand) – Coin Device	3
Theft (grand) – Motor Vehicle	32
Theft (grand) – Any Other	125
Motor Vehicle Theft	267
Counterfeit/Forgery	135
Fraud – Swindle/False	49
Fraud – ATM/Credit Card	9
Fraud – Impersonation	4
Fraud – Welfare Fraud	1
Fraud – Wire/Computer	0
Embezzlement	61
Stolen Property – Buy/Sell	49
Criminal Mischief	80
Drugs – Sell/Buy/Transport	*973*
Drugs – Paraphernalia	166

FIGURE 2.4. Bookings by Charge in Duval County Jail, July–August–September 1991 (*Ten most frequent offenses in bold and italic type*).

Offense	Number
Non-Forcible Sex	48
Obscenity – Phone/Porn	4
Gambling	6
Sex – Commerce/Prostitute	251
Liquor Violations	248
Weapons Violation	251
Traffic (not including DUI)	2,505
Driving under the Influence	783
Breach of Peace	141
Disorderly Intoxication	469
Worthless Checks	317
Other Offenses	2,666
Unknown UCR Code	139
TOTAL	**13,756**

(The reader should recognize these were charges, not convictions. Approximately half of the felony charges would not be sustained.)

FIGURE 2.4 continued.

Here is a list of the charges for which I found individuals had been arrested and "booked" into the Duval County Jail (Jacksonville, Florida) during three months in 1992.

The 10 most frequent charges for which individuals were jailed in the new Duval County Jail are shown in Figure 2.5.

Though very little of this police activity had to do with violent or serious crime, the perception cultivated by local officials was one of an out-of-control violent crime rate calling for more law enforcement

Offense	Percentage of all Arrests
"Other"	18.4
Traffic (excluding drunk driving)	16.3
Shoplifting	9.1
Driving under the Influence	7.0
Assault (simple)	6.6
Drug Sale/Purchase	6.0
Assault (aggravated)	5.0
Disorderly Intoxication	3.0
Worthless Checks	3.0
Burglary	3.0

FIGURE 2.5. Ten Most Frequent Charges in Duval County Jail.

armamentaria and larger jails. The figures available never bore out this contention.

Although gross figures showed a 31 percent increase in crime between 1988 and 1991 (years during which local authorities were engaged in an aggressive jail building program), when arrests were broken down by offense, quite another pattern emerged. Though 3,273 more persons were arrested from July through September of 1991 than during the same three months in 1988, 85 percent of the increase fell under two categories: traffic (excluding drunk driving) and other, a loosely defined category that included such crimes as "feeding of alligator or crocodile," "resisting without violence," "trespassing," "nonsupport," "feeding unsterilized garbage to animals," "contempt," "impersonating a massage license holder," and 2,990 others.

Here are a few examples:

- A young African-American man suffering from asthma and pneumonia who had been in the jail 22 days on $1,500 bond. He had been jailed on a "capias" (violation of probation) for not paying $35.00 in court costs on a four-month-old petit theft (shoplifting) charge. While in jail he had lost his job as a truck driver.
- An unemployed 25-year-old African-American male jailed for "petit theft" and kept there for want of $353 bond. The police arrest report stated, "Investigation revealed that suspect walked into Woolworths then suspect went to the candy isle [sic] and picked up two Snickers valued at $1.58. Suspect was observed by store security placing the items in bag without paying for the merchandise. Suspect was apprehended by store security and held for police. Suspect had to be physical [sic] restrained by store security since suspect was uncooperative."
- A 38-year-old African-American electronic engineer – well-dressed, middle-class – jailed for " ... 'allowing an unauthorized operator to drive'.... The suspect, who owns the listed vehicle, allowed the co-defendant to drive his car. She did not have a driver's license and NCIC advised that her license was suspended for failing to pay traffic fines. He was arrested."
- A 21-year-old African-American woman student arrested for "driving with license suspended," "violation of right of way," "no proof of license," "failure to use seatbelts," and "failure to yield at an Intersection." Her license had been suspended for failure to pay traffic

fines. When arrested, note was made of the fact that she had two children with her, ages 1 and 3, "not in restraints," and a child age 4 "not
in a seat belt." No note was made of what happened to the children
as the woman was taken to jail.

- A frail 81-year-old African-American man arrested for "gambling" (that is, playing cards for money with friends on his front
  porch).

- A mentally disordered 59-year-old African-American man arrested for
  "breach of peace" at the main gate of a nearby naval base. He had
  tried to enter the base, refused to leave.

- A 30-year-old man in the jail after having been released from a
  Florida state prison two weeks earlier where he served six years. He
  was out three days and as per the law went to the police station
  to inform them that he was back in town. He was arrested on the
  spot. He had apparently not paid a four-year-old traffic fine. He was
  in state prison when the warrant had been issued and was unaware
  of it.

These patterns weren't confined to Duval County. Studies in jurisdictions as disparate as Rochester, New York,[65] and Los Angeles[66] showed
similar patterns. An interesting glimpse at what was happening emerged
in Michigan.

In 1993, the Michigan Council on Crime and Delinquency issued a
report on arrest trends in that state that found, while index (felony)
crimes actually *decreased* by 12 percent between 1981 and 1991, the total
number of arrests had increased substantially – concentrated mainly on
lesser offenses. Nearly 9 out of 19 persons arrested in Michigan in 1991
were arrested for nonviolent offenses, nonindex offenses accounting for
78 percent of all the arrests in the state during 1991. Arrests for these

---

[65] Report to Monroe County Bar Association Board of Trustees, *Justice in Jeopardy*, May
1992.
[66] Austin, James, *Los Angeles County Sheriff's Department Jail Population Analysis and
Policy Simulations*, San Francisco, California: National Council on Crime and Delinquency, August 21, 1992.
 In this study, the NCCD researchers found that of the 168,400 bookings into the
Los Angeles County Jail in 1991, the most frequent offense was motor vehicle violation
(22 percent), followed by drug "possession" (19 percent), driving under the influence
(8 percent), theft (7 percent), and assault (5 percent).

lesser offenses increased 46 percent between 1981 and 1991.[67] Even of reported index crimes (those classified as serious by the FBI), a relatively small percentage were listed as violent (12.5 percent in 1991).[68]

What about the differences among rural, suburban, and urban areas? When comparing reported index crimes from rural areas with those from Wayne County (Detroit), there were some differences. However, given the economic disasters in the city, they were not all that striking. For example, larceny accounted for 60 percent of the reports in rural areas and 44 percent in the city. Burglary accounted for 26 percent of the rural reports and 20 percent of reports in the city. Aggravated assault made up 6 percent of the rural reports and 8 percent of the city reports. Reports of rape (2 percent), robbery (0.6 percent), and homicide (0.1 percent) totaled about 3 percent of all crime reports in rural areas. These same offenses accounted for about 10 percent of crimes reported in the city (rape, 1 percent; robbery, 7.8 percent, and homicide, 0.3 percent).[69] The most telling difference between urban and rural area crimes involved robberies. The fact remained that ninety percent of rural arrests and 82 percent of city arrests had virtually nothing to do with violent crime.

In 1992, Pennsylvania State University's Center for the Study of Law and Society completed a study for the Pennsylvania Sentencing Commission comparing "offender processing" in 1980 with 1990.[70] While there had been a negligible 2 percent increase in convictions for violent crime in the decade between 1980 and 1990, there was a *20 percent drop* in those being processed into the prison system for violent offenses, whereas those brought into the state's prisons for property crimes *increased 72 percent*.

Similar patterns prevailed among drug offenders. There had been an 8 percent increase in those charged with drug sales between 1980 and 1990, but there was a 500 percent increase in those charged with *possession* of drugs. Whereas there was a 112 percent increase in those convicted

---

[67] Research and Evaluation Division, Michigan Council on Crime and Delinquency, *Trends in the Michigan Criminal Justice System: From Crisis to Chaos*, Lansing, Michigan, March 1993, p. 26.

[68] Index crimes are the eight offenses selected by the FBI as indicators of serious crime in the nation. The index offenses include aggravated assault, arson, burglary, homicide, motor vehicle theft, larson, rape, and robbery.

[69] Michigan Council on Crime and Delinquency, op. cit. pp. 23–24.

[70] Steffensmeier, Darrell, "Incarceration and Crime: Facing Fiscal Realities in Pennsylvania," Pennsylvania Commission on Sentencing, September 1992.

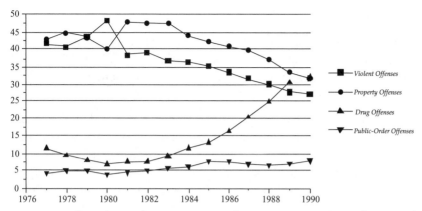

FIGURE 2.6. Percentage of new court commitments to state prisons, by type of offense, 1977–1990. *Source:* National Prisoner Statistics and National Corrections Reporter.

of drug sales, there was an 863 percent increase in those convicted of possession. This was consistent with national statistics on state prison admissions. The percentage of individuals sent to prison for violent crimes fell progressively between 1980 and 1990.[71]

Among inmates making up the daily population of state prisons (as distinct from new admissions), there was also a substantial (21 percent) *drop* between 1980 and 1990 in putatively violent inmates.[72]

Despite findings such as these, the mavens of the Right continued to hawk the view that most of the inmates in state prisons were violent – a dishonest practice that continues to excite them to this day. Even in the heyday of the ideologically inspired Reagan–Bush Justice Departments, the highest figure the in-house researchers could produce regarding the percentage of violent inmates in state prisons was 46.6 percent.[73]

---

[71] D. Gilliard, "Prisoners in 1992," Bureau of Justice Statistics, May 1993, NCJ-141874, Appendix, Table 1, p. 10. The percentage of new court commitments for violent offenses to state prisons had generally fallen over the prisons decade and a half. For example, 42% of new commitments to state prisons were violent in 1997, whereas that figure had fallen to about 27% by the early 1990s.

[72] Ibid. p. 10.

[73] U.S. Department of Justice, Bureau of Justice Statistics, *Correctional Populations in the United States, 1991*, NCJ-142729, Washington, D.C.: U.S. Government Printing Office, 1993, Table 4.3.

Overkill

What about those African-American adults who, after being arrested, were jailed, duly convicted, and sentenced? Even among the "guilty" black men, a disturbing pattern emerged in Duval County:

- An 18-year-old African-American sentenced to 45 days for "petit theft." He had been charged with having taken one cigarette out of a pack on a store shelf, smoking it, and returning the pack to the shelf. While awaiting sentencing, the bond had been set at $1,503 or $150 cash. He was unable to come up with the $150 and sat in the jail until his trial.
- A 32-year-old homeless African-American man sentenced to 1 year for burglary, having taken two clocks from a rescue mission. He was caught running away with the clocks and charged with a third-degree felony.
- A 31-year-old African-American sentenced to four months in jail for taking a pair of sunglasses from a store. He was originally charged with petit theft, but the charge was amended to first-degree misdemeanor.
- A 37-year-old unemployed African-American man sentenced to 150 days in jail for nonpayment of child support.
- A 32-year-old African-American man sentenced to 60 days for shoplifting a package of lunch meat.
- A 29-year-old African-American man sentenced to 60 days for petit theft from a gas station convenience store, having put food items into his pants pocket.
- A 25-year-old African-American given 60 days in jail for walking out of a store wearing a pair of tennis shoes for which he had not paid.
- An 18-year-old African-American sentenced to 60 days for selling fake "crack" to vice police for $20. After the sale, he rode off on his bike, but was later apprehended.
- A clearly psychotic 54-year-old African-American male sentenced to 60 days for "trespassing" and "resisting arrest without violence." He had been harassing customers at a convenience store and refused to leave.
- A 65-year-old African-American man sentenced to 60 days for "attaching a license tag not assigned" and "driving with a suspended license." (The license was suspended for not paying a fine.)
- A 34-year-old African-American sentenced to 60 days for shoplifting a package of meat from a supermarket. Pending sentencing, he had been

home, having paid the $150 cash bond. He returned to court for his sentencing and jailing.

Absent some unusual condition, in very few of these cases, would a white person of moderate means with adequate legal representation expect to be jailed. It would be a fluke – as it were, "pure and simple." The same could not be said of a black male, even given moderate means.[74]

This is not to suggest that some action could not have been taken in each of the aforementioned cases. The matter of whether confinement in an expensive maximum-security jail was ultimately the most productive approach is open to question, however.

In those rare cases in which black men were allowed an "alternative" to incarceration, similar overreaction emerged. In the "home detention" program, for example, an electronic bracelet was attached to the person's ankle whereby he or she was unable to leave home without alerting a central computer system. Leaving home resulted in a new charge, usually followed by an additional term of imprisonment.

Here are some of the African-American males sentenced to this "alternative":

- A 72-year-old man sentenced to one year for driving under the influence on his moped. He was allowed into the program due to his age and poor health (arthritis). Unable to work, he was placed on 24-hour curfew. He lived alone with his dog.
- A 43-year-old man sentenced to four months for resisting arrest without violence. He was a first offender and practicing attorney. While on home detention he lived with a friend and maintained dual custody of his 5-year-old daughter.
- A 22-year-old placed on home detention and charged with sale and possession of crack cocaine. He was placed on the program due to a handicap. He had been shot and totally blinded. He was undergoing eye surgery while in home detention. He lived with and was cared for by his girlfriend and their two children.
- A 25-year-old sentenced to 30 days for petit theft and resisting and opposing a police officer. He was in the advanced stages of Hodgkin's disease and while on home detention had to be rushed to a hospital emergency room on two occasions to be resuscitated. The young man died one week prior to the expiration of his 30-day sentence.

[74] Chiricos, Theodore G. and William D. Bales, "Unemployment and Punishment: An Empirical Analysis," *Criminology*, Vol. 29, No. 4, November 1991.

At best, the justice system was engaged in some kind of overkill. Was this an anomaly confined to one southern jail? Unfortunately, it wasn't. A large study by Rutgers criminologist Todd Clear and his associates of more than 7,000 probationers in six jurisdictions found precisely the same patterns with reference to those who were brought to jail for violating the conditions of their probation. As the authors commented:

> The relatively minor nature of most probationer violations and the small proportion of violators overall help to highlight the unnecessary costs that would surely be incurred if new programs such as intensive supervision and electronic monitoring are instituted for traditional probation populations instead of for those individuals – higher-risk felons diverted from prison – for whom they were intended. For the risks posed by the 7501 probationers studied here, such controlling strategies would have been excessive.[75]

In Duval County, local authorities had forged a path that led to the arrest and jailing of a substantial part of the white underclass and virtually every potential arrestee among African-American young men in the county. What was going on here?

The gross overrepresentation of African-American men in the jail was greatest among those accused of the puniest offenses. Most were dragged into the justice system charged with minor misdemeanors and lesser non-violent felonies. Though black males made up only 12 percent of the county's population, they constituted 71 percent of those jailed for misdemeanors – by far the largest group of offenders arrested and jailed in the county. Two-thirds of those who received jail sentences for misdemeanors in Duval County were African-American. Whatever was going on here didn't have to do with violent crime.

The practice of arresting minorities for petty public order charges came with a very specific and old tradition. Citing the studies of Donaldson on the Negro migration of 1916 to 1918,[76] Brown noted that

> ...one of the reasons why Blacks migrated to the North in large numbers was their resentment of the law enforcement tactics of Southern county and police officials – that is, these officials were paid so much per head for every man they arrested. As a result, large numbers of Black men were rounded up for petty infractions of the law such as littering and disorderly conduct. Others were arrested on various charges of suspicion.

---

[75] Clear, Todd R., Patricia M. Harris, and S. Christopher Baird, "Probationer Violations and Officer Response," *Journal of Criminal Justice*, Vol. 20, 1992, p. 1.
[76] Donaldson, H., op. cit. pp. 415–16.

Heavy fines were often levied for such small violations and frequently those who could not pay were imprisoned. Carlton[77] notes that at the turn of the century, Black men were often picked up in Louisiana when the labor market was in low supply and workers were needed for road work, ensuring that poor or working-class black males would have to spend time in prison. Black men were picked up in this fashion in Louisiana when the labor market was in short supply and workers were needed for road work.[78]

Many of these practices continued to dog black men as they moved to the North during the great migration earlier in the twentieth century. Studies in Pittsburgh showed a near doubling of arrests of blacks for the petty offenses (disorderly conduct, drunkenness, and the crime of "suspicion") over one seven-month period during 1914–15 versus the same period in 1916–17.[79]

A Department of Labor study revealed that in 1916 and 1917, black men in Cleveland, Ohio, were routinely arrested by police and sent to prison on the charge of "suspicion."[80] "It was," as Brown commented, "this type of action by police that accounted for much of the 'Negro Crime' reported during this period (in the 1920s) in the United States."[81]

In the 1980s and 1990s, as resources were progressively withdrawn from programs associated with the "root causes" of crime (e.g., poverty, unemployment, racial bias, breakdown of the family), a prosecution-driven system arrived on the scene, claiming expertise in solving theretofore intractable crime problems, while militantly ignoring the profound social disruptions from which they had sprung.

It had a narcotic effect on the middle class of the nation not unlike that attributed by conservatives to the poor under the welfare state – in effect, feeding an unnatural dependency on another government bureaucracy. This time, the criminal justice system aggressively took up the slack for the family, for the churches, and for other traditional community agencies and individuals by slapping down the helping hand and extending the

---

[77] Carlton, Mark T., *Politics and Punishment*, Baton Rouge, Louisiana: Louisiana State University Press, 1971.

[78] Brown, Shirley Ann Vining, *Race as a Factor in the Intra-Prison Outcomes of Youthful First Offenders*, unpublished Ph.D. thesis, Sociology, Ann Arbor: University of Michigan, 1975.

[79] Epstein, Abraham, *The Negro Migrant in Pittsburgh*, New York: Arno Press, and *The New York Times*, 1969, pp. 46–54.

[80] Tyson, F. D., *Negro Migration in 1916–17*, Report of U.S. Department of Labor, Washington, D.C.: Government Printing Office, p. 141.

[81] Brown, Shirley Ann Vining, 1936 – *Race as a Factor in the Intra-Prison Outcomes of Youthful First Offenders*, Ph.D. thesis, Sociology, Race Relations, 76–9354, Xerox University Microfilms, Ann Arbor: University of Michigan, 1975.

strong arm of law enforcement. The only tangible result was a further erosion of civility.

Forgotten in all this was the possibility that the criminal justice practices used with such abandon might eventually touch the majority in some more direct fashion. As Princeton Professor of Humanities Alexander Nehamas put it:

> ...the mechanisms used to understand and to control marginalized and ostracized groups (are) also essential to the understanding and control – indeed, to the constitution – of "normal" individuals. Thus, the constant surveillance of prisoners that replaced physical torture as a result of penal reform came to be applied also to schoolchildren, to factory workers, to whole populations (and, we might add, to average citizens, whose police records, medical reports and credit ratings are even today becoming more available and more detailed).[82]

What the white majority had prescribed for the African-American male in the American justice system would eventually reach a larger host group. Where might all this arresting and jailing of the poor lead? More importantly, what would the long-term consequences be for a society that used its justice system so readily and so heavy-handedly with its black population? Were there to be similar police presence and practices in the white suburban communities, how many citizens might be netted there?[83] Occasionally, the dismal prospects fell out of the closet.

Well into my tenure as the jail monitor, I was taken aback to find that in Duval County, with its 700,000 inhabitants, the local police maintained 330,000 active criminal records. On any given day, there were 75,000 outstanding (unserved) arrest warrants for persons charged with

[82] Nehamas, A. "The Examined Life of Michel Foucault: Subject and Abject," *The New Republic*, February 15, 1993, pp. 30–31.

[83] In a recent article on common offenses committed by the average citizen, two staff reporters for the *The Wall Street Journal* admitted to having committed at least 16 crimes (of 25 "common offenses") carrying maximum jail terms of 15 years and fines as much as $30,000. The common offenses included such things as "gambling illegally, drinking in public, engaging in prohibited sex acts, speeding, buying stolen goods, lying on an application, patronizing a prostitute, possessing marijuana, etc." A not insignificant number of the poor and minorities are arrested and jailed for precisely these and similar common offenses. (Adler, Steven and Wade Lambert, "Common Criminals: Just About Everyone Violates Some Laws, Even Model Citizens – Many Often View Legal Rules as Foolish or Intrusive, but Careers Can Be Hurt," *The Wall Street Journal*, March 12, 1993, p. A1, A4.)

misdemeanors and 10,000 warrants for those charged with felonies. There were an additional 82,000 Duval County citizens eligible for arrest on any given day for driving with suspended licenses.[84]

On one of my visits to Jacksonville, I turned on the local TV evening news to find the Sheriff announcing "Operation Safe Streets" – a massive effort by police to arrest and jail the approximate 82,000 citizens thought to be driving with suspended licenses. As the Sheriff put it, "If you are bent on a life of crime, we will deal with you severely. We have your pictures." The implications of defining one in five in a county's adult population as "bent on a life of crime" went unaddressed.

Thirty years earlier, President Lyndon Johnson's Commission on Law Enforcement and the Administration of Justice found that almost half of all the arrests in the United States had to do with lesser offenses. That percentage had not changed much by the mid-1990s. As Peter McWilliams noted in 1994, " ... Roughly half of the arrests and court cases in the United States each year involve consensual crimes – actions that are against the law, but directly harm no one's person or property except, possibly, the 'criminal's.'"[85]

McWilliams' argument was a familiar one. Earlier debates in the 1960s and 1970s were couched in terms of "victimless" crime and policies of "radical nonintervention" originally advanced by Edwin Schur and others.[86] The absolute numbers of persons being arrested and jailed for these and other lesser offenses had increased dramatically by the early 1990s. Four million people were arrested each year for consensual crimes, with minorities grossly overrepresented.

Lest the reader think I exaggerate, here is one day's list of unserved arrest warrants I chanced upon one day in the jail (see Fig. 2.7). The police were assigned to find, arrest, and jail these individuals. This particular batch of warrants had been issued for offenders who had failed to appear in court. For most of these individuals, the question was not whether society had a right to expect accountability of them, but whether arrest

---

[84] Most licenses had been suspended for nonpayment of traffic fines or for matters such as not notifying the Department of Transportation of a change of address.

[85] McWilliams, Peter, op. cit. p. 1.

[86] Schur, Edwin M., *The Americanization of Sex,* Philadelphia, Pennsylvania: Temple University Press, 1988. *Crimes without Victims: Deviant Behavior and Public Policy,* Englewood Cliffs, New Jersey: Prentice-Hall, 1965; and Hugo Adam Bedau, *Victimless Crimes: Two Sides of a Controversy,* Englewood Cliffs, New Jersey: Prentice-Hall, 1974.

and jailing were the only means to that end, or whether they might not, indeed, compound the problem in many of these cases.[87]

When the justice juggernaut is wheeled out into the streets, it tends to crush those who are more easily identifiable by their race and socioeconomic status than by their criminal behavior. Sustained law enforcement intrusion into the lives of urban African-American families for mainly minor reasons left the inner cities with a classic situation of social iatrogenesis – a "treatment" that maims those it touches – exacerbating the very social pathologies that lay at the root of much crime.

Along the way, it spawned a justice industry fully capable of producing sufficient numbers of new clientele to validate its need and justify its growth. The "hostile procedure" of criminal law carried its own virus for

[87] The "failure to appear" phenomenon placed what was happening in bold relief. The arrest warrants had been sought because of a policy emanating from the State's Attorney's office. He saw it as a way to maintain what he called the integrity of the system. However, it was also clear that a few simple administrative procedures could have appreciably lowered the failure to appear rates without resort to arrest.

It was the practice in Duval County of requiring arrestees who had been brought to the jail to call the court clerk's office the following day to find out the date of their court hearing. Though about 90 percent did so, a small percentage did not. Given the somewhat disorganized lives of many of those who were being routinely jailed, this should not have come as any surprise.

Most of those who didn't show up for their court hearing had not jumped bail. It was more likely to be a matter of negligence, forgetfulness, inability to schedule one's life, losing a paper that instructed them to call back, etc.

A 1982 national study concluded that willful failures to appear (in which the defendant absconded or had to be returned by force) did not exceed 4 percent of all released defendants, including those who committed crimes as disparate as felonies and misdemeanors. (Pryor, Donald E. and Walter F. Smith, "Significant Research Findings Concerning Pretrial Release," *Pretrial Issues,* Washington, D.C.: Pretrial Services Resource Center, February 1982, p. 4.1.) A 1990 study revealed that as many as 24 percent of all released felony defendants failed to make their scheduled court appearances, though only about 8 percent remained fugitives. More interestingly, those charged with the putatively lesser felonies and released on recognizance or unsecured bond had the highest rates of failure to appear. Persons charged with violent offenses were more likely to appear for their scheduled court hearings. (U.S. Dept. of Justice, Bureau of Justice Statistics, *Felony Defendants in Large Urban Counties, 1990,* NCJ-141872, Washington, D.C.: 1993, p. 11). My impressions from the Duval County, Florida, system suggest that half or more of these releasees would subsequently have had their cases dismissed or reduced to misdemeanors.

Some jurisdictions (for example, Alexandria, Virginia) had found that giving the defendant a specific date for his or her court appearance at the time the person was released from jail dramatically cut the failure to appear rate. Similarly, a reminder mailed or phoned to the defendant a few days before the court date appreciably lowered the rates of failure to appear.

Simple Assault	2
Breach of Peace	10
Consumption of Alcohol on Vendors' Premises	3
Consumption of Alcohol on City Property	10
Damage to Public Lands	1
Disorderly Intoxication	1
Dog at Large	1
Dog Running Loose without Leash	1
Dogs Prohibited on Beach	3
Drinking in Public	25
Driving on Prohibited Ocean Front Dune within 1000′ of Water	1
Driving Other Than Where Vehicles Are Permitted	1
Employee in License Premises	1
Failure to Transfer Title/Registration	1
Fishing without a License	4
Harvest of Redfish in Closed Season (Oversize Red Fish)	1
Harvesting Shellfish Prohibited Area	1
Illegal Dumping	1
Lewd and Lascivious Behavior	2
Loitering/Prowling	6
Molestation of Nesting Birds	1
Offering for Lewdness	1
Open Containers in Vehicle	1
Operation of Unnumbered or Unregistered Vessel	1
Operating a Wrecker without Registering with Sheriff	1
Opposing Police Officer	1
Petit Theft (mostly shoplifting)	44
Possession of Firearm with Altered Serial Number	1
Possession of Alcoholic Beverages by Person under 21	12
Possession of Alcohol in City Park	5
Possession of Controlled Substance	1
Possession of Drug Paraphernalia	5
Registration Not Properly Displayed	1
Retail Theft	2
Resisting Arrest without Violence	2
Saltwater Harvesting without License	1
Sale of Alcoholic Beverages to a Person under 21	3
Soliciting for Prostitution	5
Trespassing	4
Trespassing on School Property	1
Truancy	2
Violation of Adult Entertainment	3
No Inoculation, Registration, City Tags (dog)	1

FIGURE 2.7. Failure to Appear Arrest Warrants, Duval County.

later mischief, which, in a perverse turn, demanded more police, arrests, prosecutors, and prisons.

What results from the widespread intrusion of the criminal justice system into the lives of so many local citizens? For one thing, it guarantees that a substantial part of the population will have a viable criminal history record. Take, for example, the "end of sentence" phenomenon that characterized at least one-third of the arrestees brought into the jail in an average year.

The end of sentence phenomenon was an intriguing set of practices born of administrative necessity and bordering on the surreal. A large group of sentenced inmates stay in the jail a relatively short period of time. This consists of those who are arrested and, at their first or second hearing in court, plead "guilty," are forthwith sentenced to time served, and released. In pleading guilty, these individuals immediately have a conviction added to their criminal record. In many cases, particularly among the more indigent, it is questionable whether they are, in fact, guilty. The guilty plea is often the only means by which impoverished detainees can avoid a longer stay in prison. The delay between an arrest and a disposition can be long, even for a minor offense or one in which the case is subsequently dropped or the charge lowered.

Though a person arrested and jailed might initially deny the charges, the message is gotten across before the first court hearing that pleading "not guilty" will result in being returned to the jail until such a time as counsel can be appointed and a court date scheduled – conceivably weeks or months. Bond in most of these cases is low – under $2000 (requiring $200 or less and a bondsman). Usually lacking property as collateral (even if the arrestee managed to come up with the 10 percent), such inmates are unlikely to find an accommodating bondsman. These defendants learn that simply pleading guilty to the charge will result in their being immediately sentenced, given credit for time served in jail, and released. Understandably, most take the quicker exit from jail. It makes its own kind of warped sense.

About 40 percent of all the releases from the jails in Duval County annually were end of sentence releases. The majority served sentences of less than a week. The charges included offenses such as loitering, disorderly intoxication, theft of a single pack of cigarettes, theft of a pencil and mascara worth less than $5.00, driving with a suspended license, no driver's license and making threats, possession of a marijuana cigarette, eluding and public drinking on a bicycle, driving with a suspended license (for having an expired tag), playing a radio too loudly, ordering a steak in a restaurant without money ("I tried to leave because I knew I didn't have any money"), trespassing (a young man had refused to leave the apartment of the man he had been living with), and allowing dog to run at large.

In the ideal world envisioned by those who planned these moral dilemmas and awkward confrontations, most of the aforementioned individuals would be better off jailed or extruded further from civil society. Unfortunately, given our present milieu, I fear most Americans would probably agree.

3

Unanticipated Consequences

On March 6, 1990, an 18-year-old African-American man was acquitted of a felony by a black jury in the District of Columbia. That would not have been unusual. However, something else was afoot in this courtroom. As *The Washington Post* described the scene:

One young juror was crying when the verdict came. The prosecutor gasped as it was read. The crashing sound in the courtroom was the defendant, whose elation propelled him backward over his chair.[1]

Three weeks later, a letter arrived at D.C. Superior Court. It was from one of the jurors who wrote that though most of the jury believed the defendant to be guilty, they had bowed to those who "didn't want to send anymore Young Black Men to Jail."

The incident was an unsettling example of one of the unanticipated consequences of "wars" against crime. It would be repeated in a number of jurisdictions nationally.[2] In communities in which so many families

---

[1] Gellman, B. and S. Horwitz, "Letter Stirs Debate after Acquittal: Writer Says Jurors Bowed to Racial Issue in D.C. Murder Case," *The Washington Post*, March 29, 1990, p. A1.

[2] According to nationally syndicated columnist Samuel Francis, "...in Smith County, Texas black jurors recently admitted that their decision to deadlock a verdict in the trial of a black defendant was influenced by an earlier trial in which white jurors declined to indict a white policeman for the shooting of a bedridden black woman during a drug raid. The policeman claimed the shooting was accidental, and the jury believed him." Francis commented that, "Whether that was right or not, it had nothing to do with the black jurors' decision in the later, entirely separate case....From Fulton County, Ga., come several similar incidences of racially motivated decisions by black jurors in cases involving black defendants. At least six federal court cases since March have ended in mistrials, and each one involved racially divided juries. 'In each case,' reports Lisa

have seen their sons, brothers, fathers, and friends dragged into the justice system, the idea of galvanizing and organizing the residents against the "criminals" – as though they were outsiders and enemies – is naive. The expectation that the average citizen in an inner-city neighborhood will inform on young men in trouble so they might be arrested and jailed is equally naive. The cumulative effect of the massive intrusion of the criminal justice system into the community had come to be seen by many as equally destructive and threatening as the harm done by most offenders.

The depth of the alienation could be found in an informal survey of affluent African-Americans in Los Angeles taken by *The Wall Street Journal*. It revealed that many well-off blacks saw injustice in the ways in which the justice system treated the white policemen who were convicted of beating Rodney King versus those charged with beating the white truck driver, Reginald Denny. Though most whites saw no comparison in the two cases, among blacks, poor and affluent, another message was taken away.

John W. Patton, an affluent 40-year-old black senior litigator for Litton Industries Inc., "when asked about justice for people who, like him, are black," told *The Journal* reporter, "The justice system just doesn't work when we're involved, unless it's justice on our heads." The reporter summarized the matter this way:

Mr. Patton's view of the law, despite his current success, may forever be colored by an experience he had in Cleveland about 28 years ago, when he and a friend were stopped by three police cars as the two men drove down the street in an older auto. The officers leaped out, guns drawn and barking instructions: 'Driver, put your hands on the wheel', said one. 'You! Put your hands out the window', another snapped at Mr. Patton. The pair was then ordered out of the car and told to 'assume the position'.

'When we asked why they'd done this', he recalls, 'they said it was because one of us was sitting in the back seat and that made us look like we were about to commit a robbery'.... Even now, years later, Mr. Patton believes that most police officers see the profile of a potential criminal as 'any black male.' There is 'nothing to prevent that from happening to me now', he says, adding: 'You can't even imagine all the ways a black man can be killed where a white man would not even be at risk'.[3]

Kaufman of the Fulton County Daily Report, 'black jurors appear to have refused to convict black defendants.'" (Francis, Samuel, "Criminal Justice Hues and Cries," *The Washington Times*, September 4, 1994.)

[3] Holden, Benjamin A. "Harsh Judgment: Many Well-Off Blacks See Injustice at Work in King, Denny Cases," *The Wall Street Journal*, Vol. 122, No. 8, August 10, 1993, p. A1.

Six months after the 1992 Los Angeles riots, the residents of economically strapped South Central Los Angeles turned down a $1 million
federal anticrime "Weed and Seed" grant, in the process jeopardizing an
additional $18 million the federal prosecutor said was targeted for social
services. Local African-American Councilman Mark Ridley-Thomas representing the district told the City Council:

My fear is that (the grant) will widen the chasm between police and the community
– against a backdrop of what can still be described as a volatile situation.... In
fact... the Weed portion of this program has been imposed on communities of
color with the purpose of incarceration and not rehabilitation.

The federal prosecutor was to have overseen the process. A local community leader who had attended the meetings in which the anticrime
strategies were outlined said that the plan was really about "seeding"
the community with informers and "spies" who would identify young
black men for eventual arrest and imprisonment. The contrasting views
on "Weed and Seed" were best summarized by the Los Angeles-based
African-American Urban Strategies group in these statements:[4]

President George Bush (January 27, 1992)

Weed and Seed works this way: First, we join federal, state and local forces to
"weed out" the gang leaders, the violent criminals, and the drug dealers who
plague our neighborhoods. When we break their deadly grip, we follow up with
part two: we "seed" those neighborhoods with expanded educational opportunities and social services. But key to the seed concept will be jobs generating
initiatives such as Enterprise Zones.

The Urban Strategies Group, Labor/Community Center (September 1992)

Weed and Seed works this way: First, it imposes a federal police presence in inner
city, low-income neighborhoods that violates the civil rights and civil liberties of
community residents. Then, it commandeers existing federal social service programs and places them under the authority of the Department of Justice, the FBI,
and the Immigration and Naturalization Service. Then, it subordinates the eco-
nomies of low-income target areas to the enterprise zone concept so that the labor
and resources of the community serve the interests of business. In short, the federal Weed and Seed program is a move towards the imposition of a police state
on the public life of low-income communities of color.

As a result of this gap in perceptions, a code of silence pervaded many
high-crime areas – not so much a result of intimidation of witnesses

---

[4] *A Call to Reject the Federal Weed and Seed Program in Los Angeles,* Van Nuys, California: Urban Strategies Group of the Labor/Community Strategies Center, 1992.

by criminals (as it is so often portrayed by police and the media), but rather as a defense against intimidation by outsiders who represent a law enforcement model that is seen as potentially more destructive to individuals and families in the community than out-of-control crime. Only those who have been involved in the most egregious violence are likely to be reported to the police by community residents.

A week after completing a year that logged a record number of murders, the city of Richmond, Virginia, provided another example of the level of alienation between law enforcement and the community. The police indicated that of the 117 murders committed in that city in 1992, at least 20 of the murderers were known by police but no one in the community was willing to identify them for fear of retribution from those they might identify. Another explanation seemed more likely.

Three days following another homicide in Richmond, a security guard was gunned down execution style in a McDonald's parking lot. The killing occurred in full view of "hundreds" of teenagers, yet *not a single witness was willing to cooperate with police at the scene.* An angry chief of police called it a "conspiracy of silence." True to form, the city manager called for an ordinance that would allow Richmond police to round up witnesses and hold them for as long as 60 hours as a way of getting information. He admitted he made the proposal "out of absolute, total frustration."[5]

With the United States coming out of the brief depression immediately following World War I and about to enter the Great Depression, the great University of Chicago social psychologist George Herbert Mead first posed the central dilemma presented to those who would use the justice system to negotiate what he referred to as the social settlement – a dilemma that plagues governments run increasingly by lawyers who seem, at times, constitutionally unable to recognize the limitations of their models.

As Mead conceived it:

We assume that we can detect, pursue, indict, prosecute, and punish the criminal and still retain toward him the attitude of reinstating him in the community as soon as he indicates a change in social attitude himself, that we can at the same time watch for the definite transgression of the statute to catch and overwhelm the offender, and comprehend the situation out of which the offense grows.

But the two attitudes, that of control of crime by the hostile procedure of the law and that of control through comprehension of social and psychological conditions, cannot be combined.

5 *The Washington Post*, January 12, 1993, p. D1.

To understand is to forgive and the social procedure seems to deny the very responsibility which the law affirms, and on the other hand the pursuit by justice inevitably awakens the hostile attitude in the offender and renders the attitude of mutual comprehension practically impossible[6] (emphasis added).

Mead hoped that the newly invented juvenile court would breach the wall of ignorance he saw in adult justice procedure. In juvenile court, we would, for the first time, be able to consider theretofore "irrelevant" factors associated with delinquency and crime – the familiar root causes that so agitate conservatives, such as unemployment, health problems, emotional disturbance, disorganized communities, socially debilitating environments, poor education, family disorganization, and socioeconomic pressures.

Mead's vision gave sense to the comment attributed to Harvard law professor Roscoe Pound some 30 years after its founding, that this event was as significant in the history of Western jurisprudence as the signing of the Magna Charta. Mead's hopes were never realized and Pound's assessment of the potential of the court fell far short of the mark Mead outlined.

The juvenile court immediately began mimicking adult justice procedure, and was eventually characterized by the U.S. Supreme Court as embodying the worst of both worlds – punishment called treatment, with few rights. Mead and Pound were on to something, however. They recognized the potential that lay dormant in the conception of the juvenile court.

Despite the fact that the juvenile court has seldom allowed itself more than a fleeting glimpse of its original promise, it continues to represent a threat to the legal system. So long as it exists, there is always the remote possibility that, Phoenix-like, it might one day rise from the ashes and overwhelm us all with reason and decency. It is why we still hear a constant drumbeat from prosecutors and politicians calling for its abolition. Meanwhile, the destructive adult criminal justice model continues apace unchallenged and the juvenile court apes it as never before.

The Very Long Arm of the Law

Here is how a reporter described a model class being conducted in a majority black local high school just outside Washington, D.C.:

---

[6] Mead, G. H. "The Psychology of Punitive Justice," *The American Journal of Sociology,* Vol. 23, 1917, pp. 577–602.

With his fingers laced behind his head and the Prince George's County police officer grabbing hard at the pager clipped to his waistband, the smile disappeared from 17-year-old Carl Colston's face.

Later, Colston described his thoughts as the officer frisked him. "You feel uncertain. You don't know what they are going to do."[7]

The courses were sponsored by the county police, educators, the local chapter of the National Association for the Advancement of Colored People, and the black lawyers' association and represented an attempt to teach people how they are to handle themselves if stopped by police. "I have been pulled over by the police numerous times," said Hardi Jones, president of the county NAACP.

It was an odd admission – though an entirely common experience for a black man in the United States. The classes constituted a bizarre reality. So many black youths and young men were being brought into the justice system that it seemed a good idea to "train" them for the experience – whether or not they had broken the law. So many were being brought into the system for so many minor reasons that it had been trivialized to the point of irrelevance.

The scope of the problem was brought home to me in Duval County (Jacksonville), Florida. The sheer numbers of those going through the jail suggested that a considerable percentage of the county's citizens – most of them falling at the lower end of the socioeconomic spectrum – had active criminal records of some type on file. Among African-American males over age 35, the percentage probably exceeded 80 percent.[8]

The practice of arresting black men for "suspicion," more contemporaneously labeled as engaged in "furtive movements" comes with a tortured tradition. One reason black men migrated to the North earlier in the century, was precisely to flee the law enforcement tactics of southern sheriffs and local police who were commonly paid by the head for every black man they arrested. They were routinely rounded up for petty infractions like littering, disorderly conduct, on the charge of "suspicion." Black men were picked up when the local labor market was in short supply and workers were needed for plantation or road work.

These practices dogged black men as they moved to the North during the great migration in the early 20th century. Pittsburgh for example,

---

7 "The Dreaded 'Encounter' with Police," *The Washington Post,* January 18, 1994, Metro Section, p.1.
8 Miller, Jerome, *Report of Jail Monitor on Duval County Jails,* June 1993 (filed with Federal Court, Middle District of Florida, Jacksonville).

nearly doubled arrests of blacks for "disorderly conduct, drunkenness, and "suspicion" during seven month period in 1914. In fact, these kinds of arrests made up the bulk of black men jailed at the time.

Paradoxically, nearly a century later, the practice was revived under different circumstances. New York City's "Stop and Frisk" practice is a case in point. Black men who looked "suspicious" were regularly "stopped" and "frisked" as a common police tactic. The rationale was that the dramatic drops in crime in NYC during the preceding decade and a half were primarily due to aggressive police tactics.

However, little evidence could be adduced that this was true. Crime fell at similar rates in cities across the country, most of which didn't engage in NYC's aggressive police practices. Many questioned the tactic – which entered the police lexicon as a variation on a theretofore common practice in the failed "drug wars."

Between January 2006 and March 2010, the police had made nearly 52,000 stops in an 8 block area in Brooklyn, entering each "stopped" individual into a police database.

According to *The New York Times*, this amounted to, "(N)early one stop a year for every one of the 14,000 residents of this area. Fewer than 9 percent of the stops were based on a 'fit description.' It was far more likely that the police would list "furtive movements" as the reason for the stop.

This would normally be seen as "intrusive" – and certainly would be called that in most communities. However, more significantly, something over a quarter of all the "stops" in the black community were labeled "aggressive." During these encounters, police regularly brandish a revolver and a hesitant or objecting person can find himself forcibly thrown face down to the pavement. One would be hard-pressed not to conclude that subjecting something over a 150,000 citizens of the city to this kind of handling might ultimately carry some negative "unanticipated consequences" for police-community relations.

4

Race Baiting and Kitsch

Of Tufthunters and Toadies

Despite their reputation for civility and a sense of the proper, Victorians could be blunt when the occasion fit. They had a series of expressions that aptly described a certain type of politico, referring to such an individual as a "tufthunter," or perhaps, a "cringing parasite and toady" – all apt descriptions of the contemporary American politician when he or she turns to matters of crime.

Crime has seldom been more effectively exploited than in recent years. It has become a metaphor for race, hammered home nightly on TV news and exploitative crime shows replete with the images of dark-skinned predators.

Crime has never eluded the reach of politicians who may want to posture on race without ever having to say its name. It provides the ideal venue for the "rhetorical wink" – defined by former Clinton appointee-to-be Lani Guinier as a process "whereby code phrases give a well-understood but implicit meaning while allowing the speaker to deny any such meaning."[1] Ms. Guinier made the unforgivable error of saying "race" out loud.

Though there may have been some ambivalence in using to the "wink" when it came to welfare, it was all but blinding when conversation turned to matters of crime. It gave greater return at less risk.

---

[1] Guinier, Lani, "Clinton Spoke the Truth on Race," *The New York Times*, Op-Ed, October 19, 1993, A29.

Patrick Moynihan's original treatise on welfare had an obvious racial focus (that is, "The Negro Family"). However, white liberals were uncomfortable with it. Only when crime was tied to the single-parent black household did his analysis gain widespread acceptance. Escalating the same set of dynamics, Charles Murray's rationales in *Losing Ground* weren't accepted by liberals until they were associated with inner-city crime. Hovering over it all was Murray's long-time obsession with race.[2]

---

[2] In the wake of his book on welfare, *Losing Ground,* Murray embarked on a new project. As *The New York Times* put it: "One thing Charles Murray knows how to do is generate controversy. In 1984, his book 'Losing Ground' argued that social programs did more harm than good and proposed, as 'a thought experiment,' that the country simply abolish them.... That may not be Mr. Murray's last uproar. Now at the American Enterprise Institute, a public policy research center ... he sits at an important crossroads of ideas and politics. Collaborating with Richard Herrnstein, a Harvard psychologist who has in the past been in the center of disputes about heredity and intelligence, he is asking one the most explosive questions a social scientist can pose: whether there are differences in intelligence between blacks and whites that help explain differences in their economic and social standing."

The *Times* went on to note that Murray had difficulties in obtaining support for his project from various private "think tanks," though apparently, many toyed with the idea. Because he had obtained a grant from the conservative Milwaukee-based Bradley Foundation, he was offered an office at the more liberal Brookings Institution, which, according to Brookings president Bruce MacLaury, could do so without facing the question of whether to place him on its staff. MacLaury added that the racial aspects of the research would have made the decision to offer him (Murray) a staff position more difficult. Murray's project was turned down by "his friend and fishing partner," Ed Crane, president of the libertarian Cato Institute. "It's not an area that I wish to get involved in," said Mr. Crane, who was otherwise full of praise for Mr. Murray's work. When *The Times* interviewed Murray in 1990, he was at the American Enterprise Institute. Up until that time, he had been with the conservative Manhattan Institute, but the conservative policy research group was reluctant to follow him into this thicket, and he left, after an eight-year association, taking with him an annual foundation grant of $100,000.

The *Times* summarized the issues in this way: "'This book is not about blacks and whites,' he (Murray) says when asked about the current work. It is mostly about the tensions between America's egalitarian philosophy and the unequal way in which talents are distributed, he said.... Mr. Murray's collaborator in the new research, Professor Herrnstein attracted national attention in 1971 when he predicted that as society became more meritocratic, individuals with low I.Q.'s would congregate on the bottom of the economic scale, intermarry and produce offspring with low I.Q.'s ... this year, in *The Public Interest*, a conservative journal, he (Murray) attacked a report by the National Academy of Sciences on the state of black America. He said the report had overemphasized racial discrimination in explaining the status of blacks and had ignored 'intractable race differences' in I.Q. test results." (DeParle, Jason, "Washington at Work: An Architect of the Reagan Vision Plunges in to Inquire on Race and I.Q.," *The New York Times*, November 30, 1990, p. A22.)

A year later, Murray and Herrnstein were teaching a course entitled "Human Ability and Public Policy: Reconciling the Ideal of Equality and the Reality of Differences" at the

David Duke, former leader in the Louisiana Ku Klux Klan and American Nazi Party, in his 1992 Louisiana race for the U.S. Senate, garnered an overwhelming majority of white votes statewide by focusing on crime – avoiding all but the slightest direct mention of race. The demagoguery had its roots in the post-Reconstruction period. As the sociologist, Shirley Brown, noted,

> After the (Civil) War, the crime problem in the South became equated with the "Negro Problem" as Black prisoners began to outnumber White prisoners in all Southern prisons...the terms "slave," "Negro," and "convict" were interchangeable.[3]

By the 1990s, what was begun in the South had overtaken much of the nation. The caricature of the big-time (that is, African-American) drug dealer riding around in a BMW had replaced the Reagan-era welfare queen as the political currency of choice. It was one of those urban myths characteristically reserved for minorities – in this instance, that of the young African-American male as a predator.

As *The New York Times* television critic, Walter Goodman, put it,

> ...the suspects seen on television being arrested in muggings and shootings are almost always black men in their teens and '20s, and they figure hugely in the prevailing anxiety among blacks as well as whites over personal safety.
>
> ...The rules of journalism require that violent crimes be covered, but it is the rules of the tabloids that require them to be covered prominently, frequently and graphically.... Their thirst for blood is unshakable. If a fresh murder is not available, a nasty accident will serve.... The attention given to crimes of violence turns reality into the surreal. Positive stories don't lend themselves easily to the hysterical language of television reporters, whose vocabularies are not by and

University of Denver. The course, picketed by about 40 faculty members and graduate students, was described by International Studies professor Alan Gilbert as "pseudo-scientific advocacy for eugenics...associated with Nazism...and based on fallacies about IQ testing." Murray, then described as a fellow of the American Enterprise Institute, said, "I've never had people picket me before, but they were polite pickets. They did not chant slogans or obscenities." In writing of the incident, the conservative *Washington Times* noted, "The two professors believe individuals and ethnic groups are unequal in intelligence, and suggest that social and economic inequality results from racial and genetic differences rather than social factors." (Innerst, Carol, "Teaching of Racial Inequality Raises Ire," *The Washington Times*, January 16, 1991, p. 3.)

The Murray/Herrnstein book was published in September of 1994. Asked earlier about what the book might say on race and crime, Murray told an associate that it would, for the most part, reiterate some of the findings from Wilson and Herrnstein's 1985 book on crime and race, *Thinking about Crime.* described later herein.

[3] Brown, Shirley, op. cit. pp. 18–19.

large, extensive (what would they do without the words "tragic" and "shocking" and "brutal"?) where daily life becomes a theater of horror.[4]

Creating Moral Panics

Sociologist William Chambliss cited the 1964 presidential campaign of Barry Goldwater as having successfully distilled the essential elements of a classic moral panic on violent crime and making it the cornerstone of his political campaign. Here's how Goldwater expressed it:

Tonight there is violence in our streets, corruption in our highest offices, aimlessness among our youth, anxiety among our elderly... security from domestic violence no less than from foreign aggression, is the most elementary and fundamental purpose of any government.[5]

He then placed violent crime in the obligatory racial context by tying it to the civil rights movement. As he put it,

Our wives, all women, feel unsafe on our streets. And in encouragement of even more abuse of the law, we have the appalling spectacle of this country's Ambassador to the United Nations (Adlai Stevenson) actually telling an audience – this year, at Colby College – that, "in the great struggle to advance human civil rights, even a jail sentence is no longer a dishonor but a proud achievement." Perhaps we are destined to see in this law-loving land, people running for office not on their stainless records but on their prison record.[6]

Chambliss also made note of the historic tendency of "moral panics" to be tied to ethnic and racial oppression – regularly targeting groups perceived as associated with welfare, immigration, or crime.

Although Goldwater blatantly mixed crime with race, he was undone by a greater panic among middle-class white males at that time – the Vietnam War. Nevertheless, the 1966 Republican congressional campaign built on the themes introduced by Goldwater.[7]

The Nixon presidential campaign took the same path in 1968 – linking riots and disorder associated with assassinations of Martin Luther King and Robert Kennedy to violent crime – all with a distinctly black face to it. Nixon's campaign manager and Attorney General designate, John

---

[4] Goodman, Walter, *Critic's Notebook:* "Crime and Black Images in TV News," *The New York Times,* December 23, 1993.

[5] Quoted in Cronin, Thomas E., Tania Cronin, and Michael Milakovich, *United States Crime in the Streets,* Bloomington, Indiana: Indiana University Press, 1981.

[6] *The New York Times,* September 4, 1964, p. 13.

[7] Chambliss, op. cit. p. 22.

Mitchell, led the charge on the Johnson administration's Justice Department for its putative permissiveness of crime – conflating his accusations with criticism of the Warren Supreme Court.

For the first time in 20 years, "crime, lawlessness, looting, and rioting" were bundled together and seen by 29 percent of public opinion poll respondents as one of the most important problems facing the nation.[8]

The process was repeated a quarter century later when, on the Sunday preceding President Clinton's first State of the Union speech, he again introduced crime as a major national issue. A *New York Times*/CBS poll had revealed that 19 percent of the respondents cited crime and violence as the single greatest problem facing the nation. However, *The Times* noted contradictions in the poll.

The frustration about violence could be based on unfounded fears. Despite studies showing that crime had generally held steady in the past year, 73% said crime had increased in the country, and 58% said crime had risen in their own communities.

Yet surprisingly, there has been no appreciable increase in the past 20 years in the degree to which people say they fear walking at night within a mile of their homes.[9]

In the weeks following the president's speech, crime moved higher in the polls and became a defining issue. It reinforced Chambliss' conclusion that crime was being deliberately molded into a major issue, not on its merits, but through manipulation by politicians, Justice Department-funded researchers, and a media increasingly surviving on the sensational. As he put it:

The campaign of conservative politicians supported by media coverage of crime and the law enforcement establishment's non-stop propaganda campaign succeeded in raising crime as a major issue for the American people.[10]

While Bill Clinton was waging his own "war on crime," Richard Morin, director of polling for *The Washington Post*, was calling crime a "hot" issue. Whereas only 5 percent of those interviewed saw crime as a major concern in July of 1993, by November, that percentage had risen to 21 percent – rating crime as the nation's biggest problem. By mid-January of 1994, it had risen to 31 percent, with fully half of those interviewed listing crime among the country's two top problems.

---

[8] Ibid. p. 26.
[9] *The New York Times*, Sunday, January 23, 1994, p. 16.
[10] Chambliss op. cit. p. 28.

However, Morin also saw it as an artificially created crisis with a political purpose:

Helped along by the news media and a conjunction of tragic incidents, public concern about crime has risen in the polls from one of many American worries to the No. 1 concern. And suddenly in the White House and on Capitol Hill, the cry of "three strikes and you're out" is echoing down the corridors of power – and the politicians aren't talking baseball

Yet there's plenty of cause for pause when listening to all this tough talk about crime. Inconveniently the available evidence suggests that concerns about crime are soaring at precisely the same time that nearly every major type of crime is going down.[11]

Morin cited the disconnect between the image and reality, quoting University of Texas professor of communication Maxwell E. McCombs ("a pioneer in the subject of agenda-setting by the media"), who compared the hysteria over crime to the "journalistic feeding frenzy over the drug problem in the late 1980s":

The New York Times discovered drugs and thereafter many news organizations discovered it. . . . The reality was that nothing had changed regarding the incidence or use of drugs. The high spike of public concern was very much driven by media concern.[12]

Noting that the media directed, shaped, and inflated public concern, McCombs concluded that the staying power of the crime issue would probably depend upon how long the media remained interested in crime stories.[13] He had no idea at the time that, with the advent of 24/7 cable TV, the media would remain interminably "interested."

There were immediate results. The fear fed a particularly vicious $22.5 million Senate Crime Bill most notable for being passed without benefit of hearings.

Race Baiting

Political race baiting on crime was lifted to the level of art in the 1988 Bush–Dukakis presidential campaign. The TV visage of a stereotypical black criminal walking away from a Massachusetts prison to rape and assault a white woman while on furlough was very powerful indeed – packing into a single hazy montage, the savage in pursuit of

---

[11] Morin, Richard, "Crime Time: The Fear, the Facts: How Sensationalism Got Ahead of the Stats," *The Washington Post*, Sunday, January 30, 1994, "Outlook Section," p. C1.

[12] Ibid. p. C1.

[13] Ibid. p. C2.

white women and the "bleeding heart," perhaps less than the stereotypically macho "Texas-tough" governor. It was a metaphor with deep roots and a long tradition, particularly in the South. Only "toughness" could redeem matters.

Indeed, a recent study of the brutal treatment traditionally doled out in Texas prisons suggests that this major theme of toughness in southern, and specifically Texas, prisons left a considerable mark on American corrections in general.[14] Noting there was always "tough" in southern prisons – but then, there was "Texas Tough," a particularly egregious and commonly personalized type of violence. As Perkinson studied the Texas prison practices spanning more than a century, he concluded that the criminal justice system in that state was unusually harsh and racially driven, with roughshod legal proceedings, racial subjugation, corporal punishment, and unpaid field labor that had persisted into the twenty-first century. He quotes one investigation having described the system as "probably the best example of slavery remaining in the country," noting that "[p]lantation prisons at Sugarland, Huntsville, and elsewhere (had) preserved the lifeways of slavery in carceral amber."[15]

Not coincidentally, the emerging neoconservative crime expert John Dilulio liked the Texas model – writing a tome on "governing prisons" – using the management system he saw and approved of in Texas as to be emulated nationwide.[16]

The Willie Horton ad was so successful in the Bush–Dukakis campaign that Bush's campaign manager, Lee Atwater, facetiously proposed nominating Willie Horton as Dukakis' running mate. As his campaign manager, Susan Estrich, later wrote, it was "a tribute to the Bush campaign's effectiveness, if not its judgment, that in many ways that is what Willie Horton became."

Washington Post reporter, E. J. Dionne, noted that the Estrich–Atwater exchange, "embodied more than three decades of political argument and posturing around the race issue."[17]

Estrich described the effect in these terms: "The symbolism was very powerful. You can't find a stronger metaphor, intended or not, for racial hatred in this country than a black man raping a white woman."[18]

---

[14] Perkinson, Robert, *Texas Tough: The Rise of America's Prison Empire*, New York: Metropolitan Books – Henry Holt & Company, 2010.

[15] Ibid. p. 6

[16] Dilulio, John, *Governing Prisons: A Comparative Study of Correctional Management.*

[17] Dionne, E. J., op. cit. p. 78.

[18] Ibid. pp. 77–78.

But law and order posturing on race wasn't confined to Atwater. Many overlooked the fact that it was then-presidential candidate Albert Gore who first raised the Willie Horton issue during his 1988 New York Democratic primary race with Dukakis.

It was a righteousness, not so much of the victim, as of an army of poseurs and stand-ins who found ratings, votes, and no-risk heroism in immersing themselves in a peculiar kind of third-party ire – transforming human tragedy into a series of cheap playlets that seldom rose much above the level of a second-rate soap opera.

Ever vigilant for these trends, however, politicians fell in line to mouth self-righteous inanities as a means of avoiding those complex issues that might dim the public fervor for retribution or cause some to take pause.

Caught up in the same hysteria, police and prosecutors grew skillful in engaging the media, not so much to serve the needs of effective enforcement as to reinforce the destructive rubrics of what had become a racially defined ritual – without ever having to mention race. Major actors in the justice system – police, prosecutors, judges – could be regularly counted upon to perform their roles with the unctuous hyperbole of a Victorian stage actor summoning up the then-popular vision of the criminal as a Lombrosian "monster."

Backing the performances stood a bureaucracy for control and repression unparalleled in American history, having as its central, largely unuttered task, the apprehension, labeling, sorting, and managing of the absolute majority of young African-American males.

The compulsive self-righteousness driving this was uncomfortably reminiscent of that which afflicted the German middle class earlier in the twentieth century – a phenomenon of which the Danish sociologist Svend Ranulf took note as he looked across the border into pre-war Germany in 1938, seeing:

...a disinterested disposition (to punish), since no direct personal advantage is achieved by the act of punishing another person who has injured a third party. It is furthermore a disposition which is not equally strong in all human societies and indeed seems to be entirely lacking in some, and this precludes the explanation that it might be prompted by the expectation of protection for one's own life and property in return for the protection extended to others, for why should the cogency of such an argument be stronger in some societies than in others?... moral indignation (which is the emotion behind the disinterested tendency to inflict punishment) is a kind of disguised envy.[19]

---

[19] Ranulf, Svend, *Moral Indignation and Middle Class Psychology: A Sociological Study*, Copenhagen: Levin & Munksgaard, Ejnar Munksgaard, 1938, p. 1.

It was a variation on a theme later set by historian Peter Gay in his discussion of the "pathologies" that periodically afflict certain segments of public discourse – in this case, crime and punishment. Quoting Jeremy Bentham ("Men punish because they hate; crimes they are told, they ought to hate."), Gay noted:

> The desire for revenge may have its own uses; it generates the energy to pursue the criminal. But the extreme punishments now in place only overbalance the victim's pain against the pleasure that society squeezes from his sufferings. "Whence originated the prodigal fury.... It is the effect of resentment which at first inclines to the greatest rigour; and of an imbecility of soul, which finds in the rapid destruction of convicts the great advantage of having no further occasion to concern one's self about them." (Preface to *A Fragment on Government* [1776; ed. F. C. Montague, 1891], p. 104.)[20]

By the early 1990s, the country was caught up in a world of crime kitsch – peopled by coifed TV hosts and news readers shedding crocodile tears over the current state of the country while turning human complexities into a series of third-rate soap operas. It has been a highly successful exercise in its own terms. It served the purpose of shielding the citizenry from the uncomfortable realities that birth and nurture crime, while encouraging them to join in maudlin spectacles that further dulled their capacity for civic responsibility.[21]

As TV critic Janet Maslin saw it, the American public had immersed itself in "escapist trivia as a means of avoiding real discourse."[22] National Public Radio's Garrison Keillor put it more bluntly:

> Every murder turns into 50 episodes. It's as bloody as Shakespeare but without the intelligence and the poetry. If you watch television news you know less about the world than if you drank gin out of a bottle.[23]

As citizens sought to substitute portrayed scenarios over authentic experience, the seeds for the culture of kitsch took root. People were more liable to shed what the Czech novelist Milan Kundera limned the second tear:

[20] Gay, Peter, *The Cultivation of Hatred: The Bourgeois Experience Victoria to Freud*, New York: W. W. Norton & Co., 1993, p. 146.

[21] The reader is reminded that the term crocodile tears means more than simply play-acting one's grief. It is a predatory exercise arising out of the myth that the crocodile cries as it devours its victim.

[22] Maslin, Janet, "In Dirty Laundryland: A Day with Jenny, Phil, Sally, Maury, Oprah et al.," *The New York Times*, Sunday, October 10, 1993, Section 9, p. 7.

[23] "News from Lake Wobegon," on National Public Radio's *Prairie Home Companion*, December, 1993.

Kitsch causes two tears to flow in quick succession. The first tear says: How nice to see children running on the grass! The second tear says: How nice to be moved, together with all mankind, by children running on the grass. It is the second tear which makes kitsch, kitsch.[24]

It was a wallowing in emotion that led nowhere – what William James described as "the weeping of a Russian lady over the fictitious personages in the play while her coachman is freezing to death on his seat outside."[25]

James spoke to the darker implications of all this becoming a national characteristic. The need to detach oneself from unpleasant realities and to see matters in kitsch-like ways runs deep. Woe betide whoever might question these perceptions by dragging before the public any unpleasant reminders that would tie personal concern to civic responsibility.

This is what the criminal represents to a society – a reminder that all is not well. He must therefore be quickly invalidated and driven from view lest we become aware that we all may have a share in the deviance.

Kundera put it pungently:

Kitsch is the absolute denial of shit, in both the literal and figurative senses of the word; kitsch excludes everything from its purview which is essentially unacceptable in human existence. . . . Kitsch is the aesthetic ideal of all politicians and all political parties and movements. Whenever a single political movement comes to power, we find ourselves in the realm of totalitarian kitsch. . . . When I say "totalitarian," what I mean is that everything that infringes on kitsch must be banished for life. . . . In this light, we can regard the gulag as a septic tank used by totalitarian kitsch to dispose of its refuse . . . kitsch is a folding screen set up to curtain off death.[26]

The art of the Third Reich was a carnival tour of kitsch.

The Nelson Eddy Effect

As the trappings of the central actors in the criminal justice drama grew more florid, it was tacit admission that less and less was happening on the crime front. During my years in the U.S. Air Force medical service corps, a close friend and orthopedic surgeon occasionally shared his observation that after 18 years in the military he had noticed that whenever wars with other nations flagged, the uniforms of military officers got more extravagant.

---

[24] Kundera, Milan, *The Unbearable Lightness of Being,* New York: Harper Collins, 1984, p. 251.
[25] Barzun, Jacques, op. cit. p. 68.
[26] Kundera, Milan, op. cit. p. 251.

Simply enlisting made one eligible for an array of epaulets, medals, stripes, and braid, whether or not one had done anything personally to deserve them. "Were we to enter a long stretch of peace," he once commented, "our Generals would start to look like Nelson Eddy in *The Chocolate Soldier.*"

My friend's observation was a variation on the theme that when truly serious criminal activity goes unaddressed, the formal trappings of criminal justice assume greater importance.

One need only look at the military garbing of small-town sheriffs. In Jacksonville, Florida, where I functioned as the "monitor" for the federal regarding county jail overcrowding, the Sheriff had awarded himself five stars – comparable to the Supreme Commander in Western Europe during World War II.

Indeed, across the country, assorted local minions of law and order played increasingly at being Green Berets and manning military-like police SWAT teams, while pistol-toting probation officers entered and exited offices located in a plethora of Speer-like edifices springing up across the country, labeled justice centers or new-generation jails. It all carried a surreal quality. As the architecture grew more kitschy, the roles of the major actors in the criminal justice drama were romanticized beyond recognition.

The image of the policeman as one of a "thin blue line" holding back the tide of criminals ready to engulf the citizenry; the prison guard working under conditions of stress and danger while he watches over depraved criminals; or the prosecutor as the ethically driven, conscience-ridden personage of the TV crime show – all ape reality.[27]

---

[27] In an inside look at how prime-time "reality-based" cop shows "effortlessly smooth out the indiscretions of the lumpen detectives and make them into heroes rushing across the screen . . . because this is what the viewers and advertisers have come to expect," the reader is referred to an intriguing article by a Debra Seagal, former "story analyst" for the American Broadcasting Company's show, *American Detective.* As Ms. Seagal wrote, "Just before going home today, I noticed a little list that someone had tacked up on our bulletin boards to remind us what we are looking for: DEATH, STAB, SHOOT, STRANGULATION, CLUB, SUICIDE." Ms. Seagal then gave the following example of the "reality-based" approach to police work:

The tape I saw today involves a soft-spoken thirty-something white male named Michael who gets busted for selling pot out of his ramshackle abode in the Santa Cruz mountains. He's been set up by a friend who himself was originally resistant to cooperating with the detectives. Michael has never been arrested and doesn't understand the mechanics of becoming a C.I. (confidential informant). He has only one request: to see a lawyer. By law, after such a request the detectives are required to stop any form of interrogation

(*continued on p. 72*)

A policeman is at half the risk of death or injury while on the job than a farmer, and considerably less so than a heavy-construction worker,

(*continued from p. 71*)
immediately and make a lawyer available. In this case however, Commander Brooks knows that if he can get Michael to flip, they'll be able to keep busting up the ladder and, of course, we'll be able to crank out a good show.

So what happens? Hunched in front of my equipment in the office in Malibu, this is what I see, in minute after minute of raw footage:

[Michael is pulled out of bed after midnight. Two of our cameras are rolling and a group of cops surround him. He is entirely confused when Brooks explains how to work with them and become a confidential informer.]

MICHAEL: Can I have a lawyer?... I don't know what's going on. I'd really rather talk to a lawyer. This is not my expertise at all, as it is yours. I feel way outnumbered. I don't know what's going on...

BROOKS: Here's where we're at. You've got a lot of marijuana. Marijuana's still a felony in the state of California, despite what you may think about it.

MICHAEL: I understand.

BROOKS: The amount of marijuana you have here is gonna send you to state prison... That's our job, to try to put you in state prison, quite frankly, unless you do something to help yourself. Unless you do something to assist us...

MICHAEL: I'm innocent until proven guilty, correct?

BROOKS: I'm telling you the way it is in the real world.... What we're asking you to do is cooperate... to act as our agent and help us buy larger amounts of marijuana. Tell us where you get your marijuana....

MICHAEL: I don't understand. You know, you guys could have me do something and I could get in even more trouble.

BROOKS: Obviously, if you're acting as our agent, you can't get in trouble....

MICHAEL: I'm taking your word for that?...

BROOKS: Here's what I'm telling you. If you don't want to cooperate, you're going to prison.

MICHAEL: Sir, I do want to cooperate...

BROOKS: Now, I'm saying if you don't cooperate right today, now, here, this minute, you're going to prison. We're gonna asset-seize your property. We're gonna asset-seize your vehicles. We're gonna asset-seize your money. We're gonna send your girl-friend to prison and we're gonna send your kid to the Child Protective Services. That's what I'm saying.

MICHAEL: If I get a lawyer, all that stuff happens to me?

BROOKS: If you get a lawyer, we're not in a position to wanna cooperate with you tomorrow. We're in a position to cooperate with you right now. Today. Right now. Today...

MICHAEL: I'm under too much stress to make a decision like that. I want to talk to a lawyer. I really do. That's the bottom line.

[Commander Brooks continues to push Michael but doesn't get far.]

MICHAEL: I'm just getting more confused. I've got ten guys standing around me....

BROOKS: We're not holding a gun to you.

MICHAEL: Every one of you guys has a gun.

(*continued*)

roofer, or coal miner (the most dangerous job). Likewise, being a prison guard brings about as much risk of injury or death as being a teacher or a nurse. Despite the occasional tragedy, a policeman or policewoman is at no more risk of a fatal injury while on the job than an electrician or construction work supervisor. A farmer, fisherman, trucker, or logger has double the risk of a policeman of suffering a fatality while on the job. A construction worker has two and a half times the risk and a taxi driver is four times more likely to be killed while on the job than a policeman

(*continued from p. 72*)

BROOKS: How old is your child?

MICHAEL: She'll be three on Tuesday.

BROOKS: Well, children need a father at home. You can't be much of a father when you're in jail.

MICHAEL: Sir!

BROOKS: That's not a scare tactic, that's a reality.

MICHAEL: That's a scare tactic.

BROOKS: No, it isn't. That's reality... And the reality is, I'm sending you to prison unless you do something to help yourself out...

MICHAEL: Well, ain't. I'm also innocent until proven guilty in a court of law?... You know what, guys? I really just want to talk to a lawyer. That's really all I want to do.

BROOKS: How much money did you put down on this property?... Do you own that truck over there?

MICHAEL: Buddy, does all this need to be done to get arrested?...

BROOKS: Yeah. I'm curious – do you own that truck there?

MICHAEL: You guys know all that.

BROOKS: I hope so, 'cause I'd look good in that truck.

MICHAEL: Is this Mexico?

BROOKS: No. I'll just take it. Asset-seizure. And you know what? The county would look good taking the equity out of this house.

MICHAEL: Lots of luck.

[*Commander Brooks continues to work on Michael for several minutes.*]

MICHAEL: I feel like you're poking at me.

BROOKS: I *am* poking at you.

MICHAEL: So now I really want to talk to a lawyer now.

BROOKS: That's fine. We're done.

[*Brooks huffs off, mission unaccomplished. He walks over to his pals and shakes his head.*]

BROOKS: That's the first white guy I ever felt like beating the fucking shit out of.

Ms. Seagal then concludes, "If Michael's case becomes an episode of the show, Michael will be made a part of a criminal element that stalks backyards and threatens children. Commander Brooks will become a gentle, persuasive cop who's keeping our streets safe at night." (Seagal, Debra, "Tales from the Cutting-Room Floor: The Reality of Reality-Based Television," *Harper's*, November 1993, pp. 54–55.)

or policewoman.[28] Moreover, despite the hype about violent crime in the 1980s and 1990s and the putative danger to law enforcement officers, policing got progressively *less* risky over those two decades.[29]

Contemporary prosecutors, both federal and state, have never much resembled the media image first portrayed in its most idealized form in the 1990s by Michael Moriarty on the National Broadcasting Company's then-new series, *Law and Order.* In reality, however, prosecutors both then and now are largely indistinguishable from run-of-the-mill "pols," with the possible exception that they are afforded more resources and staff than most as they go about their business of getting a "win" or maybe a shot at higher office.

Among the better examples of contemporary crime kitsch is the so-called victims' movement, which, in its attempts to focus attention on legitimate concerns, has courted a mélange of hangers-on ready to trade rehearsed outrage for thoughtful consideration.

It would be difficult to find an element of the criminal justice system more exploited and dripping in kitsch than the so-called victims' movement. It fosters and wallows in the most saccharine elements of what Kundera labeled totalitarian kitsch – a situation in which everything that infringes on kitsch must be banished for life. It is based in, and draws its emotional sustenance from, a peculiar kind of revenge – described by writer Alexander Theroux – that "like hemorrhoids, seems to have been created to locate in one particular place one particular pain to absolve the body in all other places of all other pains." It's the kind of revenge that can never be satisfied – ultimately compulsively revictimizing the victim.

The major political effect of the victims' movement has been to feed the national hysteria in the process, destroying more individuals than it purports to salvage, through stoking a series of poorly conceived revengeful legislative proposals.

The movement does, however, provide bold outlines for carefully fashioned entertainments for a TV crime series – hosts playing to the worst impulses of audiences primed to scream on cue over another's tragedy.

---

[28] Jack, Tracy A. and Mark J. Zak, "Results from the First National Census of Fatal Occupational Injuries, 1992," *Compensation and Working Conditions,* U.S. Dept. of Labor, Bureau of Labor Statistics, December 1993, Table 5.

[29] In 1990, there were 65 felonious deaths among the 600,000+ federal, state, and local "sworn" law enforcement officers. This represented a 40 percent drop from the number of such deaths (104) in 1980. This drop occurred despite the fact that the number of police in the country had grown by at least 20 percent in the intervening years.

The format has spawned a not-insignificant number of professional victims who travel the circuit peddling their troublesome wares.

Occasionally, the need to sustain the stereotype of the criminal gets out of hand and becomes embarrassingly obvious. Take for example, a front page February 1993 story in *USA Today*. The story about gang violence was capped with a large photo of five young, armed African-American males identified as gang members. The central figure in the photo had a string of cartridges hung bandoleer style over his shoulder as he looked menacingly into the camera.

A few days later, it was revealed that the young men had been brought to the reporter by a community activist who was under the impression that *USA Today* was doing a story on a handgun "turn-in" program. The young men had originally come for the interview unarmed, whereupon the reporter drove them across town to locate any guns they might be able to find with which to pose for the photo for the story – headlined, "Gangs put L.A. on edge." When the young man who had issued the original invitation to the press saw the *USA Today* story and photo, he could only say, "I am sick. I can't sleep. They didn't want to talk to me. They called me names. They think I set them up. I may not even be able to live here anymore. Where can I hide?"[30]

The effect on crime of all this *sturm und drang* has been minimal. However, the social detritus left behind has been considerable. Arrest and jailing are now routinely proposed as the optimum means of dealing with a growing range of personal, economic, and social problems. From family breakdown to alcoholism, drug addiction, welfare, homelessness, mental illness, child abuse, or school failure, all are presented as fit for criminal justice handling that demonstrably routinely exacerbates the problem to be addressed – often turning violent in the process.

After the burning and looting subsided in Los Angeles in the spring of 1992, politicians of both parties were crawling over one another to assign "root causes." The hope was that the serious problems in urban America would either go away or the residents would remain settled until after the election. That hope was dashed in a few hours, with ominous portents for other cities around the nation. Then-Los Angeles Police Chief, Daryl Gates, blamed criminal gangs. President G. H. Bush's press secretary, Marlin Fitzwater, attributed the riots to wrong-headed social welfare programs from a quarter century earlier.

---

[30] Kurtz, Howard, "Did *USA Today* Shoot Straight: Photo of Armed Gang Didn't Tell Whole Story," *Washington Post*, February 18, 1993.

Then-Vice President Dan Quayle suggested that the urban poor had lost their moral fiber because of the social permissiveness of the 1960s – using as an example, the acceptance of a single mother on a TV sitcom. Having adopted a strategy to court alienated middle-class white voters, then-Democratic presidential candidate Bill Clinton called for a tough-sounding but virtually irrelevant federal crime bill.

President Bush unveiled the Justice Department's new "Weed and Seed" program. The idea was to "weed out" the criminals (and, as is the case with weeds, presumably to dump them in collective trash containers called prisons), while "seeding" the urban environment with enterprise and investment. Two weeks after the riots, Bush showcased his Weed and Seed initiative, sandwiching in a visit to the poor, black "Hill" neighborhood of Pittsburgh between a speech to law enforcement officials at the Washington Monument's Sylvan theater and a $1,000 a plate dinner meeting with Pennsylvania Republicans.

At the Washington affair, he had said, "We must show less compassion for the criminal and more for the victims of crime." But that note didn't play so well in urban Pittsburgh. "We need your help beyond the weeding part," said Bunny Carter, head of the Three Rivers Employment agency. "We need more support in the seeding part." A local barber named Napoleon Buice spoke up in a halting voice to tell Bush, "There's people out in the Hill. There's drug addicts out in the Hill that need help. And there are intelligent boys out there who don't have any hope." The president responded by committing $1.1 million in federal funds for law enforcement in Pittsburgh. There were no specific commitments for social programs.

A similar model begun a few months earlier in the District of Columbia had allocated $1 million for a troubled community in the northeast sector of the city. It was a variant of Weed and Seed. However, of the $1 million, $700,000 was allocated for police overtime and $96,000 for surveillance equipment, cameras, zoom lenses, and scopes for night vision. The only identifiable funding for non-police activity was $28,000 for a performing arts and basketball program at a local school. Clearly, more effort would be directed at weeding than at seeding.

There was little reason to believe things would improve in urban areas. George Santayana's characterization of a fanatic as one who redoubles his efforts when he has lost sight of his goal accurately described the nation's self-defeating dependence upon the justice model. The greater the failure, the more demand for increased firepower and harsher punishments from politicians of both parties.

As the 1992 presidential race swung into gear, it was the successful African-American lawyer, lobbyist, and chairman of the Democratic
National Committee, Ron Brown, who wrote:

Let's get it all out on the table. Race and crime. Kerosene and a match. Bush and
Horton. Republicans since Richard Nixon have "used" crime as an issue 'better'
than we Democrats have. They've "tied" it well to racial fears and stereotypes,
and that has won them many votes.[31]

Then, in a parody of a Broadway show tune, Brown belted out his
version of "Anything you can do, we can do tougher" – noting that
Democratic leaders in Congress had proposed 15,000 more federal prison
cells than the Bush administration had requested.

Striking the same rich political vein, liberal Massachusetts Democratic
Congressman Barney Frank wrote an Op-Ed piece for *The New York
Times* in which he said, in part:

Race and crime together show the "notsaposta" syndrome at its worst. Liberals
are notsaposta take note publicly of the fact that young black males commit street
crimes in a significantly higher proportion than any other major demographic
group.... We liberals have allowed ourselves to be restrained from saying what
the public at large wants – and has every right – to hear: that people who assault,
rape, rob, or otherwise terrorize others are bad people from whom the innocent
majority must be protected.[32]

To a degree of course, Frank was right. However, given the history of
the politics of race and crime in this country, there may have been more
merit to being "restrained from saying what the public at large wants to
hear" on crime than either Frank or Brown cared to acknowledge.

The political attractiveness of being tough on black men was amply
demonstrated by all the major candidates opposing President Bush in the
1992 election. Bill Clinton had already proven his willingness to be tough
by taking a break from his New Hampshire primary campaign so he might
preside over the execution of a severely brain-damaged black man. Third-
party presidential candidate H. Ross Perot hinted at similar draconian
measures with reference to defendants accused of drug offenses. Using
the war analogy on a *Today Show* appearance, Perot anticipated the
future by noting that drug offenders should be treated like prisoners of
war, with no bail and no release, apparently until the "war" is over.

[31] Brown, Ronald H. "Republican Baloney on Crime," *The Washington Post*, 1992.
[32] Frank, Barney H., "Race and Crime: Let's Talk Sense," *The New York Times*, Op-Ed,
January 13, 1992, p. A15.

Describing the soft-authoritarian government of Singapore as a vision of the future, Perot mused that dealing with the drug problem in the United States "won't be pretty."

He'd have to see if citizens "had the stomach" for his unspecified solutions. Given whose communities would likely be cordoned off for house-to-house searches, whose doors would be broken down, and whose young men would meet the hangman, the majority of Americans just might have "stomached" such extreme measures.

William Barr, the Attorney General in the George H. Bush administration, gave a hint of the pattern likely to be followed when it came to draconian punishments. Of the 14 cases approved for capital prosecution by General Barr (under the drug laws) during the last 10 months of the Bush administration, 13 involved minority defendants.[33] However, it was good politics. Why?

Again, it was Mead who succinctly summarized the uncomfortable reality as he saw it:

[The] attitude of hostility toward the law-breaker has the unique advantage of uniting all members of the community in the emotional solidarity of aggression. While the most admirable of humanitarian efforts are sure to run counter to the individual interests of very many in the community, or fail to touch the interest and imagination of the multitude and to leave the community divided or indifferent, the cry of "thief" or "murderer" is attuned to profound complexes, lying below the surface of competing individual efforts, and citizens who have [been] separated by divergent interests stand together against the common enemy.

There is nothing in the history of human society nor in present-day experience which encourages us to look to the primal impulse of neighborliness for such cohesive power. The love of one's neighbor cannot be made into a common consuming passion.[34]

Mead's prescient words were written long before the advent of the electronic media with its recognition that passions are easily fed and high ratings garnered when matters of crime and punishment are generously spiced with young, black, and brown faces paraded across TV screens night after night in news broadcasts and exploitative crime shows such as *48 Hours, Street Stories, America's Most Wanted, Cops,*

[33] National Legal Aid and Defender Association, *Capital Report,* January/February 1993, No. 29, p. 4, Washington, D.C.

[34] Mead, George H., in his essay, "The Nature of the Past," originally published in 1929, reprinted in Rack, Andrew J. (ed.), *Selected Writings: George Herbert Mead,* Chicago: University of Chicago Press 1981, p. 591.

A Current Affair, and Inside Edition. In an earlier age, such sensationalism was mostly confined to a few tabloids or magazines such as *The Police Gazette.* No more. In many ways, it defines our society.

Feeding a Culture of Neglect

Shortly after his inauguration, President Nixon brought Harvard professor Daniel Patrick Moynihan into the White House as his special assistant for domestic affairs. Previously, an assistant secretary of state in the Johnson administration, Moynihan had produced an internal report entitled "The Negro Family," which called attention to what he saw as the disintegration of the black nuclear family into a "tangle of pathology."

Though heavily criticized by African-American leaders, Moynihan's controversial thesis conditioned much of the national debate on welfare and crime for the next two decades. A Democrat, and occasionally uneasy in the role in which he had been cast, Moynihan became something of a hero to the newly burgeoning neoconservative movement, which would reach its apotheosis in the Reagan administration.

At the time, as urban geographer Susan Roberts noted, the idea of a "city life cycle" infused most of the debate on urban policy.[35] Tracing that concept to the politics of welfare, Roberts observed:

During the 1970s and early 1980s, the city life cycle idea is found peppered throughout debates on urban policy and in policy documents themselves. In particular, the city life cycle idea found favor among modern conservatives. The New Right, represented in journals such as *Commentary* and *The Public Interest,* used the city life cycle idea and the related but more vague urban death thesis. The organicism of the idea at first seems far away from the grinding economism of the New Right, but, in fact, the two are compatible. This compatibility is based on similar conceptions of the economy, politics, and place.[36]

As the geographer, P. E. Peterson summarized discussions at that time:

For many analysts, especially those with training in economics, the incapacity of cities to redistribute goods and services [wa]s not a cause for alarm. The... drift toward retrenchment [wa]s accepted not just as inevitable but as simply desirable. For these scholars industrial societies [were] plagued by the negative impact on societal productivity of an inefficient public sector. The issues simply require(d) "benign neglect."[37]

---

[35] Roberts, Susan, "A Critical Evaluation of the City Life Cycle Idea," *Urban Geography,* Vol. 12, No. 5, 1991, pp. 431–49.

[36] Ibid. p. 440.

[37] Peterson, P. E., *City Limits,* Chicago: University of Chicago Press, 1981, p. 214.

A variation on the theme of planned shrinkage was proposed by the journalist Roger Starr who, along with Charles Krauthammer, James Q. Wilson, Moynihan, and Charles Murray, served on the "publication committee" of Irving Kristol's journal, *The Public Interest*. Here's how he crafted the idea:

We could simply accept the fact that the city's population is going to shrink, and we could cut back on city services accordingly, realizing considerable savings in the process.[38]

The influential conservative journalist, Marvin Stone, proposed that the big cities be left to die,[39] while the British magazine, *The Economist*, in considering the deterioration occurring in the South Bronx, was more direct:

The bleak truth is that this is the natural and inevitable consequence of a shrinking city. The destruction, poverty and hopelessness that cluster around the burnt-out wrecks is abhorrent. That something should be done to stop it is the immediate reaction. That something should be done to speed it up is nearer the mark.[40]

It was within this kind of intellectual and historical context that Moynihan had made his call for "benign neglect." Though Moynihan himself later disavowed the views of the neoconservative writer Charles Murray that the antipoverty programs of the Great Society had, in fact, *caused* most of the problems in the urban areas, Murray's social prescriptions flowed directly from Moynihan's social diagnosis. Welfare and crime were but two sides of the same coin. Though a plug nickel, it was highly negotiable currency in the contemporary world of politics, race, and crime.

It was President Nixon's Attorney General, John Mitchell, who advised observers to "watch what we *do*, not what we say." It proved to be good advice not only with reference to that administration but over the next two decades. It was better said in the New Testament, "By their fruits you shall know them." Behind the cacophony of threat and law and order rhetoric, the politics of crime proved finally to be the politics of race.

One of the greatest myths promulgated by the Right during the 1980s and early 1990s was that the United States went through a "permissive" period in criminal justice in the 1960s and early 1970s, eschewing

[38] Starr, Roger, "Making New York Smaller," *The New York Times Magazine*, November 14, 1976, p. 32.

[39] Stone, Marvin, "Let Big Cities Die?" *U.S. News and World Report*, August 8, 1977, p. 80.

[40] Where Do We Go Next? A Survey of New York City, *The Economist*, March 25, 1978, p. 10.

punishment and focusing on rehabilitating juvenile and adult offenders. True, for awhile it was chic to talk about progressive alternatives such as "diverting" young offenders from the justice system, using only "least restrictive" means consistent with public safety, and touting ideas such as the deinstitutionalization of reform schools, and the creation of community-based alternatives. It was largely blather. Though there may have been a period of neglect masquerading as permissiveness, there was never a time of major investment in options or alternatives to routine criminal justice handling.

Having served at the cabinet level for three governors and having run 2 of the 10 largest states' youth correctional agencies (Massachusetts and Pennsylvania) and another's child welfare agency (Illinois), I learned long ago to trust the old saw that the only way to judge commitment to a policy was to follow the budget. When that exercise is completed, one can only conclude that even in the heyday of putative permissiveness, 90 percent to 95 percent of justice budgets went to arrest, prosecute, and imprison offenders. Alternative diversionary and rehabilitative programs were, at best, small appendages to the massive state institutional budgets geared to incapacitate and deter.

The truth is that there never was a shining hour in justice in the United States in which there was even minimal retreat from basic reliance on jails, prisons, and detention centers. So many semantic games were played that the public (and the media) mistook the rhetoric for reality. With the abandonment of the rehabilitative ideal, national justice policy was redirected from disciplining an incorrigible population to managing a disposable one. It helped ever so much if it were quietly understood by all that the bulk of eligible clientele would be black or brown.

President Johnson's Crime Commission had called for the nation to take a different direction. It stressed the need for prevention programs, development of alternatives, and diverting the young from the justice system whenever possible within the constraints of public safety. With a war in full swing in Vietnam, there was little stomach for inflated rhetoric on a parallel war on crime. Wars on errant citizens would have to wait.

James Vorenberg, the executive director of the Johnson Commission, summarized its goals in this way – "to show how police, courts, and correctional agencies could *both reduce crime and treat people more decently (by lowering) the level of hostility between the police and young people, particularly blacks*" (emphasis added). Here was a highly placed representative of a national administration actually suggesting that we needed to treat young African-American offenders decently while we set about stemming crime. It was not to be.

Though planners like Vorenberg and the criminologists who acted as consultants to the Johnson Commission conceived this promising new anticrime initiative, it never got off the ground. The legislation that resulted from the Commission's recommendations was passed. However, it fell to the Nixon administration to implement it. As then-Attorney General John Mitchell, who had led the strident 1968 law and order campaign for Nixon (and who, himself, would eventually end up in prison), told a House subcommittee, "No problem is of higher priority than the ever increasing crime in our nation."

Crime increased 30 percent during the first three years of the Nixon administration. As the war in Vietnam wound down, it was a propitious time to wind up a new war on crime. The Nixon-appointed administrators of the newly established Law Enforcement Assistance Administration began by funding the very approaches the Johnson Commission had sought to undo. As an article published in *The Nation* in late 1970 put it, "The Cops Hit the Jackpot."[41]

Colorado was purchasing everything from patrol cars and snowmobiles to personal police uniforms. Mississippi used the federal monies to buy more service weapons, radios, automobiles, night sticks, handcuffs, and station wagons for Parchman prison, even while its state police department remained segregated.

Georgia's police departments used their federal money to buy 569 mobile radio units, 85 automobiles, 50 fingerprint and ID kits, 57 cameras, 9 typewriters, 64 firearms of unspecified caliber, 8 mace units, 18 pairs of handcuffs, 41 fire extinguishers, 8 evidence lockers, and 14 helmets. Georgia authorities projected that they would need federal money to buy at least 1,300 additional police cars by 1975. It was all penny ante to what would follow.

In his 1984 broadside attack on social welfare programs, even Charles Murray admitted that when it came to federally funded anticrime programs, conservatives had won the day:

But, which way to go? Get tough? (the conservative prescription). Or attack the problem at its roots (the liberal prescription)? The conservatives (and apparently much of the electorate) got what they wanted, a program that would try to strengthen the hand of the law enforcers in catching criminals. The dollar commitment to these (anti-crime) efforts followed the familiar curve. In 1950, the

[41] Goulden, Joseph, "The Cops Hit the Jackpot," *The Nation*, November 23, 1970.

combined budget of the Department of Justice and the FBI was $455 million in 1980 dollars. The combined figure climbed steadily but slowly through the 1960s (as in other instances the increase in expenditures lagged behind the increase in rhetoric), standing at $1.2 billion in 1969, the first year that LEAA's budget was added in. Within only three years, the total had nearly doubled to $2.3 billion.[42]

Annual funding for the Department of Justice, FBI, and Law Enforcement Assistance Administration eventually reached more than $3.4 billion before disillusionment with LEAA set in during the late 1970s and its allocations were cut. By 1980, annual funding was at $2.6 billion.

In the last year of the Nixon administration, a concerned Vorenberg wrote:

It would be a tragic mistake to assume that we can look to the law-enforcement system to control crime... The view that the level of crime is determined less by law enforcement than by the extent to which we make life worthwhile for those at the bottom of the economic and social ladder is not a partisan one.[43]

Noting that the Johnson Commission had among its members such staunch conservatives as then-Secretary of State William Rogers and Nixon's Supreme Court Justice Lewis Powell, Vorenberg wrote that these men:

...[had] no doubt whatever that the most significant action that can be taken against crime is action designed to eliminate slums and ghettos, to improve education, to provide jobs, to make sure that every American is given the opportunities and freedoms that will enable him to assume his responsibilities.

Vorenberg then accurately predicted where things would head:

The country seems to be proceeding on the contrary assumption. Against the background of the tremendous increase in crime committed by blacks, whatever notions of fiscal soundness or social justice are thought to underlie the Administration's apparent acceptance of Daniel P. Moynihan's proposal for "benign neglect" of blacks, that policy seems almost certain to have disastrous effects on crime.

In a style that was to become *de rigueur* in an increasingly politicized Justice Department, after Vorenberg's comments appeared in the *Atlantic*,

---

[42] Murray, Charles, *Losing Ground*, New York: Basic Books, 1984, pp. 121–22. In subsequent years, even Murray's "familiar curve" would be outdone in federal spending on anticrime efforts, with $11 billion allocated to the drug war alone in 1992.

[43] Vorenberg, James, "The War on Crime: The First Five Years," *Atlantic*, February 1971.

the Center for Criminal Justice that he headed at Harvard Law School was threatened with loss of its Justice Department grants.[44]

Two decades after his original call for benign neglect of urban areas, Daniel Patrick Moynihan (by now a Senator) looked out again upon the urban terrain and, in a highly publicized and well-marketed article in *The American Scholar,* suggested that America's troubles resulted from the fact that our society had become too tolerant of uncivil and criminal behavior.[45] James Q. Wilson was saying much the same thing – giving the subject an ever so slight genetic (and, by implication, racial) twist.[46]

Moynihan's thesis, drawn from the work of the nineteenth century French sociologist Emile Durkheim and the contemporary American anthropologist Kai Erickson, was that a society can only stand so much social deviance. When overloaded with unacceptable behavior on all sides, it redefines matters, making acceptable what was formerly unacceptable to keep social deviance within bounds and at a relatively fixed level. In a related speech appropriately entitled "Toward a New Intolerance" delivered before the Association for a Better New York and published in the neoconservative journal *The Public Interest,* Moynihan amplified his views in this way:

(When) I settled down to work on the *American Scholar* article(,) . . . I remembered the St. Valentine's Day Massacre. I have a *World Book Encyclopedia,* a wonderful thing. I looked it up. The St. Valentine's Day Massacre in 1929 in Chicago has two entries in the *World Book Encyclopedia.* Two. Along with the Battle of Thermopylae and things like that. The country was outraged. Al Capone had sent four of his men dressed as police. They rubbed out seven of Bugsy Moran's men.

---

[44] I was on the Massachusetts committee that oversaw the distribution of LEAA funds in that state. As Vorenberg (who was also on the committee) left a meeting the week his critical *Atlantic* article appeared, he noted that he had to leave early to stem an attempt to cut the funding to the Center for Criminal Justice by the administrators at LEAA, who were unhappy with his comments.

[45] Moynihan, Daniel P. "Defining Deviancy Down," *The American Scholar,* Winter 1993, pp. 17–30.

[46] Wilson, James Q., *The Moral Sense,* Mankato, Minnesota: The Free Press, 1993, p. 137.
    Among the obscure findings Wilson manages to work into this latest book is one by psychologists Allison Rosenberg and Jerome Kagan that suggests that "most very inhibited Caucasian children have blue eyes while most very uninhibited ones have brown eyes. . . . " Wilson uses the finding to bolster his views on the genetic and temperamental foundations of human morality. In any other context, the Kagan findings would be simply interesting or unremarkable. However, in the context of some of Wilson's other writings on race and I.Q. and, by implication, race and crime, Kagan's findings take on the more ominous potential for misuse and misinterpretation.

All adults; they knew what they were up to and in for. But it shocked the country. We changed the Constitution. We said this was not acceptable behavior.[47]

Moynihan went on to decry a contemporary society that had lost its sense of outrage. Citing Wilson, he noted that "Los Angeles has the equivalent of a St. Valentine's Day Massacre every weekend." In an article in *The New Republic* subtitled "The New Assault on Bourgeois Life," neoconservative columnist Charles Krauthammer took up Moynihan's thesis enthusiastically, describing current (ostensibly liberal) social reformers as having created a "vast project . . . (in) the moral deconstruction of middle-class normality."[48] (At the time, Moynihan, Wilson, Murray, and Krauthammer all served on the publication committee of *The Public Interest*).

In some ways, of course, Moynihan was correct. However, not entirely. The overall national homicide rate (that crime most likely to be reported and the best barometer of violence in a society) was as high in 1929 as it was in the late 1980s.[49] Of particular relevance to the racial issues implicit in Moynihan's discussion was the fact that homicide rates among African-American males (as measured by victimization rates) were higher in the putative halcyon days of the early 1930s than they were throughout most of the 1980s and early 1990s. Homicide rates for nonwhite males spanning the half century from 1930 to 1990 reached their all-time high in this country in 1934 – after having soared earlier in the century and equaling or outstripping recent growth in violent crime (see Fig. 4.1).[50]

---

[47] Moynihan, Daniel Patrick, "Toward a New Intolerance," *The Public Interest,* No. 112, Summer 1993, p. 121.

[48] Krauthammer, Charles, "Defining Deviancy Up: The New Assault on Bourgeois Life," *The New Republic,* November 22, 1993, p. 22.

[49] Reiss, Albert J. Jr., and Roth, Jeffrey A., *Understanding and Preventing Violence,* Washington, D.C.: National Academy Press, 1993, p. 50. (The authors update the earlier trends outlined by Hollinger cf. below.)

For an interesting discussion on the validity of recorded homicide rates as the most reliable crime indicator, the reader is referred to Dane Archer and Rosemary Gartners' reference summary of worldwide data on crime. As to the validity of recorded homicide rates, they comment:

"The finding that serious offenses are relatively immune to under-reporting has particular significance for the offense of homicide . . . evidence on this question appears to be consistent and persuasive: homicide is the most valid of offense indicators in that official statistics on this offense are immune to under-reporting." (Archer, Dane and Rosemary Gartner, *Violence & Crime in Cross-National Perspective,* New Haven, Connecticut: Yale University Press, 1984, p. 35.)

[50] Reiss, A., op. cit. (see Figure 2–1, p. 51).

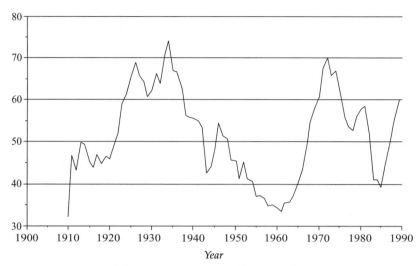

FIGURE 4.1. Homicide Rates for Nonwhite Males 1910–1990. *Source:* Adapted from Paul Hollinger, *Violent Deaths in the United States: An Epidemiological Study of Suicide, Homicide and Accidents* (New York: Guilford Press (1987), pp. 209-10; and Albert J. Reiss and Jeffrey A. Roth, *Understanding and Preventing Violence* (Washington, D.C., National Academy Press), p. 50.

A study of suicide, homicide, and accidents spanning the years 1900 to 1985 revealed that the rates of homicide victimization for nonwhite males were about as high in 1934 as they were in the late 1980s.[51]

It's likely that a significantly higher percentage of black males were killed in the 1920s and 1930s by white men than was probably the case in the late 1980s and early 1990s, when it appeared that black victims of homicide were more likely to have been killed by other blacks. It puts Moynihan's thesis in a somewhat different light, however. Though he may have been correct in his view that the 1934 St. Valentine's Day Massacre galvanized the white majority to do something about violent crime, there appeared to have been no equivalent national "sense of outrage" over the fact that black men were being killed at the highest rates registered in the post-emancipation era. Moynihan implied that the nation responded to the St. Valentine's Day Massacre by sending a strong message that the country would not allow the violence to continue. As he would have it, in effect, the citizenry stood up and said, "No more!" refusing thereby to

[51] Hollinger, Paul C., *Violent Deaths In the United States: An Epidemiologic Study of Suicide, Homicide, and Accidents*, New York: Guilford Press, 1987, pp. 209-10.

ignore or "define down" the violence. In reality, something quite different happened.

The nation's response to the Chicago incident was *not* to get tougher (for example, to put more police on the streets, stiffen laws, or lengthen criminal sentences). Rather, the government defined down deviance by legalizing behaviors that had, for the previous 14 years, been held to be illegal, by repealing Prohibition.

In contrast, "outrage" over violent crime in the 1990s arising out of turf battles over drug dealing was directed in precisely the opposite direction than in the 1930s. Ever-larger police task forces were put on the streets, ever-wider ranges and types of nonprescription drugs proscribed, and ever-harsher sentences imposed for their possession or sale – with African-Americans and Hispanics disproportionately targeted. This "zero tolerance" approach to deviance brought profound changes in police procedures and criminal laws enacted in the wake of the hysteria attending the war on drugs.[52]

As so often is the case, criminal justice stratagems aimed at the poor and minorities have a way of coming back to bite their handlers. For example, mandatory sentencing went unrecognized so long as it was confined primarily to young black and Hispanic offenders and perhaps a few "white trash." However, when a few white college students, teachers, businessmen, and others began to be handled in this way, a new sense of outrage was heard from previously silent legislators.

If the past is prelude, the question of whether mandatory sentences are repealed will have virtually nothing to do with their ineffectiveness in deterring crime. Rather, the issue will be decided on the basis of how many middle- or upper-middle-class whites are at risk. The social policy lesson to be taken from all this is as old as the Salem witch hunts. Reform comes only when those who make and employ the laws are, themselves, in danger of falling prey to them.

Although Moynihan had drawn his thesis from the nineteenth century French sociologist Emile Durkheim's theory, he acknowledged but

---

[52] As writer Peter McWilliams points out, by 1993, there were more people in federal prison for drug violations than the total federal prison population when President Reagan first declared war on drugs in 1982. McWilliams goes on to summarize a number of cases notably egregious in their viciousness – including the storming by 38 officers from 8 different government agencies of the house of a 61-year-old man and his wife (killing the man) who was suspected of growing marijuana – though none was found. (McWilliams, Peter, *Ain't Nobody's Business If You Do: The Absurdity of Consensual Crimes in a Free Society,* Los Angeles, California: Prelude Press, 1993, pp. 9–12.)

downplayed Durkheim's more important point – that should actual criminal behavior recede, new crimes would be legislated to ensure that new demons can be easily identified by the populace as the enemy.[53]

This is not to suggest that American society had at any point freed itself of crime. However, there is ample evidence that during the years in which crime rates were falling, the criminal justice system had a life of its own – growing or receding, at times exponentially – unrelated to patterns of criminal behavior.

During the past four decades, the tendency has been to cast the net of justice control ever more widely into communities where, in the past, other agents of social control traditionally addressed these matters (for example, family, church, school, etc.). The criminal justice saturation of minority urban areas was strongly supported by the majority white population, most of whom lived elsewhere.

Indeed, in light of the victimization surveys that, for 20 years, had found a stable or falling crime rate, one could make the argument that the swath cut by the justice system had little to do with stemming violent or serious crime. Rather, it chipped away at the edges, bringing millions of African-American and Hispanic young men accused of lesser offenses formally into the justice system – individuals who, in earlier times, would more likely have been dealt with informally, by friends, families, churches, schools, and other traditional groups and other agencies of socialization. All this had little to do with defining down or overlooking deviance. Precisely the reverse was happening. Indeed, arrest statistics suggested that among African-Americans and the poor, very little was being overlooked.

It remained for the Reagan and Bush administrations and a cowed Democratic Congress to deliver the final *coup de grace* to any brief flirtations with reason and decency in controlling crime. Federal, state, and local funding for justice (police, judicial, prosecutors, public defenders, and corrections) rose from about $11.7 billion in 1972 to $62 billion by 1988. In 1981, there were 54,422 employees in the U.S. Justice Department. By 1992, there were almost 100,000. In 1988, $3.1 billion was going to the federal war on drugs alone. By 1989, it was $4.7 billion and by 1992, the federal government was spending $11 billion annually. In the hysteria surrounding crime in 1993, the Democrat-controlled U.S. Senate passed a $22.5 billion Crime Bill. It was a remarkable phenomenon.

---

[53] Durkheim, Emile, *The Rules of Sociological Method*, London: The Free Press of Glencoe, Collier-MacMillan Ltd., 1946 (originally published in 1885), pp. 68–69.

Meanwhile, as the cities continued their downward spiral and social welfare programs fell more deeply into national disfavor, policymakers of both the Left and the Right turned to the justice system to pick up the pieces. As plans were being made to drastically curtail welfare, the amount of federal, state, and local funding directed at pursuing, catching, and punishing offenders grew exponentially. Whatever remained of the social safety net was being effectively replaced with a dragnet thrown so widely over the urban areas that it would eventually catch most of the young black and brown men who lived there.

The centerpiece of law enforcement was its preoccupation with highly visible groups who could be relatively easily and, if possible, *publicly* arrested. The crown jewel was the handcuffed black youth or young man paraded before TV cameras so all might behold this symbol of lawlessness and disorder. It all had less to do with stemming crime than with providing a rite of public castration for the entertainment of the white majority.

The symbolism was nowhere more visible than in the liberal version of the same rite – embodied in the rush to create so-called boot camps as a means of disciplining young offenders. The fact that there was not a wisp of evidence they deterred, rehabilitated, or provided a real alternative to prison was beside the point. The ritual translated into a gripping TV image.

Genuine rehabilitation generally is thought to flow from relationships and some predisposition to care on the part of those who dispense it. That is now impossible. Indeed, we have reached a point at which rare or occasional concern must be camouflaged in pseudo-macho rhetoric. Boot camps confirm the metaphor of the black man in need of taming – one whose "reform" rested in his keepers' ability to make him run, jump about "double time," and, on command, spout back "Yes Sirs!" and "No Sirs!" as ersatz "drill instructors" heap abuse on their charges.

The fact that such stratagems had no effect on recidivism was beside the point. The *image* was correct, evoking appropriate sound bites from any politician who might wish to relieve himself of his opinions on crime and punishment.[54]

---

54 The fact that there is virtually no *credible* research to suggest that this type of handling "reforms" delinquents is beside the point. It is a matter of image, of looking tough on crime. It meets the majority's criteria for the proper political image on crime, no less than the unshaven face of Willie Horton met the same need. The military long ago learned that the boot camp was not likely to rehabilitate a young offender, despite the folk myths to the contrary. It is the major reason the military stopped taking in anyone with even the most minor record of criminal behavior. However, one might be tempted to support

The Great Divide

The Wall Street Journal suggested that the Los Angeles riots placed in stark relief, the divisions between black and white, rich and poor, suburban and urban:

> ... growing up in the 1960s and 1970s, liberal children of conservative parents vowed they would be different. In fact, many of them have become so detached that the cognoscenti have a phrase for them: "People Like Us," or "PLU's ... It means "People Like Us" as opposed to "People Like Them" – who we find threatening. It's a term of distinction, exclusion and lately, it stresses defensiveness and escapism.[55]

The major source of information about, or contact with, violent crime for most Americans comes from TV. The media images that fuel the fear of crime among suburban and rural citizens (the groups least likely to be victimized by violent crime) have also made them willing to support extreme tactics of crime control (threatening basic democratic traditions in the process), so long as these measures are seen as primarily being aimed at minorities living in urban locations (those most likely to be victims of serious crime). It defined what the majority meant when it called for law and order. It also fed a sense of unity and cohesion based in hostility directed at an identifiable enemy. It was a smooth way to go for politicians.

Noting the great gap between the public's perception of crime and realities of crime, *The Wall Street Journal* headlined a front page article on the subject, "People with the Least to Fear from Crime Drive the Crime Issue." The *Journal* cited a 1992 survey by the Joint Center for Political and Economic Studies that found that suburban upper-income blacks were more likely to see crime as a critical issue than were low-income blacks in urban areas.[56] As if to reinforce this view, in the New York mayoral election of 1993, those boroughs with the highest crime rates and in which citizens were the more likely to be victimized by violent crime voted for the incumbent David Dinkins, rejecting the harsh law

---

boot camps for young inner-city youths were they authentic – that is, were they, as in the military, followed by intensive training in a trade or occupation, with guaranteed employment with full benefits, including retirement at age 38, to be followed with a pension.

[55] Ron Suskind, "Islands in a Storm: As Urban Woes Grow, 'PLUs' Are Seeking Psychological Suburbia," *The Wall Street Journal*, Vol. 219, No. 96, 1992, p. 1.

[56] McQueen, Michel, "Political Paradox: People with the Least to Fear from Crime Drive the Crime Issue," *The Wall Street Journal*, August 12, 1992, p. A12.

and order rhetoric of Rudolph Giuliani while the whiter and the more removed voters were from high crime areas, the more likely they were to vote for Giuliani.

It was not unlike the image conjured up in Richard Nixon's 1968 law and order campaign against Hubert Humphrey – the visage of a predatory black man ready to do violence to whites. With this visage before them, hundreds of suburban whites bought guns in the wake of the Los Angeles riots, even though the disturbances never came close to their neighborhoods. All this, despite the fact that even in the 75 largest urban counties (most likely to have greater concentrations of African-American citizens), more than 80 percent of both white and black murder defendants had victims of the same racial background and 8 of every 10 murder victims were killed by relatives or acquaintances.[57] As Northeastern University criminologist James Fox commented, "One of the worst things affecting our feeling of safety was probably the development of the video camera."[58]

University of Pennsylvania communications researcher George Gerbner, who had collected data on 20 years of television and movie violence, noted that "violence on television is vastly exaggerated compared to real life and has a totally different demography." Noting that there were an average of six to eight acts of violence per hour in prime time with two murders per night, Gerbner was less concerned that this might stimulate real-life violence than he was alarmed with how it exaggerated "feelings of insecurity, dependence and fear" – mostly among middle-class whites.

The political and policy implications of this were immense. While black ghetto residents identified jobs or the economy as their first concern, suburbanites saw it as violent crime.[59]

As *The New York Times* noted, urban residents who were the most likely to have to contend with real-life crime seemed more able to separate fact from fantasy.[60] When it came to developing policy and legislation to combat crime, those who were least likely to be victims of serious crime ended up defining the debate while those most likely to be personally victimized by crime were, for the most part, excluded. Had they been included, it is more likely the discussion would have centered more on so-called root causes, particularly aimed at unemployment. In effect, the

[57] Dawson, John and Barbara Boland, *Murder in Large Urban Counties, 1988*, Bureau of Justice Statistics Special Report, May 1993, pp. 1, 3.
[58] McQueen, Michel, op. cit. p. A14.
[59] Ibid. p. A12.
[60] Meier, Barry, "Reality and Anxiety: Crime and the Fear of It," *The New York Times*, February 18, 1993, p. A14.

philosophy of crime control came to be one of finding the best means of dealing with "people like them" (primarily, as portrayed on TV news and tabloid shows).

For the media, the disintegration in the inner cities was less a problem than an opportunity for an extended series of crime shows. Indeed, slowing the crime was beside the point.[61] Any indication that crime rates

---

[61] Indeed, some commentators on contemporary journalism are of the opinion that we have already passed the point of no return when it comes to media exploitation of events – and concomitant disinterest in facts. Commenting on the whole sorry spectacle, John Leo, the syndicated columnist and contributing editor to *U.S. News and World Report* said:

These are embarrassing days for the news business. *Dateline NBC* rigged a GM pickup to explode helpfully on camera. *USA Today* suspended a reporter for staging a front-page photo of ominous gunbearing gang members. The young men had been sent home to get their guns for the picture. And a PBS documentary on how black troops freed Jews from Dachau and Buchenwald was pulled for review when news broke that some members of the black regiment involved said they had never been anywhere near either camp.

In all these cases, the question is whether this is inaccuracy or deception. As the media have rehashed the deceptive explosions on *Dateline NBC*, the consensus seems to be that this was a lapse from the standards of TV news.

But what if it wasn't a lapse? What if it was a preview of what news is destined to become as images, story line, and emotional impact begin to erode the old commitment to literal truth? Richard Reeves, a syndicated columnist with good contacts in the world of TV, explicitly makes this argument.

Mr. Reeves says the old guard has disappeared from TV news, and the business is now in the hands of a new generation. They don't think of themselves as reporters or producers, but as "filmmakers" with little interest in words, and heavy interest in dramatic effect. To Mr. Reeves, the GM truck explosions are a watershed event, "the end of the old standards, those old journalism ethics imposed, sometimes quite hypocritically, by print journalists."

He thinks deceptive stories on TV, like the first homeless people on our streets, are being treated as isolated problems instead of the beginning of a major trend. *CBS News* was accused of staging combat scenes in Afghanistan. *ABC News* "re-enacted" a scene that nobody ever proved was enacted at all – a U.S. diplomat taking a briefcase full of money from Soviet agents. These events put NBC's current problems in perspective.

Obvious competitive pressures have a lot to do with this corner-cutting trend in journalism. The world of TV journalism is an overheated, fragmented one with no old-line, stable corporate cultures to fall back on. The old-guard CBS reporter with a guaranteed lifetime job and no ratings problems could sit around pondering standards and the lessons of Edward R. Murrow. The new guard has to produce, drive the ratings, or get out. People don't get fired for getting facts wrong or misplacing a few Idaho fish. They get fired for falling to No. 3.

When Mr. Reeves says the new guard is made up of completely different people, he is echoing many criticisms of young, aggressive producers who don't get much guidance or mentoring these days. "These are the vidkids who know much more than us about filming, editing, and graphics," said one veteran TV executive. "But they aren't very

might, indeed, be dropping would be counterproductive to the whole exercise. It was the scent of the hunt that excited us. Catching the "most wanted" had quietly become a pop culture industry, and if the despised could be seen to have a black face, the distinctions were elemental and the remedies gratuitously vicious.

familiar with the basic rules of journalism. If you don't vigilantly supervise, they'll come back with stuff that sets your hair on end."

University of New Hampshire professor of communication Joshua Meyroswitz put it more succinctly:

They tend to have an image-based standard of truth. If I ask, what evidence supports your view or contradicts it, they look at me as if I came from another planet. It's very foreign to them to think in terms of truth, logic, consistency, and evidence. (Leo, John, "Lapse or TV News Preview?" *The Washington Times*, Op-Ed, March 5, 1993.)

5

The Search for the Criminaloid

Stalking the Criminal Brain

In 1985, a University of Florida sociology professor was engaged in a hallway conversation with the head of the Department of Psychiatry when the discussion took a quirky turn. The psychiatrist casually remarked that another professor had been collecting portions of the amygdala from the remains of prisoners recently executed in Florida's electric chair. He emphasized the point by remarking that the brain samples were "in a bucket upstairs" in the same building in which the two were chatting.

The sociologist, somewhat taken aback at the revelation, remarked on it to his class later that day. As it happened, a reporter from Jacksonville's *Florida Times Union* was auditing the course and the secret was out. It was later revealed that the professor had made private arrangements with the state's medical examiner to have the brains saved for her after the autopsies. Releases and permissions had not been sought from the families of the deceased and the whole matter had been kept sub rosa. The professor planned to study the brain slices to assist her in finding organic markers of a murderer.

When the incident of the purloined brains was made public, Florida corrections authorities stopped the practice. Florida State University criminologist C. R. Jeffery, who had long held that the future of criminology lay in pursuit of "genetic codes and brain codes," responded to a front page story in the *Tallahassee Democrat*:

... I assume this means that the causes of crimes are social and not biological: Even the conservative James Q. Wilson now recognizes this role of biology in criminal behavior.[1]

Jeffery was right in his assessment of Wilson, and indeed, one could reasonably argue that slides of brain sections might conceivably be of some limited value in understanding some types of violent behavior. The professor who had accumulated the brains hoped they might provide hard evidence of head trauma due to gross physical child abuse – brain lesions that might be related to the loss of inhibition, as some researchers had suggested, were common in some individuals who had committed certain kinds of homicides.[2]

Given the pervasive hostility in the courts toward narratives of physical and sexual abuse in the early lives of so many of those convicted of violent crimes, the professor apparently concluded that were she able to come up with an identifiable marker in the brain, it might be partially exculpatory or mitigate the likelihood of the death penalty being applied. The idea that brain injury or disease might explain even less specific situations of violence was not new. Indeed, in the wake of the urban riots of the 1960s, Drs. Vernon Mark, W. H. Sweet, and Frank Ervin published their view of this problem in the *Journal of the American Medical Association,* headlined "Role of Brain Disease in Riots and Urban Violence."[3] They suggested that many of those who engaged in violence during urban riots of the late 1960s suffered from brain diseases – and needed to be diagnosed "before they contribute to more tragedies." The fact that the doctors were primarily, if not exclusively, referring to black males when they related brain disease to inner-city riots was not mentioned.

---

[1] Jeffery, C. R., "Look beyond legal question of brain study," Letter to the Editor, *Tallahassee Democrat,* October 14, 1985.

[2] Lewis, D. O., J. H. Pincus, et al. "Neuropsychiatric, Psychoeducational, and Family Characteristics of 14 Juveniles Condemned to Death in the United States," *American Journal of Psychiatry,* Vol. 145, No. 5, May 1988. In a summary of their research, Lewis Shanok and Balla conclude that "if genetic factors play any role at all in delinquency, they are more likely to involve the inheritance of special vulnerabilities to maladaptive behavior in the nature of susceptibility to disorganized thought processes or to attentional and perceptional disorders. Only when such diverse kinds of vulnerabilities are environmentally influenced toward an antisocial set of behaviors may delinquency result." (Lewis, D. O., S. S. Shanok, and D. Balla, "Parents of Delinquents," in Lewis, D. O. (ed.), *Vulnerabilities to Delinquency,* New York: SP Medical and Scientific Books, 1981, p. 289.)

[3] Letter to Editor, *Journal of the American Medical Association,* Vol. 201, 1967, p. 895.

The treatment this diagnosis would warrant was not specified until three years later, when Mark and Ervin called for establishing a federal hospital for the "sociobiological study of violent persons." They outlined their approach in this way:

This study must be aimed at (1) establishing the physical and social causes for such behavior; (2) developing reliable early warning tests for violence; (3) assessing presently available methods of treatment, including medical and surgical therapies; and (4) establishing community facilities to help violent persons – facilities that also might be used for medical and sociological studies.[4]

Surgical procedures such as implanting electrodes deeply in the brain and removal of parts of the amygdala were among the options recommended.[5]

Where would all this lead in terms of social policy? In this case, it almost led to the establishment of a federal prison (Butner, North Carolina) where, it was proposed, brain surgery – lobotomies and amygdalatomies – could be performed on selected offenders, not exclusively those identified by the violence of their crimes but also as a means of dealing with individuals whose aggressiveness had made them management problems within the correctional bureaucracy itself.[6]

---

[4] Mark, Vernon H., and Frank Ervin, *Violence and the Brain,* New York: Harper & Row, 1970, p. 65.

[5] None of these suggestions came without a certain amount of political and personal baggage. In the late 1980s, Dr. Mark also led the movement in Philadelphia calling for a total quarantine of persons with AIDS. The ubiquitous image of the criminal as monster merges with other apparently primal fears. As a film reviewer for *The New York Times* noted in her review of the first Dracula film, *Nosferatu*: "The enduring power of 'Nosferatu' is more than a testament to Murnau (the filmmaker). It also suggests the depth and complexity of the vampire myth, which adapts to every era and genre. The disease-carrying hero can refer to the bubonic plague or to AIDS; his state of eternal unrest holds meaning for the religious and the godless; he is often alluring and repulsive at once. Vampires are shape shifters, in the symbolic as well as the physical sense." (Caryn James, "'Nosferatu,' the Father of All Horror Movies," *The New York Times*, April 2, 1993, pp. C1 and C19.)

[6] Moran noted that "... a brief look at penal history reveals that it was under the banner of humanitarian concerns that involuntary sterilization of the mentally ill, mentally defective, the epileptic, sex offenders, 'degenerates,' syphilitics, and the so-called hereditary criminal were undertaken. Lobotomy, electrical shock, and preventive incarceration of the 'dangerous classes' were likewise practiced as preferable penal substitutes." Moran added, ":... crime and the criminal become a status rather than a behavior." This was precisely the goal of Carl Schmitt, Nazi Germany's leading constitutional lawyer, when he proposed the theory of a priori culpability. According to Schmitt, a criminal was not necessarily one who committed an illegal act, but one whose character and personality rendered him a criminal. (Moran, op. cit.)

Mark and Ervin were not the only ones to suggest that urban violence might be profitably dealt with through psychosurgical means. As psychiatrist Peter Breggin noted, in an unpublished speech in 1973, Dr. Ernest Rodin, neurologist in charge of Detroit's Lafayette Clinic Project, had strongly recommended the use of psychosurgery on prison inmates. Rodin argued that children of limited intelligence tended to become violent when treated as "equals." Touting what he called an authoritarian life style, Rodin declared:

Tolerance and encouragement of free thought is probably excellent for the high IQ bracket, but not advisable for the lower one, and one is reminded of the Roman saying: "Quod licet Jovi non licet bovi" (what is allowed for Jupiter is not allowed for the ox). The problem is that the ox may not recognize himself as an ox and demand Jupiter's prerogatives.[7]

As Breggin commented, "Rodin liked the ox image. Much violence could be avoided by castrating 'dumb young males' who riot."[8] Rodin expanded on the ox metaphor:

Farmers have known for ages immemorial that you can't do a blasted thing with a bull except fight or kill and eat him; the castrated ox will pull his plow; try to ride a young stallion and you will gladly settle for a gelding or a mare. It is also well known that human eunuchs, although at times quite scheming entrepreneurs, are not given to physical violence. Our scientific age tends to disregard this wisdom of the past...[9]

While Rodin also advocated psychosurgery, he felt that without castration it was likely to be ineffective:

As a result [of the psychosurgery], the now hopefully more placid dullard can inseminate other equally dull young females to produce further dull and aggressive offsprings.[10]

None of this is to suggest that pathology in the brain had no relevance to violent crime. Indeed, in the 1990s, clinical studies by medical researchers Dorothy Otnow Lewis and Jonathan Pincus were suggesting that a significant number of men on death row who had histories

---

7 Rodin, E., *A Neurological Appraisal of Some Episodic Behavioral Disturbances with Special Emphasis on Aggressive Outbursts*, Exhibit 3 for American Orthopsychiatric Association, *Kaimowitz v. Dept. of Mental Health*, Civil No. 73–19, 434-AW (Cir. Ct. Wayne Co. Mich., July 19, 1973).

8 Breggin, Peter, "Psychosurgery for Political Purposes," *Duquesne Law Review*, Vol. 13, 1973, p. 853.

9 Rodin, E., op. cit. p. 13.

10 Ibid. p. 14.

of gross physical and ruminative sexual abuse had also suffered head trauma with identifiable brain lesions, particularly in the temporal lobe – that section of the brain that ostensibly controls the ability to inhibit one's impulses. According to Lewis and Pincus, an unhappy confluence of childhood abuse combined with demonstrable insults to the brain seemed related to an individual's ability to inhibit aggressive or sexual impulses given certain conditions.[11] However, in addition to neurological tests and brain scans, Pincus and Lewis presumed interest and motivation on the part of researchers to expend time and effort to fully investigate and compile corroborated facts regarding the personal and family history.

Having myself prepared mitigative studies on dozens of defendants facing execution, I had learned through bitter experience that these kinds of medical and personal narratives are difficult to uncover and were seldom developed in even the most high-profile capital cases (with the exception of those few defendants who came from families of wealth). As the mother of one of those whose brain had been appropriated in Florida commented to me, "I probably would have given them permission to take his brain, but I wish someone would have spent some time talking with him while he was still alive." What she didn't understand is that looking too closely at her son, his background, his community, his family, or his life experience is an extremely dangerous exercise for those in search of monsters. In contrast, the search for the criminal *brain* provides blessed reassurance that the monster doesn't potentially reside in us all.

I found it common that in death penalty cases, even the most attenuated and incomplete social histories of defendants were seen by prosecutors to represent a threat to their case. Pulling out every stop to discredit or disregard this kind of information, they were willing to go to extraordinary lengths to keep such material out of the hearing of juries. This frantic fight had virtually nothing to do with the truth or pursuing justice. Rather, it seemed more geared to keeping the ritual in place, which, in capital cases, above all is about the business of demonization.

Following Washington State's 1993 execution by hanging of Westley Allan Dodd, who had been convicted of sexually molesting and murdering three children, Dr. Jerry Dennis, the medical director of that state's Western State Hospital, requested Dodd's brain. Dennis wanted to widen the search for "criminal man" by conducting brain scans and extracting vials of the dead man's blood to detect any gene oddities. As Dennis put

---

[11] Lewis, Dorothy and Jonathan Pincus.

it, "He (Dodd) was certainly a pedophilic and sociopathic personality. We want to enhance our understanding of these kinds of disorders."[12]

Having worked on a large number of death penalty appeals and sentencings, there was a time when I would have welcomed some revelation that a criminal gene, a brain lesion, or "bad blood" might explain the violence – reasoning that such a finding might mitigate the rush to execute. If the person were truly "born that way" surely we couldn't hold him as responsible as someone without the abnormality. I would have been wrong. The way the nation has headed, it is more likely that were a brain section to conclusively reveal a "marker" for the murderer, be it genetic or a result of child abuse, it would probably only seal the fate of the condemned – damaged goods to be done with.

Indeed, it had become common, if not chic, to claim a genetic link for a wide variety of human problems and behaviors. More interesting than the extravagant claims of having located the genetic situs of a specific kind of behavior was the fact that so much was claimed for so few demonstrable results. In June 1993, *The Scientific American* published the following "Lack-of-Progress Report" on the state of behavioral genetics up to that date:

Crime: Family, twin and adoption studies have suggested a heritability of 0 to more than 50 percent for predisposition to crime. (Heritability represents the degree to which a trait stems from genetic factors.) In the 1960s researchers reported an association between an extra Y chromosome and violent crime in males. Follow-up studies found that association to be spurious.

Manic Depression: Twin and family studies indicate heritability of 60 to 80 percent for susceptibility to manic depression. In 1987 two groups reported locating different genes linked to manic depression, one in Amish families and the other in Israeli families. Both reports have been retracted.

Schizophrenia: Twin studies show heritability of 40 to 90 percent. In 1988 a group reported finding a gene linked to schizophrenia in British and Icelandic families. Other studies documented no linkage, and the initial claim has now been retracted.

Alcoholism: Twin and adoption studies suggest heritability ranging from 0 to 60 percent. In 1990 a group claimed to link a gene – one that produces a receptor for the neurotransmitter dopamine – with alcoholism. A recent review of the evidence concluded it does not support a link.

Intelligence: Twin and adoption studies show a heritability of performance on intelligence tests of 20 to 80 percent. One group recently unveiled preliminary

---

[12] Glamser, Deeann, "Killer's Brain Causes Clash," *USA Today*, April 1993.

evidence for genetic markers for high intelligence (an IQ of 130 or higher). The study is unpublished.

Homosexuality: In 1991 a researcher cited anatomic differences between the brains of heterosexual and homosexual males. Two recent twin studies have found a heritability of roughly 50 percent for predisposition to male or female homosexuality. These reports have been disputed. Another group claims to have preliminary evidence of genes linked to male homosexuality. The data have not been published.[13]

As I edited the last chapter of the first edition of this book, another behavioral genetics news story related to crime appeared in the major newspapers of the country. It referred to the work of a group of Dutch and American researchers who studied a Dutch family with a history of erratic and hostile behavior. The scientists claimed to have identified a tiny genetic defect that appeared to predispose some men toward aggression, impulsiveness, and violence.[14] Hans Brunner, the lead author of the study and a geneticist at University Hospital in Nigmegen, the Netherlands, told *The New York Times* that whereas, "Other studies have implicated biological and inherited factors.... This is the first that actually pinpoints a specific gene and a specific mutation within that gene."[15] Comparing the monamine oxidase A genes in 5 "afflicted" and 12 "nonafflicted" males in the family, the scientists found a difference in a single "point mutation" in a single building block among the thousands that make up the gene among those who appeared to manifest aggressive or impulsive behavior. Admitting that they did not know the exact mechanism of the disorder, the researchers hypothesized that lacking the metabolic enzyme, the brains of the afflicted men contained excess deposits of powerful signaling molecules such as serotonin, dopamine, and noradrenaline. A surplus of these neurotransmitters was hypothesized as stimulating erratic and hostile behavior.

Dr. Xandra O. Breakefield, an associate neurogeneticist at Massachusetts General Hospital in Charleston, cautioned that even in a seemingly straightforward case such as an enzyme disorder, the spectrum of the behaviors in the five afflicted men could not be explained by a single genetic defect alone:

---

[13] Horgan, John, "Trends in Behavioral Genetics: Eugenics Revisited," *The Scientific American*, Vol. 268, No. 6, June 1993, pp. 122–31.

[14] Brunner, Hans G., et al., *Science*, November 1993.

[15] Angier, Natalie, "Study Finds a Genetic Flaw That May Explain Some Male Violence," *The New York Times*, October 22, 1993.

Different members of the family behave differently. Some are functioning quite well, and one is married, has children and a job. Obviously how this syndrome is manifested as a behavior depends on many factors.

Dr. Jonathan Beckwith, professor of microbiology and molecular genetics at Harvard Medical School, noted that this study, like others before it, did not adequately define what was meant by aggressive behavior:

It's been a long-term problem in this area, an insufficient characterization of the behaviors you're looking at. . . . That's one reason why there have been so many announcements of genes that have later been retracted. There's often a lot less here than meets the eye.

Perhaps more interesting was the researchers' conclusion that the particular type of enzyme deficiency they had found in a Dutch family would afflict no more than 1 in 100,000 people. As Dr. Emil F. Coccaro, director of clinical neuroscience research at the Medical College of Pennsylvania in Philadelphia commented:

. . . this is a rare disorder. It ain't the gene for all those people who are committing murder left and right.

In fact, were the study to be replicated and were the defect to be found in the general population, the enzyme would affect fewer than 1,500 males in the whole United States – most, but not all, of whom would be subject to outbursts, shouting, cursing, and occasionally assaulting persons they see as a threat. If the theory is correct, only a small minority of these would find themselves involved with the justice system.

None of this is to suggest that genes have no place in human behavior (including violent behavior) or that *homo sapiens* has no grounding in evolutionary heritage, or even that human morality itself may not draw its shape from biology. The questions are as old as Aristotle. However, the search for these common sources of our humanity has usually emanated from impulses quite different from those that historically have driven the search for our differences. Indeed, given the shaky science and the peripheral relevance of the data on differences, motivation (personal and political) ends up being the more important issue.

Stalking the Criminal Gene

The quest for "criminal man" has begun in earnest. One study of popular magazines and scientific journals revealed that between 1983 and

1988, articles attributing crime to genetics were published four times more often than they had been during the previous decade.[16] As the California African-American sociologist Troy Duster had suggested, when it comes to African-Americans and crime:

... with blacks constituting about 12 percent of the U.S. population and committing about 60 percent of the reported homicides, and with the incarceration rates reflecting the racial patterns noted above, and with our prisons getting darker and darker, it is only a matter of time before there is a convergence of the halo of the new genetics and the appropriation of that halo by other researchers.[17]

Elsewhere, Duster outlined the ways in which the numbers could be misinterpreted by those in search of the genetics of crime:

If we are ignorant of recent history, and do not know that the incarceration rate and the coloring of our prisons is a function of dramatic changes in the last half century, we are far more vulnerable to the seduction of the genetic explanation ... (the) astonishing pattern of incarceration rates by race ... should give pause to anyone who would try to explain these incarcerated. . . . The gene pool among humans takes many centuries to change, but since 1933, the incarceration of African-Americans in relation to whites has gone up in a striking manner. In 1933, blacks were incarcerated as a race approximately three times the rate of incarceration for whites. In 1950, the ratio had increased to approximately 4 to 1; in 1960, it was 5 to 1; in 1970, it was 6 to 1; and in 1989, it was 7 to 1.[18]

To a white majority standing in frantic need of a *scientific* rationale, the "genetics of crime" presents a seductively appealing refuge. The ways in which matters have been quickly twisted to these kinds of needs can be seen in the response of a number of academics to an "in-house" 1991 U.S. Justice Department study on incarcerated adults and juveniles. Allen Beck, a demographer with the Bureau of Justice Statistics, found that 52 percent of incarcerated youths and 35 percent of imprisoned adults had close relatives who had also been incarcerated. In personal interviews of a representative national sample of 2,621 teenagers in juvenile correctional facilities in 1987, 24 percent said their father had served time in jail or

---

[16] Duster, Troy, *Backdoor to Eugenics*, London: Routledge, 1990, p. 93.

[17] Ibid. p. 100.

[18] Duster noted that the drug war of the 1980s further exaggerated these differences. In Florida, admissions to state prisons tripled from 1983 to 1989. In Virginia, 63 percent of prison commitments for drugs were white, 37 percent minority. By 1989, the pattern had reversed, with 34 percent of the new commitments being white and 65 percent minority. "Yet, in this very period we find a significant increase in scientific journal articles and scholarly books (Mednick et al. 1984; Wilson and Herrnstein 1985) suggesting a greater role for biological explanations of crime." (Duster, Troy, "Genetics, Race, and Crime, Etc.," pp. 133–35.)

prison, 9 percent said their mother had been incarcerated, and 25 percent said a brother or sister had been incarcerated. Similarly, 8 percent of adult jail inmates and 7 percent of prison inmates said a parent had been incarcerated, while 29 percent and 32 percent respectively said a brother or sister had been incarcerated.[19]

These data weren't particularly new. A 1979 study had found that 40 percent of prison inmates had immediate family members (father, mother, brother, sister, spouse, or child) who had been incarcerated at some time in the past. A 1983 study had likewise found that 34 percent of jail inmates had family members who had been incarcerated. However, the 1991 study involved larger percentages of black inmates than did the earlier studies. Suddenly, the rush to genetic interpretations was unstoppable.

Fordham University Associate Professor of Law Deborah W. Denno tied the phenomenon to "hyperactivity," transmitted genetically across generations, creating a "biological predisposition to criminal behavior." "These results are stunning statistics," said the redoubtable Harvard psychologist Richard Herrnstein. The data provided fresh proof "that the more chronic the criminal, the more likely it is to find criminality in his or her relatives... (criminality) is transmitted both genetically and environmentally. So kids brought up in criminal families get a double exposure. That accounts for this enormously dramatic statistic."[20]

Marvin Wolfgang, professor of criminology and law at the University of Pennsylvania, took a somewhat different tack: "You should remember that most of these people come from low socioeconomic backgrounds, disadvantaged neighborhoods, where a high proportion of people will be sent to jail whether they are related or not." Wolfgang was conservative in his assessment. The reality was that African-Americans were being arrested in such large numbers in the inner city that a person who *didn't* know of a close relative who had been jailed or imprisoned would be an odd exception.

---

[19] Beck, Allen, *Survey of Youth in Custody, 1987* NCJ-11365, September 1988; *Profile of Jail Inmates, 1989,* NCJ-129097, April 1991.

[20] The genetic interpretations contrasted vividly with those of sociologists Ann Case of Princeton University and Lawrence Katz of Harvard. They found that one of the most powerful predictors of criminal behavior among youths was growing up in a household in which a family member was in jail. However, they saw this as a far more powerful argument for the ill effects of social contagion than the so-called genetics of crime.

(Case, Anne, and Lawrence Katz, "The Company You Keep: The Effects of Family and Neighborhood on Disadvantaged Youths." NBER Boston Youth Survey. Research supported by Russell Sage Foundation and National Science Foundation, Cambridge, Massachusetts: Bell Associates, May 1991.)

There were many possible explanations for the findings. For example, Princeton researcher Anne Case and Harvard researcher Lawrence Katz found that:

... youths who had family members in jail when they were being raised are much more likely to be involved in criminal activity....

... the links between the behavior of older family members and youths are important for criminal activity, drug and alcohol use, childbearing out of wedlock, schooling, and church attendance. We also find that the behaviors of neighborhood peers appear to substantially affect youth behaviors in a manner suggestive of contagion models of neighborhood effects. Residence in a neighborhood in which a large proportion of other youths are involved in crime is associated with a substantial increase in an individual's probability of being involved in crime... Our results indicate that family and peer influences both operate in manner such that "like begets like."[21]

The joining of race and crime got uncomfortably free-associational in early 1992, when then-administrator of the Alcohol, Drug Abuse and Mental Health Administration, Frederick K. Goodwin, relieved himself of his views on inner-city crime to a Washington meeting of the National Mental Health Advisory Council:

If you look for example, at male monkeys, especially in the wild, roughly half of them survive to adulthood. The other half die by violence. That is the natural way of it for males, to knock each other off and, in fact, there are some interesting evolutionary implications of that.... The same hyperaggressive monkeys who kill each other are also hypersexual, so they copulate more and therefore they reproduce more to offset the fact that half of them are dying.

Dr. Goodwin then drew an analogy with the "high impact [an]inner city areas with the loss of some of the civilizing evolutionary things that we have built up.... Maybe it isn't just the careless use of the word when people call certain areas of certain cities, jungles."

More disturbing than the implied racist content was the fact that an eminent health professional at the highest level of national policy formulation felt no uneasiness in making such statements in a public forum. It suggested that although he may have committed a public relations *faux pas,* he probably hadn't misjudged his audience of professionals, advisers, government officials, and policy planners, many of whom he had ostensibly dealt with in less formal interchange.

[21] Ibid.

Goodwin pretty much dismissed the idea of dealing with the social and economic causes and concomitants of crime and violence:

... if you are going to leverage that at all, in my view, you are going to leverage it through individuals, not through large social engineering of society.... [Y]ou look at genetic factors and violence and aggression which are very strong, and from the few adoption studies that we have ... If you are going to say, we have 10 million potential recipients of this intervention, forget it. If we are talking about, we might be able to hone down to something under 100,000 and then talk about interventions...

After his comments appeared in the national press, Dr. Goodwin was "demoted" by being appointed director of the National Institute of Mental Health (NIMH), where, among other things, he would oversee a recently crafted national "violence initiative" to study the causes of violent crime in the inner city. As the end of the first year of the Clinton administration approached, Dr. Goodwin was still director of NIMH, and a respected behavioral geneticist, David Rowe, was proposing an "evolved genetic theory" of delinquency, which, based in the mating strategies of such animals as baboons, monkeys, and cuckoos, would seek to identify those genes that maximize mating and minimize parenting among certain groups and individuals.

Acknowledging that his new theory was not ready to meet the needs of social policymakers, the author noted that most of the policy conclusions flowing from his analysis probably would be unacceptable to a democratic society. He then outlined the possibilities:

Whether the hypothesized trait serves a mating effort function, I am pessimistic that interventions aimed at altering family conditions so that more families exhibited the disciplined practices of intelligent, middle class parents would greatly reduce the mating effort traits of children who are at the trait extreme.... A biologically-based trait, of course, raises the possibility of using biological as opposed to social interventions. Biological interventions could take two forms. First, eugenic interventions would involve adopting public policies that control human reproduction.... Therapeutic interventions could involve administering drugs to alter nervous system functioning.... Ecological intensifiers could be another target of intervention efforts.... For example, if threshold effects are associated with population composition, one could plan communities to keep the population at risk below the threshold level ... an intervention contravening our most fundamental democratic values favoring freedom of association.[22]

---

[22] Rowe, David C., "An Adaptive Strategy Theory of Crime and Delinquency," in Hawkins, J. David (ed.), *Some Current Theories of Delinquency and Crime*, Cambridge: Cambridge University Press (1994).

The New Lombrosians

Most may have thought that the theories of the nineteenth century Italian criminologist Cesare Lombroso on the "born criminal" were long dead. Not so. Lombroso was being resuscitated in new forms to meet the current crisis among minorities in the cities. The door to the genetics of crime had been thrown open widely in 1985 by Harvard psychologist Richard Herrnstein and University of Southern California management professor James Q. Wilson. In their well-received book, *Crime and Human Nature*, Wilson and Herrnstein deftly skirted the so-called criminal gene, focusing instead on putative differences among criminals versus normal citizens and, by extension, the differences in IQ between blacks and whites.

It was another step down a path Herrnstein had set years before. Long known for his views on the heritability of IQ with particular reference to African-Americans, and a proponent of the view that American society is basically a "meritocracy," he once mused that " . . . the tendency to be unemployed may run in the genes of a family about as certainly as bad teeth do now."[23]

Following Harvard psychologist Arthur Jensen's argument that most of the difference between blacks and whites in their performance on IQ tests was genetic, in a 1971 *Atlantic* article, Herrnstein widened his concept of genetic inferiority:

The privileged classes of the past were probably not much superior biologically to the downtrodden, which is why revolution had a fair chance of success. By removing artificial barriers between classes, society has encouraged the creation of biological barriers. When people can take their natural level in society, the upper classes will, by definition, have greater capacity than the lower.

---

[23] This was a variation on earlier discussions in Northern Europe. Near the turn of the twentieth century, the German anthropologist Werner Sombart held that Jews had an innate tendency to trade, along with an abnormally strong sexual impulse. Yet, he seemed to be surprised by how his theories were taken up politically – long before the advent of Nazism, he summarized his concerns in 1911:

Of late everything that is in any way connected with the study of national and racial characters has become a toy for dilettantic whims, and more especially has the study of Jewish character been undertaken as a political sport by rude minds with blunt instincts – to the disgust and surfeit of all who are still possessed of some taste and impartiality in this unpolished age.

(Sombart, W., *Die Juden und das Wirtschaftsleben*, Leipzig, 1911, p. 296 (quoted by Svend Ranulf, op. cit. p. 54).

As Lerner observed:

To Herrnstein, then, our present society is totally "just and fair," and consequently the poor, weak, homeless, and unemployed are in their proper, biologically established place. This is so, in Herrnstein's view, because no "artificial" (societally constructed) barriers have blocked people from falling into their biologically proper role.[24]

The premise was that inner-city crime occurs for the most part among those who are left poor and jobless in an otherwise just and equal society. If particular racial groups are disproportionately arrested, therefore, there must be some genetic, ethnic, or racial flaw at work.

This conception was entirely consistent with James Q. Wilson's previously stated views of contemporary society. In a laudatory review in *Fortune* magazine of *Forbes* magazine columnist Daniel Seligman's book, *A Question of Intelligence: The I.Q. Debate in America,*[25] which held that IQ is primarily racially determined, Wilson left little doubt regarding where he stood on this crucial issue:

Indisputable facts – worry many decent people who feel that it is impolite or impolitic to acknowledge *group differences* in a society committed to the proposition that 'all men are created equal'... [The] egalitarian impulse makes such people willing victims of academic charlatans and political demagogues who argue that differences in IQ are chiefly or entirely a matter of environment[26] (emphasis added).

Characteristically, Wilson slipped over the racial issue, even though race was the central point of the book he so strongly endorsed. He suggested, however, that when it came to breeding, all was not lost for the majority – "group differences," he noted, "... depending on marriage patterns and birthrates, may well change." Wilson didn't spell out what this might mean as a matter of formal social policy. If history is any guide, the acrid smell of eugenics sifts through the air whenever the putatively more endowed turn to discussion about the marriage patterns and birthrates of the putatively less endowed. Though Wilson allowed himself sufficient "wiggle room" should such an uncomfortable subject arise, his compatriot Herrnstein was less cautious.

---

[24] Lerner, Richard M., *Final Solutions: Biology, Prejudice, and Genocide,* University Park: The Pennsylvania State University Press, 1992, p. 186.

[25] Seligman, Daniel, *A Question of Intelligence: The IQ Debate in America,* New York: Birch Lane Press, 1992.

[26] Wilson, James Q., "Uncommon Sense about the IQ Debate," *Fortune,* January 11, 1993, p. 99.

In his review of the same Seligman book for *National Review,* Herrn-stein correctly identified where the arguments were headed and waded in boldly:

Looking to a more distant horizon, Seligman considers the possibility of declining (IQ) scores from generation to generation, if people with high scores continue to reproduce at low rates. This is highly controversial, and Seligman concedes that talking about differential fertility harks back to eugenics. But before eugenics was perverted by the Nazis, it was seen by such respectable and upright people as Oliver Wendell Holmes Jr. as a matter of designing public policies to improve human hereditary endowment in humane and voluntary ways, such as dissemi-nating information about birth control.[27]

Herrnstein omitted mention of the somewhat less felicitous form of eugenics sanctioned by Oliver Wendell Holmes in the 1927 U.S. Supreme Court decision on the subject: *Buck v. Bell.* The case revolved around the constitutionality of a 1924 Virginia law that permitted the involuntary sterilization of persons in state institutions who were thought to be fee-bleminded. Justice Pierce Butler, the only Roman Catholic on the court, was also the only justice who voted against the decision.

Writing about the decision, the American historian Carl Degler observed:

From his (Holmes') treatment of the subject, it was clear that in his mind the question was not complicated. If a state may compel a young man to serve in the army in time of war, thereby putting his life in jeopardy, Holmes wrote, then it certainly ought to be able "to call upon those who already sap the strength of the state for... lesser sacrifices, often not felt to be such by those concerned, in order to prevent our being swamped with incompetence.... It is better for all the world," Holmes continued, "if instead of waiting to execute degenerate offspring for crime, or let them starve for their imbecility, society can prevent those who are manifestly unfit from continuing their kind. The principle that sustains compulsory vaccination," he concluded, "is broad enough to cover cutting the fallopian tubes... Three generations of imbeciles are enough."[28]

In the wake of the *Buck v. Bell* decision, involuntary sterilization of selected populations spread across the United States. Oklahoma had its Habitual Criminal Sterilization Act and California embarked on a 20-year program of involuntary sterilization of the institutionalized, eventu-ally sterilizing 11,000 individuals. Virginia's massive sterilization of the institutionalized provided the legal framework for early Nazi legislation

---

[27] Herrnstein, Richard J., "Subversive Intelligence," *National Review,* October 19, 1992.
[28] Degler, Carl N., *In Search of Human Nature: The Decline and Revival of Darwinism in American Social Thought,* Oxford: Oxford University Press, 1991, p. 47.

that led, first, to the sterilization of retarded children, the physically or mentally handicapped, and selected offenders.

Admittedly, the Nazis were more enthusiastic than their American counterparts, initially placing 52,000 persons under the orders to be sterilized. These planners for population improvement through eugenics gained considerable support from American advocates of eugenics. It was seen as the preferred means of improving the stock of the nation. The Nazis eventually sterilized 3.5 million persons, leading ultimately to more technically efficient methods of halting racial "degeneration."[29]

"Degeneration"

This had to do with something deeply more disturbing than simply ascribing putative genetic flaws to a particular minority. As Degler put it:

Perceiving themselves surrounded by social degeneration, particularly in the cities, many professionals and members of the intellectual elite took crime, slums, and rampant disease to be symptoms of social pathologies that they attributed primarily to biological causes – to "blood," to use the term for inheritable essence common at the turn of the century.[30]

Indeed, as Rafter has pointed out, the investigation of "degenerate" clans in the United States attracted its most fervent audience from among recognized professionals who were preoccupied with social control of the poor. These themes emerged:

Gradual rejection of the possibility that environmental factors might contribute to social problems;

Introduction of concepts from the rapidly developing field of genetics;

Increasing hostility toward the "feebleminded"; and

Ever stronger endorsement of eugenic solutions.

Those who stood most to gain from eugenics were professionals in the newly emerging business of social control – welfare workers, authors of family studies, eugenic field workers, institutional superintendents, and

[29] Duster, Troy, *Genetics, Race and Crime: Genetic Identification and Criminal Justice,* New York: Cold Spring Harbor Laboratory Press, 1992, p. 132.
[30] Degler, Carl N., op. cit.

mental testers. These groups of professionals were precisely those who contributed most to the creation of the American eugenics movement.[31]

When it came to crime and criminals, Hans Frank, the chief jurist of the early movement to halt racial degeneration in Germany and subsequently Minister of Justice in the Third Reich, said it most clearly:

> ...degeneracy is an immensely important source of criminal activity... (it) signifies exclusion from the normal "genus" of the decent nation. This state of being degenerate or egenerate, this different or alien quality, tends to be rooted in miscegenation between a decent representative of his race and an individual of inferior racial stock.... criminal biology, or the theory of congenital criminality, connotes a link between racial decadence and criminal manifestations.[32]

Though the language may differ, the conceptions were not far from those of contemporary apologists for a meritocracy obsessed with the "barbarians at the gate" – increasingly seen by the many in the majority as being of African-American or Hispanic stock. However, the concern of the elite with bad breeding among the poor had been with us long before the American eugenics movement or its appropriation by the Nazis. As the British historian Daniel Pick has observed, upper and middle-class whites had long held to the concept of degeneration among blacks:

> Lombroso's science of crime was bound up with an anthropological, evolutionary conception of "backwardness" and the primitive. In *The White Man and the Coloured Man* (1871), he (Lombroso) had confirmed that: "Only we White people [Noi soli Bianchi] have reached the most perfect symmetry of bodily form.... Only we [have bestowed]... the human right to life, respect for old age, women, and the weak... Only we have created true nationalism... [and] freedom of thought."
>
> ...inside the triumphant whiteness there remained a certain blackness. The danger was not simply external – the "Dark Continent" of Africa just beyond Sicily... Lombroso's criminal anthropology sought to help contain the threat: to comprehend it scientifically and hence exclude it politically.... The confrontation between the forces of the state on the one side and a riotous peasantry on the other amounted to civil war.[33]

Between 1880 and 1925, scientists could write about maternal instincts in women and hunting instincts in men, while stereotyping men as "unfettered by any such sentiment as sympathy, and therefore wholly

[31] Rafter, N. H., "White Trash: Eugenics as Social Ideology," *Society*, Vol. 26, No. 1, 1988, pp. 43–49.

[32] Hans, Frank, *Nationalsozialistische Strafrechtspolitik*, Munich, 1938, p. 32, quoted in Bleuel, *Strength*, p. 209.

[33] Pick, Daniel, *Faces of Degeneration: A European Disorder 1848 – c. 1918*, Cambridge: Cambridge University Press, 1989.

devoid of moral conceptions of any kind."[34] Genes were seen as determining not only intelligence, but morality and character. At the time, blacks and Asians, as well as certain Eastern European and Mediterranean whites, were all seen as falling short.

In this light, Wilson's and Herrnstein's emphasis upon the shaky concept of genetically (that is, racially) determined low IQ as a major, if not *the,* factor that most distinguishes the criminal from the rest of society is entirely reminiscent of the views of early twentieth century eugenicists such as Charles Goring, who held that "[t]he principal constitutional determinant of crime is mental defectiveness – which, admittedly, is a heritable condition."[35] Indeed, it was Goring who coined the term eugenics along with its more descriptive corollaries, race-betterment and viriculture – all part of "the science of improving stock."[36] A near-religious faith in genetics drove the Galton Eugenics Laboratory where Goring worked. Karl Pearson, the laboratory's director who most influenced Goring's work, commented that:

... it (is) quite safe to say that the influence of environment is not one-fifth that of heredity, and quite possibly not one-tenth of it. There is no real comparison between nature and nurture; it is essentially the man who makes his environment, and not the environment which makes the man.[37]

With a critical eye to certain modern-day criminological research methods, the American sociologist Pierce Beirne observed:

Goring attempted to determine the relative intensity of heredity and environment in the transmission of tuberculosis (phthisis) and insanity. His method was a correlational analysis of a random sample (the families of 1,500 nonlunatic criminals) of the general population divided into disease-present and disease-absent groups. Diseased children were significantly more likely (tuberculosis, r = 0.43; insanity, r=0.50) to have diseased parents than children in whose parents the diseases were absent. These associations, Goring concluded, showed that tuberculosis and insanity were transmitted in the same way as physical characteristics – through heredity rather than through "contagion, infection,... class distinctions or social conditions."

As Beirne summarized the research:

Discarding other possible explanations of these data, and ignoring contrary evidence, such as sewage treatment programs that reduced the incidence of

---

[34] Degler, Carl N., op. cit.
[35] Goring, Charles, *The English Convict: A Statistical Study.* London: His Majesty's Stationery Office, 1913, p. 372.
[36] Beirne, Pierce, op. cit. p. 205.
[37] Ibid. p. 198.

tuberculosis, Goring adduced, "[The] ultimate extinction [of disease] will depend upon an inherited improvement in the human stock, and not upon hygiene."[38]

Moving from genetically flawed *race* to its manifestation in the flawed *individual,* the theories and language deteriorate substantially, making things positively eerie. In effect, the hordes of whatever color were transformed into individual monsters. As Herrnstein told a *Baltimore Sun* reporter, it was no accident that the potion that changed the law-abiding Dr. Jekyll into the criminal Mr. Hyde "also made him pale and dwarfish... stooped... with a ferret, animal-like face."[39] Herrnstein's reference to the nineteenth century Jekyll and Hyde was particularly interesting, reviving, as it did, the foggy images that infected Victorians grown fearful of criminal "degenerates."

In an engrossing analysis, Pick demonstrated how the writings of Cesare Lombroso and Darwin's cousin, Francis Galton, dovetailed with the fictional netherworld of that era – including *The Picture of Dorian Gray, The Strange Case of Dr. Jekyll and Mr. Hyde,* and Bram Stoker's *Dracula*... all based in the ideas and prejudices of the time regarding the physiognomy of "degeneration."[40] Indeed, there has never been a dearth of those willing to describe criminals of whatever era as physically unattractive, animal-like, devilish appearing, or simian. Pick's analysis makes a kind of weird sense of this description by a 1940s New York prosecutor of a young Jewish offender:

He had a round face, thick lips, a flat nose and small ears, stuck close to his kinky hair. His arms had not waited for the rest of him. They dangled to his knees, completing a generally gorilla-like figure. He was, investigators concluded, "an animal in human guise."[41]

The prosecutor's homily recalled a familiar Victorian vision. As Pick noted, Oscar Wilde's Dorian Gray moved across

"this grey monstrous London," flitting between "polite" society and a grotesque East End underworld peopled by "hideous" Jews, "half-casts," opium addicts, prostitutes and alcoholics – a vast gallery of "monstrous marionettes" and "squat, misshapen figure[s]."[42]

[38] Ibid. pp. 189–90.
[39] Quoted in *Baltimore Sun*, February 2, 1986.
[40] Pick, Daniel, op. cit. pp. 155–75.
[41] Roberts, Sam, "Metro Matters," *The New York Times*, March 2, 1992.
[42] Pick, Daniel, op. cit. pp. 165–66. In his analysis of Jekyll and Hyde, Pick notes that:

   The riddle of atavism is only solved in Jekyll's final statement, delivered posthumously into the hand of his lawyer. We learn how an early recognition of the "thorough and

And when it came to flawed intelligence, who said it better than Bram Stoker, whose Dracula carried intimations of degeneration closely tied to the criminological theories of Max Nordau and Lombroso? As Pick quoted from Stoker,

"This criminal has not full man-brain. He is clever and cunning and resourceful; but he be not of man-stature as to brain. He be of child-brain in much. Now this criminal of ours is predestinate to crime also; he too have child-brain.... " The Count (Dracula) is a criminal and of criminal type. Nordau and Lombroso would classify him, and *qua* criminal he is of imperfectly formed mind.[43]

The resurgence in genetic theories of criminality in recent years is justified with the argument that more sophisticated research techniques exist now than were available to those who first searched for "criminal man." For example, Lombroso is faulted by Wilson and Herrnstein on *methodological* grounds – sampling techniques, imprecise measurement, and lack of matched samples. Modern researchers would, so the argument goes, improve the techniques. That is all to the good, but the question is hardly one of technology.[44]

primitive duality of man" had led him to transgress the bounds of chemistry, to experiment with the alchemy in a fabulous dream of separating good from evil.... Instead of the dream of transcending an animal history Jekyll discovers tragically that Hyde's "ape-like spite" is overpowering. Ever larger quantities of the antidote are needed to suppress the fiend, for as the drug wears off, "the animal within me" is once again "licking the chops of memory." Sleep itself becomes the catalyst of Hyde's liberation. Jekyll awakes to find his hands "corded" and hairy.

[43] Pick, Daniel, op. cit. p. 171.

Stoker's novel refers to Max Nordau and Cesare Lombroso, to a whole realm of investigation into degeneration and atavism which itself wavered between a taxonomy of visible stigmata and the horror of invisible maladies. There was an unresolved contradiction between the desired image of a specific, identifiable criminal type (marked out by ancestry) and the wider representation of a society in crisis, threatened by waves of degenerate blood and moral contagion.

Pick adds that Dracula's Jonathan Harker, like Lombroso and Morel, "journeys from specific images of deformity (goitre in particular: 'Here and there we passed Czechs and Slovaks, all in picturesque attire, but I noticed that goitre was painfully prevalent'), towards the citadel of full-blown degeneracy. From that early work on cretinism and goitre, a medicopsychiatric theory had emerged in which, ... the degenerate was cast as a kind of social vampire who preyed on the nation and desired, in Lombroso's words, 'not only to extinguish live in the victim, but to mutilate the corpse, tear its flesh and drink its blood.'"

[44] In a paper on this, Duster commented:

Although many are aware of the gross abuses during the early part of the century, most of the current advocates, researchers, and celebrants of the putative link between genetics and crime are either unaware of *the social context of that history*, or too quick to dismiss that history as something that happened among the unenlightened. Both formulations

For example, there is much more involved than simple differences of research methodology in Wilson's focus on the views of those who hold that certain "psychopaths" have a higher pain threshold than normal persons. Indeed, the proposition that certain types of offenders are constitutionally incapable of feeling is hardly a new one. It was first made by Lombroso, who held that:

(the criminal's) physical insensibility well recalls that of savage peoples who can bear in rites of puberty, tortures that a white man could never endure. All travelers know the indifference of Negroes and American savages to pain: the former cut their hands and laugh in order to avoid work; the latter, tied to the torture post, gaily sing the praises of their tribe while they are slowly burnt.[45]

To understand such conceptions, we need less to know about the behavior of the criminal than to identify public stereotypes and plumb the national impulse relative to those groups singled out for labeling. In 1983, University of California psychologist Sarnoff Mednick proposed to the U.S. Justice Department that he be allowed to begin testing 2,000 9- to 12-year-old boys for such markers, stating:

When frightened or otherwise emotionally aroused, normally calm individuals will evidence episodes of volar sweating. This sweating moistens the skin with a salt solution that increases its electrical conductivity.... If a weak current (generated by a battery) is leaked through the fingers we can monitor the electrical resistance (or its inverse, conductance) of the skin to the passage of the current. If we stimulate the individual to become emotionally aroused (e.g., shoot off a gun behind his back) his ANS (autonomic nervous system) will activate his volar sweat glands. The skin will be suffused with perspiration, which will increase it(s) conductance; if we are monitoring this conductance on a polygraph we will see an excursion of the pen that (all other things being equal) will be proportionate to the extent of ANS arousal experienced by our subject. Subjects who are relatively unaroused by stimulation will produce little or no pen excursion. Individuals who are highly aroused by the gunshot will evidence a substantial pen excursion. The extent of the pen excursion can be calibrated so that it can be expressed in electrical units of conductance. This process yields an objective score that reflects, at least to some substantial extent, the subject's degree of emotional arousal and ANS activation.

miss the special appeal of genetic and eugenic explanations to the most privileged strata of society, those who lay claim to the legacy of enlightenment. It was the President of Stanford University, respected bankers and politicians, governors, university professors, and other respected professionals who favored sterilization of the "lower forms" of human life, well into the middle part of this century.

(Duster, Troy, "Genetics, Race, and Crime," op. cit. p. 130).
[45] Lombroso.

Much of the work reported ... involved prisoners as subjects. The prisoners are typically divided and compared on the basis of assessed psychopathy level, seriousness of criminality, recidivism, or some combination.[46]

Those youngsters of most concern, that constantly rediscovered "new breed" of unfeeling juvenile delinquents, seem inevitably to be found to reside among the minority populations of whatever era. Indeed, Wilson and Herrnstein came perilously close to positing these kinds of arguments for crime in New York and had gotten away with it with surprisingly little criticism. Then-New York Mayor Ed Koch was particularly taken with their analysis. He reviewed *Crime and Human Nature* for the Heritage Foundation's house organ – *Policy Review* – under the title, "The Mugger and His Genes." As he saw it:

[Wilson and Herrnstein's] central thesis is that certain individual biological – indeed genetic – traits can barely be changed if at all.... The authors find only marginal roles for schools, neighborhoods, peer group values, television violence, and job market conditions as causes of crime.[47]

In an unusual two-part review on separate evenings on National Public Radio's *All Things Considered*, NPR correspondent Nina Totenberg hailed Wilson and Herrnstein's book in near-Olympian terms.

However, psychologist Leon Kamin was more than disparaging in his review in the *Scientific American*:

Wilson and Herrnstein tread delicately when writing about race and crime, but not delicately enough. They state: "If blacks are more likely to have an impulsive temperament or a somewhat lower measured IQ, these traits may be the result of patterns of prenatal care as well as of inheritance." They then cite research to show that blacks are less "normal" than whites in their personality test scores, have lower IQs, and are more likely to be of low birth weight. Criminals, remember, are said to be impulsive and unintelligent.[48]

Kamin characterized Wilson and Herrnstein's work as one in which:

Tiny snippets of data are plucked from a stew of conflicting and often nonsensical experimental results. Those snippets are then strung together in an effort to tell a convincing story, rather in the manner of a clever lawyer building a case. The data do not determine the conclusions reached by the lawyer. Instead the conclusions

---

[46] Mednick, Sarnoff and Katherine Van Dusen (Social Science Research Institute, University of California), Proposal – "Early Identification of the Chronic Offender"; submitted to U.S. Department of Justice, Office of Juvenile Justice and Delinquency Prevention, August 15, 1983, pp. 21–22.

[47] Koch, Ed, "The Mugger and His Genes," *Policy Review*, Winter 1986.

[48] Kamin, Leon, Review of *Crime and Human Nature*, *The Scientific American*, February 1986.

toward which the lawyer wants to steer the jury determine which bits of data he presents.[49]

In a curious and unusually defensive reply, Wilson and Herrnstein focused on Kamin's implied criticism of their motives:

... he (Kamin) believes we are agents of a Reaganite "ideological bent" ... This is patent nonsense, for which he can adduce not a shred of evidence ... one of us (Herrnstein) has been engaged in an effort to improve educational attainment among children in a developing country by supplying instructional materials, and the other (Wilson) has been part of an effort to extend, improve and refine preschool education for disadvantaged children.[50]

In his rejoinder, Kamin rubbed salt in the wounds:

I was pleased to learn ... that Professors Wilson and Herrnstein have each engaged in efforts to improve education for the disadvantaged. I should like to believe it was their absorption in such worthwhile activity that prevented them from taking the time to prepare a serious reply to my criticism of their book.

Noting that he had read "a few hundred" of the studies cited by Wilson and Herrnstein, Kamin concluded:

It is hard for me to believe Wilson and Herrnstein have actually read those papers. The kinds of misrepresentations ... include the description by Wilson and Herrnstein of a control group that did not exist, the reporting of statistically nonsignificant results as if they were significant, the citing of a preliminary study as if it were definitive (without mention of later, larger and better-controlled studies from the same laboratory, which produced contradictory outcomes), and so on.... Based on a sample of a few hundred cases, I soberly report my judgment that very few of Wilson and Herrnstein's citations are accurate, and that still fewer are adequate.[51]

However, there was little doubt that Wilson and Herrnstein had tapped a rich vein in the American psyche while providing popular support to a growing movement within American criminology symbolized by Florida State University criminologist C. Ray Jeffery, who, as president of the *American Society of Criminology* in the late 1970s, had sought to lead that organization in genetic directions. Jeffery also posited a connection between criminal behavior and low IQ – which he saw as primarily genetically determined. His anticrime proposals were based in what he called biosocial criminology. They included stratagems such as cybernetics and

49 Ibid. p. 24.
50 Wilson, James Q. and Richard Herrnstein, Letter to the Editor, *The Scientific American*, May 1986, p. 6.
51 Kamin, Leon, Reply, *The Scientific American*, May 1986, p. 7.

psychopharmacology, with Jeffery arguing that the punishment of the criminal must be calibrated to the work of behavioral genetics.

Like Wilson and Herrnstein, Jeffery confined his genetic arguments to working-class criminals, aggressively denying that genetics had any relevance whatsoever to white-collar offenders. As Jeffery put it:

> . . . white collar crime should be regarded not as a problem in criminology but as a problem of politics and economics.[52]

This is consistent with Wilson and Herrnstein's conception of a meritocratic world. Indeed, Herrnstein had been more blunt regarding where all this was leading, urging policymakers " . . . (to consider) the possibility that the different outcomes [in intellectual achievement, criminality and health for blacks and whites] are also the product of differing average endowments of people." Herrnstein was not alone in this. Racial arguments regarding crime in the inner city based on racially determined IQ were being boldly advanced by others. Take, for example, this comment of the Johns Hopkins sociologist Robert Gordon:

> . . . black–white IQ difference exists even before pupils enter school. . . it is not changed in the course of schooling, . . . it has not decreased over time despite the substantial reduction of black–white differences in the amount of schooling attained. It is time to consider the black–white IQ difference seriously when confronting the problem of crime in American society.[53]

The irony of this crop of genetic claims is that virtually none were being made by molecular geneticists.[54]

---

[52] Quoted in Platt, Anthony and Paul Takagi, "Biosocial Criminology: A Critique," *Crime and Social Justice,* Vol. 11, Spring/Summer 1979, p. 8.

[Kamin, an irascible individual with little regard for academic niceties when discussing behavioral genetics, exposed the fabricated twin studies of the British scientist, Sir Cyril Burt, who had posited dramatic racial (genetic) differences in IQ.]

[53] Gordon, Robert, "SES versus IQ in the Race-IQ-Delinquency Model," *International Journal of Sociology and Social Policy* Vol. 7, no. 3, 1987, pp. 91–92.

[54] Duster, op. cit., pp. 94–95.

As Duster somewhat wryly observed:

Edward Wilson is an entomologist who made his reputation studying insect societies. Yet, he got the Pulitzer Prize for publishing a book applying a genetic theory to social life of humans. . . . Arthur Jensen, who vaulted to national fame with a claim on the relationship between genetics and intelligence, is an educational psychologist. Seymour Kety is a psychiatrist, and is one of the leading figures in the world espousing the genetics of schizophrenia. David Rowe and Sarnoff Mednick, who argue the genetic basis for crime, and (H. J.) Eysenck, who argues the genetic basis of psychopathology and intelligence, are all psychologists. Richard Herrnstein is a Harvard psychologist who has not only argued the genetics of intelligence, but has even speculated that someday, "the tendency to be unemployed may run in the genes." Herrnstein recently teamed with James

The potential of the IQ test for identifying and keeping the rabble at bay was recognized from its inception. Stanford University psychologist Lewis Terman, who introduced the *Stanford-Binet* test and the *Terman Group Intelligence* tests into the U.S. Army in 1920, was a member of the team assembled to assess the results of California's massive sterilization of the mentally retarded between 1909 and 1927. This group issued a series of reports that concluded that involuntary sterilization of selected offenders and patients in California had produced "the first comprehensive 'proof' that sterilization was cost-effective and posed no significant medical harm to the institutionalized persons at whom it was aimed." Others on the team included David Starr Jordan, the president of Stanford University, and S. J. Holmes, a geneticist at Berkeley.[55]

Labeling the Deviant

Historically, the labels we have attached to those viewed as social deviants – from witches, to moral imbeciles, to constitutional psychopathic inferiors, to sociopaths, to those unresponsive to verbal

---

Q. Wilson, a political scientist, to write a book that asks for a more sympathetic reading of the possible "biological roots of an individual's predisposition to crime"....Each of these men lays considerable claim, and most have achieved considerable attention in the popular media postulating the importance of heredity in the explication of human behavior.

55 Reilly, P., *The Surgical Solution: A History of Involuntary Sterilization in the United States,* Baltimore, Maryland: Johns Hopkins University Press, 1991.
   As Duster has noted, these pronouncements came in the heyday of the eugenics movement, "sure that feeble-mindedness, degeneracy, and criminality were inherited." In 1912, the American Breeders' Association, an organization of farmers and university-based theoreticians, created a Committee to Study and to Report on the Best Practical Means of Cutting off the Defective Germ Plasma in the American Population. It was a five-man committee, chaired by a prominent New York attorney and having among its membership a prominent physician from the faculty at Johns Hopkins...and read in part:
   Biologists tell us that whether of wholly defective inheritance or because of an insurmountable tendency toward defect, which is innate, members of the following classes must generally be considered as socially unfit and their supply should if possible be eliminated from the human stock if we would maintain or raise the level of quality essentials to the progress of the nation and our race:
   The Feeble Minded, the Pauper class (pauper families through successive generations); Criminaloids (persons born with marked criminal tendencies); Epileptics, The Insane (excepting certain forms of acute insanity showing no hereditary taint); The Constitutionally Weak, or asthenic class; those predisposed to specific diseases or the diathetic class; the Congenitally Deformed, and those having defective sense organs, such as the deaf-mutes, the deaf and the blind...
   Duster, Troy, "Genetics, Race, and Crime: Recurring Seduction to a False Precision," op. cit.

conditioning – flow less from research concerns than from the needs of prevailing ideology. The need, in the words of the late British psychiatrist Ronald Laing, is for "social prescriptions."

However, labeling offenders gets particularly dicey for a democratic society when a substantial percentage of a particular racial group begin finding themselves eligible for diagnoses such as psychopath, sociopath, or antisocial personality – attributions barely one step removed from a more atavistic nomenclature – savages, animals, and monsters. The currently fashionable static psychiatric labels are, however, being massively applied to African-American males in the hundreds of thousands by psychiatrists, psychologists, and social workers who are directly or indirectly associated with the justice system. It is no accident that side by side with political demands for harsher handling and mandatory sentences for offenders we would re-emphasize the use of static psychiatric labels that, in practice, minimize developmental conceptions of human behavior and, for the most part, ignore individual, family, or social history.

In 1984, Harvard law professor and psychiatrist Alan Stone warned the profession about the "invidious aspect" implicit in the diagnosis of the so-called sociopath as defined by the official *Diagnostic and Statistical Manual (III)* of the American Psychiatric Association. The criteria could, in effect, be applied to a large percentage of inner-city black males. They include truancy, delinquency, running away from home, thefts, vandalism, school grades below expected, and repeated sexual intercourse in a casual relationship. As Stone points out, *"The existence of only three of these factors (before age 15) is sufficient to establish the disorder in this age group."*

If the male over age 18 is unemployed; is not a responsible parent; refuses to accept social norms; maintains attachments to a sexual partner; fails to meet financial obligations; doesn't plan ahead; or shows a disregard for the truth or "recklessness," he is to be diagnosed a sociopath. As Stone concluded, "whatever scientific value the diagnosis of sociopath may have, there can be little question that the urban poor and racial minorities will be swept into this diagnostic category . . . the DSM-III may well introduce . . . racism."[56]

Such rationalizations have already been enshrined in some state laws and indeed, carry life or death implications. For example, in Texas, a diagnosis of sociopath or antisocial personality is in itself an "aggravating" factor to be weighed by the jury in deciding whether the defendant

---

[56] Stone, Alan A., *Law, Psychiatry and Morality: Essays and Analysis,* Washington, D.C.: American Psychiatric Press, 1984.

deserves the death penalty. Indeed, a "down home," friendly middle-aged Texas physician earned himself the title Dr. Death for his ability to convince juries that certain defendants were incorrigible psychopaths and thereby incurable and appropriate for execution. On occasion, he rendered his diagnosis without ever meeting or interviewing the defendant – but by observing him in the courtroom during the trial.

These racially biased markers of psychopathy are relatively benign compared with the genetic markers of criminal predisposition yet in store for the black male. Such efforts also come with a long tradition. In the early and mid-nineteenth century, Charles B. Davenport looked for the genetics of nomadism, shiftlessness, and thalassophilia – the love of the sea in naval officers. He tied thalassophilia to a sex-linked recessive trait since it was almost always expressed in males. Samuel Cartwright sought to prove that Negroes consume less oxygen than white people and suffer from drapetomania – an insane desire to run away – a medical diagnosis of the early nineteenth century applied to runaway slaves.[57]

The relationship of such diagnoses to contemporary social structures and politics is always close. As the reform-minded liberal, Frederick G. Pettigrove, Chairman of the Massachusetts Prison Commission, asserted in his 1910 report to the International Prison Congress:

One subject . . . for discussion is . . . whether or not the Negro race can be fitly governed under Anglo-Saxon law. The Fourteenth Amendment to the Constitution of the United States makes the citizens of each state citizens of the United States and precludes any discrimination on account of race. Whether this ignoring of racial differences is the best thing for the Negro in America is a question which I am sure must finally occupy the thoughtful consideration of humane and patriotic men.[58]

---

[57] Cartwright, Samuel A., "Slavery in the Light of Ethnology," in Elliott, E. N. (ed.), *Cotton is King, and Pro-Slavery Arguments* (Augusta, Ga., 1860), pp. 689–728 (as cited in Robert Proctor, *Racial Hygiene*, Cambridge, Massachusetts: Harvard University Press, 1988, p.1 3.

[58] Pettigrove, Frederick G., "The State Prisons of the United States under Separate and Congregate Systems," in Henderson, Charles (ed.), *Penal and Reformatory Institutions*, New York: Russell Sage Foundation, Charities Publication Committee, 1910, p. 88.

Pettigrove echoed an opinion outlined five years earlier in the *American Journal of Sociology* that noted that it was probably a mistake to subject these genetically less advanced individuals to the same methods of government as the rest of us. These elemental distinctions, though decidedly more subtle, drive much of contemporary criminal justice policy. [Reinsch, Paul S., "The Negro Race and European Civilization," *American Journal of Sociology*, Vol. 11, September, 1905, p. 148.]

Pettigrove's comments confirm the later analysis of Carl Degler. However, as University of Chicago professor of human development Richard A. Shweder commented in his review of Degler's book, *In Search of Human Nature:*

> .... although Darwin himself viewed racial differences as insignificant, his ideas about the biological roots of human behavior led to social Darwinism. He (Degler) believes Darwin inadvertently set loose the supernumerary imp of genic group differences by positing that savage peoples did not have the bodies to support civilization.[59]

The gut feeling among so many whites that young African-American males are some sort of different breed is in increasingly desperate need of scientific validation, lest other usually messy social arrangements demand attention. Genetic crime research aimed, as it has and will continue to be, at African-American males, will therefore continue to garner considerable support despite the fact that most studies of crime in black majority nations (absent civil wars) suggest low rates of violence overall among black men.[60]

Early Attempts at Preventing "Genetically Influenced" Crime

The first organizational effort in behalf of eugenics was a committee of the American Breeders' Association formed in 1906 "to investigate and report on heredity in the human race." The committee was expected to make clear "the value of superior blood and the menace to society of inferior blood."[61]

Involuntary sterilization was first used, not in Germany but in the United States, by the superintendent of the Cincinnati Sanitarium. At the time, sterilization meant castration. He characterized the surgical procedure as having a twofold benefit: both as a punishment and a way of helping individuals to control their criminal proclivities.[62]

The first institutional use of involuntary vasectomies on criminals was at the Indiana State Reformatory, where the procedure was performed on

---

[59] Shweder, Richard, "Dangerous Thoughts," *The New York Times Book Review,* Sunday, March 17, 1991, p. 30.

[60] For example, the homicide rate in New York City is double that of Nairobi, Kenya, or Georgetown, Guyana. New York's rate of assault is five times higher and robberies are committed at 40 times the rate of most African nations. Archer and Gartner, op. cit. "Comparative Crime Data File: Nations," pp. 173ff.

[61] Degler, op. cit. p. 43.

[62] Ibid. p. 45.

several dozen boys in an effort to prevent masturbation. As the physician who administered them off-handedly noted: " . . . it occurred to me that this would (also) be a good method of preventing procreation in the defective and physically unfit."[63]

It's something of a paradox that linking science and medicine to the justice authority of the state led to more draconian measures and punitive social policy proposals than to policies emerging directly out of a philosophy of deterrence. An example can be found in the crime remedies recommended in an influential 1928 classic, *The New Criminology: A Consideration of the Chemical Causation of Abnormal Behavior.*

The authors, Max Schlapp, a professor of neuropathology at the New York Graduate Medical School, and Edward Smith, a mystery writer, posited the theory that crime was caused by glandular disturbances resulting in chemical imbalances in the blood and lymph of the criminal's mother during pregnancy. Except for the medical jargon, Schlapp and Smith's proposals were based in the same meritocratic paradigm implicit to Wilson and Herrnstein. Unlike Wilson and Herrnstein, however, Schlapp and Smith stated clearly and bluntly where things must head if their premises were accepted.

In spite of the howls of the demos, mankind probably must go back to some sort of caste system founded on productiveness, upon ability, upon service to the state.[64]

Their recommendations were equally straightforward – euthanasia, compulsory treatment for defectives, registration, sterilization, and forced labor. The convergence of genetics with remedies so vicious in outcome is striking. One might think that if certain citizens are born with a predisposition to crime, their culpability for their delinquent acts would be somewhat mitigated. After all, a genetic predisposition would seem to drain the idea of the willfully wicked criminal of much of its power. The conception would seem to inhibit the need to run to the punishment box. In practice, just the opposite happens.

Something paradoxically, those who see criminals as greatly influenced by genetic or constitutional factors seem inevitably to end up being the strongest supporters of harsh punishment. Wilson and Herrnstein's *Crime and Human Nature* was a case in point. The authors recognize the

[63] Ibid. p. 45.
[64] Quoted in Platt and Takagi, op. cit. p. 61.

contradiction, then dismiss it, admitting that "scientific explanations of criminal behavior do, in fact, undermine a view of criminal responsibility based on freedom of action. And it is also correct that this book has taken pains to show that much, if not all, criminal behavior can be traced to antecedent conditions [Yet] we view legal punishment as essential, a virtual corollary of the theory of criminal behavior upon which this book is built."

Wilson and Herrnstein rationalize this contradiction with a reference to British legal philosopher, H. L. A. Hart, who provided

> ... an account of criminal behavior that seems to us to resolve the apparent paradox of holding people responsible for actions that they could not help committing, and to do so in a way that fits naturally with the theory of criminal behavior proposed in this book. An act deserves punishment, according to the principle of equity, if it was committed without certain explicit excusing conditions. In Hart's scheme, free will is a negative, rather than a positive, attribute of behavior. For the purposes of the law, behavior is considered "free" if not subject to these *excusing conditions*. One such condition is insanity, but there are others, such as duress, provocation, entrapment, mistake and accident.[65]

A closer reading of Hart, however, reveals that his argument was advanced in response to social theorists such as Lady Barbara Wooton who suggested that we might not be able to hold *anyone* responsible for any criminal act in the strict sense, all behavior having been preconditioned.[66] There is nothing in Hart to suggest that were the gross genetic predeterminants suggested by Wilson and Herrnstein to be proven, they would not of themselves be mitigative, if not exculpatory, of a criminal act.

Among those of a genetic bent, Wilson was not alone in his calls for harsher punishments. Four years after Wilson's highly influential 1975 book, *Thinking about Crime*,[67] was published, Professor Graeme Newman, Associate Dean of the Department of Justice at the State University of New York at Albany, was strongly asserting his belief that violent criminals were genetically flawed:

---

[65] Wilson, James Q. and Richard Herrnstein, *Crime and Human Nature*, New York: Simon & Schuster, 1985, p. 505.

[66] Hart, H. L. A., *Punishment and Responsibility*, rev. ed. 1978, Oxford: Oxford University Press.

[67] Wilson, James Q., *Thinking about Crime*, New York: Basic Books, 1975.

... there appears to be no alternative to accepting the possibility that some people may be born with a physiology that is likely to predispose them (or even in some rare cases determine them) to become killers.[68]

In 1983, Newman had proposed devising an electric shock machine to which the offender could be strapped to receive painful jolts calibrated to the seriousness of the offense and the individual's threshold of pain. Although Newman presented his punishment machine as an alternative to imprisonment, his musings carried him ominously near the concentration camp:

Obviously, prisoners cannot be subjected to the same terrible tortures in prison as Dante dreamed up for Hell or Purgatory. But it is time that we took prison seriously as a punishment, and realized that these few criminals, these bad people, have been sent there for punishment and that is what they should get... on the simplest level, it seems morally required that incarcerated murderers... should see it as quite deserving that they should risk their lives for others. Their use for risky medical research might well be justified on this basis.[69]

In his book on race and social policy, the liberal commentator Christopher Jencks appeared to recognize the dangers inherent in the genetic focus on crime:

Genetic explanations of crime also alarm us because we fear they will lead to more brutal treatment of criminals. The notion that criminals are "different" has been used to rationalize horrifying abuses in the past, and the same thing could happen again. The danger here, however, is not that a realistic understanding of genetic influences will lead us to think of criminals as subhuman, but that the mythology surrounding genetic explanations will do so. The most serious risk is that we will come to think of criminals as incorrigible.[70]

Looking at the controversial Danish "twin studies," Jencks admits that even if genes mattered, they "seem mainly to influence men's chance of committing minor offenses. There is currently no solid evidence that, if we set aside skin color, men's genes affect their chances of committing violent crimes, although such evidence may well emerge." Yet, after acknowledging that there is virtually no evidence of genes being tied to violent crime, Jencks toys with the idea that were genes to provide an explanation, the criminals might use their genes as an excuse, saying, "It's not

---

[68] Newman, Graeme, *Understanding Violence*, New York: J. B. Lippincott, 1979.

[69] Newman, Graeme, *Just and Painful: A Case for the Corporal Punishment of Criminals*, London: Harrow and Heston/Macmillan, 1983, pp. 69–70.

[70] Jencks, Christopher, *Rethinking Social Policy: Race Poverty, and the Underclass*, Cambridge, Massachusetts: Harvard University Press, 1992, pp. 110–11.

my fault I keep breaking the rules. I'm just one of those people who can't follow the rules no matter how hard I try. Some people are just born to be criminals."

Given the history of blacks in the American justice system, one could reasonably presume that any rationalization for genetic interpretation of crime among African-American males would be welcomed by a substantial proportion of the white majority. Such an explanation would give a scientific gloss to the destructive policies already in place when it comes to crime and punishment. Such vicious measures pine for equally vicious conceptions of human behavior.[71]

In some ways, Jencks' conclusions were not surprising. In his controversial book, *Inequality* (1972), he had argued against the idea that investing in special instructional programs for children in poor families and those of ethnic minorities would have any effect on equalizing income. Jencks' approach to this social problem was similar to that of Wilson's approach to crime in his blanket dismissal of preventive and rehabilitative efforts directed at offenders. The questionable science aside, the destructive implications of grounding social policy in such narrow considerations were pointed out by Harvard psychologist Jerome Kagan, who recognized the necessity of ethical "a priori assumptions" in such matters. As Kagan put it:

He (Jencks) used facts to argue that the decision to invest money in education in order to equalize income was ill founded. Although one could argue with some of the facts, even if they are valid, their utility lies in their power to refute those who want to base educational funding on a desire to reduce diversity in income. The facts do not imply that the community cannot decide, a priori, that it is still good

---

[71] Following the Atlanta riots of 1906, a substantial percentage of the white population favored openly genocidal policies toward blacks, rationalizing it as a protection for Southern white women from rape.

"The Atlanta riot of 1906 was an outgrowth of a Southern white attitude that, in Atlanta, Wilmington, and other cities, favored black genocide and rationalized it as protection for Southern white women supposedly threatened by the 'New Negro Crime,' rape, which blacks had adopted, so it was felt, in frustration over their failure to gain the social equality that had emerged as a goal during Reconstruction. Under the delusion that blacks were avid rapists of white women a leading Southern editor, John Temple Graves called for the castration of black men involved in incidents with white women, and one Georgian wanted all black women 'unsexed' to forestall the rise, so he alleged, of another generation of rapists. This was the background of the riot of September 22–26, in Atlanta, a city where white prejudice had been inflamed by an 18-month long gubernatorial election campaign featured by the Negro-baiting of top candidate Hoke Smith and brought to the point of violence by a newspaper campaign ... against a less than genuine epidemic of black rape." (Brown, Richard Maxwell, op. cit. p. 210.)

to invest in education – for self-actualization, for appreciation of science and art, or for general enlightenment.[72]

Kagan specified the relationship between scientific positivism and policy formulation in a democratic society in this way:

Where are the a priori assumptions necessary for ethical decisions to come from?...One source lies in consensual sentiment, which will change over time....Indeed, on each election day more and more moral issues are placed on the local ballot, indicating the community's receptivity to using public sentiment as a guide to ethical dilemmas....[However, it] is extremely difficult to implement that strategy more broadly in our society because of the extraordinary diversity of opinion on critical issues and a deep resistance to having legally binding propositions rest, in any way, on nonrational grounds. That is one reason why science has been placed in the position of moral arbiter. Although science can help in this role by supplying factual evidence which disconfirms the invalid foundations of ethical premises, it cannot supply the basis for a moral proposition. Facts prune the tree of morality; they cannot be the seedbed.[73]

Earlier commentators seemed more aware of these issues than many of our contemporaries. For example, the great Austrian social theorist Max Weber, though personally convinced of many of the extant theories on inheritance and behavior so common in the early 1900s, held that the potential for misuse of such vague biological and genetic views of social deviance far outweighed whatever value such knowledge might bring. It was not simply a matter of so-called political correctness. A decade before the advent of Nazism, he wrote:

I do not see how, in spite of the valuable contributions of anthropological (i.e., genetic) research, it would be possible for the time being to decide with an exactness its share in the evolution here investigated, either quantitatively or about all as regards the manner of its influence and the points where it is exerted. I do not see a basis for guesses about it. Sociological and historical research should therefore first concentrate on the task, as exactly as possible to establish the influences and causal connections which may be explained satisfactorily as reactions to external events and to the environment.[74]

---

[72] Kagan, Jerome, *Unstable Ideas: Temperament, Cognition, and Self*, Cambridge, Massachusetts; London: Harvard University Press, 1989, p. 28.

[73] Ibid. p. 29.

[74] In a classic example of Nordic understatement regarding Weber's warning, the Danish sociologist Ranulf commented in 1938, "We believe that these words have their full validity today." (Ranulf, Svend, op. cit. p. 54.) There is little in the contemporary discussion of genes and crime to suggest that the parameters of the discussion have substantially changed.

Despite the fact that they had yet to acknowledge, much less accomplish, the tasks outlined by Weber, contemporary liberal commentators continued to toy with genetic arguments for social class and, indirectly, for crime. For example, referring to Herrnstein's "disturbing syllogism" that "social standing (which reflects earnings and prestige) will be based to some extent on inherited differences among people," Mickey Kaus, then editor of *The New Republic,* appeared to accept Herrnstein's assumption that we were headed toward a "Hereditary State."[75] Despite all the qualifications and concern about what he dubbed "The Herrnstein Nightmare," Kaus, as did Jencks, imputed more credibility to Herrnstein's musings than they probably deserved, while ignoring his more extreme comments on genetics, race, and crime. One wonders whether the views expressed so clumsily by Goodwin were as foreign to white liberals as most might presume.[76]

Even those studies used most commonly to point to a genetic tie, such as those of Sarnoff A. Mednick of the University of Southern California, in which he compared the criminal records of 14,000 adopted Danish males with those of their biological and adoptive fathers, claimed no evidence of heritability when it came to violent crime. The associations related to property crimes (for example, burglary) only.

Similarly, Temple University's Joan McCord, in comparing the criminal histories of 34 pairs of genetic brothers born between 1926 and 1933 with each other and with the histories of matched subjects (analogical

---

[75] Kaus, Mickey, *The End of Equality,* New York: New Republic Books, 1992.

[76] Wilson, in his review of Kaus' book, while criticizing its hopes for social equality, upbraided Kaus' liberal critics for not accepting what is essentially Herrnstein's view of genetics and the meritocracy. Wilson leaves no doubt as to where he stands:

Robert Kuttner, writing in the *New Republic* suggests that Kaus may have become a "convert to conservative fantasies of market meritocracy or unfounded genetic theories of intelligence." Robert Scheer, writing in the *Los Angeles Times Book Review*, displays an impressive command of old-left venom. He describes the book as a self-indulgent rant of a kind one expects to find in an erotic novel and calls Kaus' proposals "harebrained" and "bizarre." Kuttner here displays an ignorance of the evidence on the heritability of intelligence that is truly remarkable. I wonder if he thinks that he is as smart as he is – and he is very smart, indeed – simply because his parents sent him to the best schools. (Wilson, James Q., "Redefining Equality: The Liberalism of Mickey Kaus," *The Public Interest*, No. 109, Fall 1992, p. 104.)

Wilson clearly has little room in his IQ lexicon for the conception of those such as psychologist Howard Gardner, who sees IQ as presently measured as being anything but predictive or helpful. (Gardner, Howard, *Ways of Knowing*, Cambridge, Massachusetts: Harvard University Press, 1989.)

brothers) with similar backgrounds, found slight, if any evidence of genetics at work.[77] Between 1935 and 1939, the biological brothers were individually matched to another child of similar age, intelligence, personality, physique, and family environment – creating the analogical brothers. All were from deprived, disorganized areas near Boston.

McCord summarized her research in this way:

The genetic brothers shared exposure to family interactions as well as genetic loading. The analogical brothers had resembled the genetic brothers during childhood, but shared no genetic material. Nor did they share households with one another.

Criminality was checked between 1975 and 1979. A man was considered to be a criminal if he had been convicted for a serious street (index) crime. There were 24 criminals among the brothers and 24 criminals among their analogs.

The matching enabled comparisons of two types. In one, the concordance of biological brothers could be compared with the concordance of analogical brothers. Brothers were considered concordant if both or neither had been convicted for an Index crime. The rate of concordance was similar: 22 pairs of biological brothers were concordant for crime and 18 of the analogical brothers were concordant for crime.

The second type of comparison considered each brother separately. Sixty-eight pairs of comparisons tested whether the difference in the number of convictions for serious street crimes was greater for the biological brothers or for a biological brother and his analog. The results showed that genetic brothers were more similar than analogical brothers among 16 pairs, but less similar among 18 pairs (with differences equal among 34 pairs). The mean difference in convictions among biological brothers was 1.4 and among analogical brothers, the mean difference was 1.5.

Together, the two studies suggest that whatever impact genetic factors have on crime is mediated through criminogenically relevant social factors.

Likewise, a study by Washington University's C. Robert Cloninger examined personality factors such as impulsivity and aggressiveness – characteristics that some claimed were partially inherited – in more than 1,000 adults of various races. He found the same proportion of these purportedly "crime-linked" characteristics in both the white and black populations. He concluded the higher rates of criminality observed among

77 McCord, Joan, "Research Perspectives on Criminal Behavior," paper presented at *American Association for the Advancement of Science* symposium, "Controversy over Crime and Heredity: An Exploration," February 15, 1993.

blacks to "be the result of socioeconomic factors or other environmental variables."

Most of the medical doctors, psychiatrists, and scientists involved in the genetic programs in the Third Reich were well into their models long before the advent of Nazism. Most were not, in fact, party members until later.[78] Though liberals seem at times, aware of the ominous potential which resides in genetic conceptions of criminal behavior, they also seem to have something approaching infinite faith in the roles of professionals and the dicta of academics. It should therefore not go unnoticed, that historically, neither professionalism nor scientific sanction have afforded insulation from racist impulse or inhumane practice.

Warren Leary, in reviewing a 1992 exhibit on scientists' complicity in Nazi-era atrocities for *The New York Times'* Science Section, commented:

---

[78] As Benno Muller-Hill, professor of genetics in the University of Cologne, discovered:

When we compare the ideological, scientific, and bureaucratic activities of psychiatrists and anthropologists (eugenicists, race-hygienists, ethnologists, behavioral scientists) we reach...a surprising conclusion: they set themselves similar goals and adopted similar positions. The anthropologists busied themselves with identifying and eliminating inferior non-Germans (Jews, Gypsies, Slavs, and Negroes), whilst the psychiatrists were busy identifying and eliminating inferior Germans (schizophrenics, epileptics, imbeciles, and psychopaths).... Psychiatrists and anthropologists competed over the vast numbers of asocial individuals to be eradicated.

... We see these cultured and learned men hesitating at times, but none the less making steady progress, step by step, along the path to the final solution. They did not all go the whole way. Those who stopped closed their eyes, or rather blinded themselves to the truth...so there came into being a remarkable community of self-blinded internal exiles coexisting with the annihilators, those who did go all the way to the final solution.

Physicians, however, didn't shrink from membership in the more militant arms associated with the final solution. Twenty-six percent of all the physicians in Germany were in the SA and 7 percent were in the SS – (seven times more often than the average for the employed male population).

(Muller-Hill, Benno, *Murderous Science: Elimination by Scientific Selection of Jews, Gypsies, and Others, Germany 1933–1945*, Fraser, George (trans.), Oxford: Oxford University Press, 1988, pp. 30–31.)

As historian Robert Proctor concluded:

Medical science did not fail Hitler.... By the beginning of 1933 (that is, *before* the rise of Hitler to power), 2,786 doctors had joined the (Nazi Physicians') League. Doctors in fact joined the Nazi party earlier and in greater numbers than any other professional group.... By 1934 the number waiting to join was so great that *Ziel und Weg* advised doctors to make no further applications until the present ones could be processed.... Nearly 40,000 physicians joined the league by 1942... by the beginning of 1943...roughly half of all physicians [belonged to the League].

(Proctor, Robert N., *Racial Hygiene: Medicine under the Nazis,* Cambridge, Massachusetts, Harvard University Press, 1988, pp. 65–6.)

[It] suggests that doctors, more than any other professional group in Germany, accepted the new order.... Being part of this system allowed doctors and scientists to get research grants, [and] receive promotions at universities.[79]

Predispositions and "Unintrusive Therapies"

In the fall of 1991, the National Institutes of Health and the University of Maryland's Institute for Philosophy and Public Policy scheduled an "invited only" 1992 conference on "Genetic Factors in Crime: Findings, Uses, and Implications." Described as a meeting that would "integrate the concerns and findings of several disciplines on a range of topics, from mathematical modeling of polygenic disorders to the courtroom use of genetic-predisposition evidence," the announcement dismissed social and environmental understandings of crime as having failed and concluded:

Researchers have already begun to study the genetic regulation of violent and impulsive behavior and to search for genetic markers associated with criminal conduct... genetic research also gains impetus from the apparent failure of environmental approaches to crime – deterrence, diversion, and rehabilitation – to affect the dramatic increases in crime, especially violent crime, that this country has experienced over the past 30 years.

... Genetic research holds out the prospect of identifying individuals who may be predisposed to certain kinds of criminal conduct, of isolating environmental features which trigger those predispositions, and of treating some predispositions with drugs and unintrusive therapies.[80]

The matters of how one isolates environmental features or which unintrusive therapies would be administered in the service of the genetics of crime were not mentioned. The lead-off speaker was to have been James Q. Wilson. Other invited participants included behavioral genetic psychologists David Rowe and Sarnoff Mednick; Peter Hoffman, technical advisor to the U.S. Sentencing Commission; psychologist Gregory Carey of the Institute for Behavioral Genetics at the University of Colorado; and investigator Robert Ressler of the FBI behavioral science unit.[81]

---

[79] Leary, Warren E., Review of Exhibit at National Museum of Medicine and Health, Science Section, *The New York Times,* November 10, 1992.

[80] University of Maryland, Institute for Philosophy & Public Policy, Fall Conference announcement, "Genetic Factors in Crime: Findings, Uses, and Implications, September 1991.

[81] For some, the conference's emphasis on genetics was not extreme enough. Johns Hopkins sociologist Robert Gordon, who was not invited, complained that the organizers deliberately excluded those who dealt directly with the question of racial heritability and differences. Ignoring the unwarranted statements included in the announcement of

As news of the theretofore low-profile conference leaked out, mainly through the efforts of Bethesda, Maryland-based psychiatrist, Peter Breggin, objections were raised by influential members of the African-American community. Two decades earlier, in the wake of the unrest following the assassination of Martin Luther King, Breggin had derailed a National Institute of Mental Health–Justice Department initiative that, among other stratagems, had suggested brain surgery might provide the best means of dealing with selected inner-city rioters.

In late July 1992, National Institutes of Health director Bernadine Healy decided to delay the grant of $100,000 for the Maryland conference, apparently in response to a large number of calls to NIH after a critical column by *Washington Post* columnist Dorothy Gilliam appeared and panelists on a black-oriented cable network program attacked the conference as racist.[82]

Professor Ronald Walters, the head of Howard University's political science department, joined the fray, commenting, "I generally don't deal in conspiracy theories," adding his concerns that there may be " . . . some willingness on the part of the scientific community to go along with this line of research."

In early September 1992, the conference was canceled. Calling the decision "an abdication of the integrity of the review process," the conference

---

the conference – all but endorsing the genetics of crime – Gordon was upset that the organizers of the conference had not directly tied the racial issue to genetics and crime. As he told John Miller, a writer for a neoconservative journal that endorsed the search for genetics of crime and deviance, "You can't argue with those ethicists because they ignore science and talk right past you." [Miller, John, "The Violent Gene," *Diversity & Division: A Critical Journal of Race and Culture*, Vol. II, No. 2, Winter 1992 (Miller, a 1992 graduate of the University of Michigan described as a "researcher" at the Manhattan Institute, also writes for the *New Republic* on this issue. Other contributors to the magazine come from such groups as the Competitive Enterprise Institute, the *National Review*, *Roll Call*, and Freedom House. The publication is copyrighted by the Madison Center for Educational Affairs. There is a curious disclaimer under the masthead of the publication, "*Diversity and Division* and its publisher, the Madison Center for Educational Affairs, have no relationship to Genetic Resources Communications Systems Inc. (GRCS) or its publication *Diversity: A News Journal for the International Plant Genetic Resources Community.*"]

[82] In announcing the delay, NIH added that a multiracial panel would be selected to reexamine the questions raised. Healy invited back three of the original peer reviewer scientists who had approved funding the conference to NIH to discuss the project. At this point, she found their support, at best, lukewarm. One of the reviewers couldn't remember the proposal and another confessed to having had second thoughts about it. In the absence of a "ringing endorsement" from the reviewers, NIH spokesperson Joanna Schneider said, "We didn't have the feeling that we could defend [the conference] against public criticism."

organizer, lawyer David Wasserman, noted that it would probably have to be given a new title. In a quick retreat from the statements contained in the earlier prospectus and brochure on the conference, he said, "We don't want people to think that we ever assumed the existence of genetic factors."

Concomitant with the planning of the University of Maryland conference, a draft report by the National Academy of Sciences' Panel on the Understanding and Control of Violent Behavior was being prepared.

News of the draft report, which called for funding a longitudinal study of violence, leaked out at about the same time the controversy over the Maryland conference surfaced. Some members of the panel and some of those who had seen the draft had indicated their unease with its genetic emphasis. As one of the individuals who reviewed the draft told me, "Frankly, I was somewhat surprised with the emphasis on genetics." A staff person speaking off the record commented, "It's work that came more out of behavioral genetics than criminology."

The summary report was published as a book entitled *Understanding and Preventing Violence* in early 1993,[83] with other volumes to follow. After reviewing it, Leon Kamin commented, "If you need to be convinced that much of contemporary social science is utterly bankrupt this is the book you've been waiting for."

Edited in the wake of the highly publicized cancellation of the University of Maryland conference, the final published version appeared to place less emphasis on genetic factors than had apparently been the case in the original draft.[84] It noted, for example, that the twin and adoptive studies "suggest at most, a weak role for genetic processes in influencing potential for violent behavior – the correlations and concordances of behavior in two of the three studies are consistent with a positive genetic effect, but are statistically insignificant."

---

[83] Reiss, Albert J. Jr. and Jeffrey A. Roth (eds.), *Understanding and Preventing Violence*, Washington, D.C.: National Academy Press, 1993.

(Released shortly after the controversy surrounding the University of Maryland conference, the report was characterized widely differently in press accounts. *The New York Times* summary saw the clear focus of the report as being on the genetics of crime. Writing in the conservative journal *Diversity & Division: A Critical Journal of Race and Culture,* then-reporter Jonathan Miller saw the report as a "de facto endorsement of the NIMH 'violence initiative.'" (At this writing, Miller was employed by, and working on projects with, Charles Murray at the Manhattan Institute.)

[84] Having been told by two readers of the draft report of its heavy genetic emphasis, I attempted to obtain a copy from staff at the National Academy of Sciences. I was told by the staff director that this would be impossible. The defensive tone of the conversation left me with the distinct impression that the draft report had become something of a political "hot potato."

However, the ambivalence of the panel when it came to race (referred to as "ethnic status") was, perhaps, best exemplified in the appendix, which summarized "some of the most important findings and theories." Though factors such as temperament, IQ, impulsivity, and family, peer, and school influences in the development of a potential for violence are briefly discussed, the writers then noted:

Non-manipulable individual factors such as sex and ethnic origin are not discussed, except insofar as they interact with other factors. It seems probable that the greater likelihood of males and blacks to commit violent offenses might be explained by reference to some of the other factors discussed here.[85]

The panel listed, among these other factors, the antisocial personality or psychopath and "physiological differences between shy and fearless children (reflecting) differential thresholds of limbic structures such as the amygdala and hypothalamus...implicating limbic structures in aggression in both animals and children."[86]

Though early childhood neglect and abuse were mentioned, the authors suggested that parental abuse of children may simply be a normal response to a child's misbehavior, with those who physically abuse their children passing on a genetic or biological predisposition to violence.[87] The authors danced ever so deftly around race, suggesting that

...children who live with parents who possess undesirable qualities (unemployed, unfair, unjust) will believe that some of these properties belong to them.... These identifications may be part of the explanation why black children are disproportionally at risk for aggressive behavior.[88]

The authors then briefly mentioned "protective factors":

For example, if low IQ predicted violence among low-income families but not among high-income families, high income might be protecting children from the effects of low IQ.[89]

The panel did not shy from proposing procedures that Kamin had described as having "a science-fiction ring about them; partly comic, partly fear-inducing":

Thus, batteries of behavioral measures can be applied as early as the age of 4 months...the infant could be exposed to unfamiliar visual, auditory, and olefactory stimuli, and various changes are taken as measures of autonomic responsivity.

---

[85] Reiss, Albert J. Jr. and Jeffrey A. Roth, op. cit. pp. 357–58.
[86] Ibid. p. 366.
[87] Ibid. p. 66.
[88] Ibid. p. 369.
[89] Ibid. p. 370.

Levels of motor activity and irritability would be quantified from videotapes. The battery would permit the detection of uninhibited infants. Or, since "saliva measures of gonadal and adrenal hormones offer reasonably accurate indicators of endocrine activity," such measures can be used "to estimate predictive relationships for violent behavior.... such relationships might be used to identify categories of youth for whom social skills training or *some other intervention* (emphasis added) might be especially effective in reducing chances of violent behavior."

Kamin summarized his impressions:

We live in a society in which large numbers of citizens, quite justifiably, live in fear of falling victim to predatory street violence. The urban centers of that society contain communities characterized by massive unemployment, unspeakably wretched housing, obscenely inadequate schools, flourishing drug markets, widespread availability of guns, alienation, and hopelessness. In the face of all this, the best and the brightest of our social scientists propose to spend 15 years and more studying the autonomic reactivity of infants and the saliva of adolescents. *O tempora! O mores!*

Finally, the panel proposed 12 "key questions" as research priorities for the future. The first question stated openly what had lain dormant, but palpable, throughout this curious report:

Do male and black persons have a higher potential for violence than others and, if so, why?[90]

Clearly, there should be nothing wrong with looking at putative racial or genetic concomitants of crime. Troy Duster had suggested that avoiding race in studies of violence and crime would be "playing into the hands of the Right Wing." He maintained that if studies properly accounted for

---

[90] Ibid. p. 380. In the early 1990s, a jointly funded U.S. Justice Department–MacArthur Foundation longitudinal study to divine the causes of criminality was being constructed in a manner that would ensure it all but ignored such crucial elements as the possible negative effects of criminal justice intrusion itself, concentrating instead upon genetics and the usual deficits in the family and community. Predictably, a major instigator and continuing adviser to the study staff was the ever-present *eminence grise* of the punitive state, James Q. Wilson.

There seemed little question that the Justice Department–MacArthur Foundation study would have the African-American male as its central focus. However, there were problems in identifying a city where there would be no objections to genetic screening of youngsters. As of this writing, the cities chosen as sites had not been formally announced, though a source close to the project indicated to me that Chicago was to be the site for the study.

racism and related factors, allegations of the propensity of blacks for criminality "will fade away into nothing."[91]

Duster was right when he suggested that the substantive evidence for a racially determined genetic propensity toward crime is meager. However, reopening the debate on crime and genes is probably more risky than Duster acknowledges. It would be less so, if the arena of crime and punishment was notable for valuing scientific findings over ideology and politics. Indeed, if national justice strategies were based on scientific outcome, we would have long ago abandoned the war on drugs and the massive use of prisons to control inner-city crime. But this is not a field driven by such realities. It is difficult enough to keep the science separate from the politics when talking about race in other social arenas, much less one in which putative law-breaking or predatory behavior has entered the scene. When the "criminal" enters on stage, minimal civility usually exits the proceedings.[92]

For this reason, I would not agree with those who hold that, with time, "the truth will out." Given the history of the past with reference

---

[91] Quoted in Hogan, John, "Genes and Crime: A U.S. Plan to Reduce Violence Rekindles an Old Controversy," *The Scientific American*, February 1993, pp. 24–29.

[92] Lerner, Richard, op. cit., pp. 86–87. Lerner cites an interesting example of this in his discussion of the Austrian Nobel laureate, Konrad Lorenz, whose biological determinism had been so consonant with the views of the Third Reich. Shortly after he received the Nobel Prize in 1973, an article by a German freelance writer, Vic Cox, living in Munich, appeared in a March 1974 issue of *Human Behavior* summarizing Lorenz' career and discussing Lorenz' Nazi past and current thinking and work. As part of that article, a passage from Lorenz' 1940 publication on "Domestication-Caused Disturbances in Species-Specific Behavior" was quoted in two places. In both places the quote was *incorrect*, containing a small typographical error in one word that nevertheless, changed the meaning of the passage. The passage was misquoted to read that Lorenz called for "a more severe elimination of the ethnically inferior than has been done so far," although Lorenz actually said: "a more severe elimination of the ethically inferior than has been done so far."

An extra *n* had been added to the word "ethical," to make the word "ethnical." Thus, we may infer that in 1940 Lorenz called for elimination – indeed, the "extermination" – of people who were ethically inferior by virtue of their genes, but that he did not call for the elimination of any particular ethnic groups that because their "race" may have been carriers of inferior genes. My inference about Lorenz's meaning is supported by his own words. Lorenz wrote a letter to *Human Behavior* to correct the typographical error and to clarify the views the misquoted passage represented. The letter, appearing in the September 1974 issue, reads in its entirety as follows:

I thank you very much for the readiness to correct what was obviously more an error of the printer than of the editor. However, I beg you to realize that changing ethical into ethnical ... makes me appear a rabid racist, which I never was. I never believed in any ethnical superiority or inferiority of any group of human beings, though I strongly hold that ethical inferiority of individuals due to heredity or to bad upbringing (lack

to this kind of research, and given the stereotypes that have dogged the black man in the American justice system for the past century and a half, it would be silly to conclude that ideology and politics would not drive the questions, influence the outcome, and determine the policies and practices.

As the infamous Tuskegee study on syphilis demonstrated, even a scientifically sound medical diagnosis attached to black men hardly guarantees a humane outcome.[93] In fact, it is clear that if "risky" medical research of any kind is to be implemented, it will more likely than not be tried on the poor, the powerless – and most specifically in this country, the poor black.

Indeed, in late 1993, as a result of declassification of previously secret documents of the Atomic Energy Commission, it came to light that at least 1,000 people had been exposed to potentially harmful doses of radiation, for the most part without their knowledge. Among the human guinea pigs were 19 mentally retarded teenaged boys at the Fernald state institution in Massachusetts who were exposed to radioactive iron and calcium in their breakfast cereal. (The study was funded in part by the

of motherly love during the first year of life) is indeed a reality, which has to be taken seriously.

I should highly appreciate it if you could include that in the intended correction.

Prof. Dr. Konrad Lorenz
Altenberg, Austria

As Lerner comments, "Although Lorenz thus insisted he was not a racist, claiming that he had never believed there was a group of humans who by virtue of the *ethnical* heredity are inferior, he did believe in 1974, and in the Nazi period, that there was a group of humans who by virtue of their *ethical* heredity are inferior. It is this group – the moral imbeciles and dregs discussed in 1940 – that should be eliminated, Lorenz believed."

93 The Tuskegee Study was run as a public health service by the Centers for Disease Control. It was designed to study the "natural course" of syphilis. Public Health Service doctors advertised "special free treatment" and after doing blood tests, selected 412 infected black men and a control group of another 200 for study. The infected men were not told they had syphilis, nor were they treated, placing entire families at risk for the disease. Since examining the corpses of the men was important to the study, the families were offered $100 in burial fees if they brought in the bodies. When penicillin was discovered in the early 1940s, thousands of returning GIs were treated for syphilis, but the Tuskegee subjects were not. Indeed, in order to prevent the possibility of treatment "contaminating" the study, the U.S. Public Health Service arranged for 50 of the infected men to be exempted from service during the war. The disease was allowed to run its course for 40 years, killing, maiming, and permanently impairing the subjects – even when the effects of the antibiotics in stopping the course of the disease had been clearly demonstrated. (Jones, James H., *Bad Blood*, New York: Free Press, 1981.)

Quaker Oats company.) Though the boys were referred to as "morons" in their records, the scientists at Harvard University and the Massachusetts Institute of Technology who oversaw the experimentation called them "the Fernald Science Club."[94]

In Memphis, Tennessee, 18 institutionalized patients were injected with plutonium and seven newborn boys, (six of them black), were injected with radioactive iron. Dr. Joseph G. Hamilton, a biologist who worked for the Atomic Energy Commission at the time, warned in a memo that the experiments might have "a little of the Buchenwald touch." As Dr. David S. Egilman, a physician who had investigated the human experimentation by the military, commented,

Based on their own documents and the history of medical ethics, they knew clearly at the time that the studies were unethical. They called this work, in effect, Nazilike. The argument we hear is that these experiments were ethical at the time they were done. It's simply not true.[95]

In light of such history, one can understand how even the most tentative musings about the genetics of race and crime might carry implications far beyond whatever small intrinsic importance they might have.

Boys with Prehensile Feet

Early in the Reagan administration, University of Southern California psychologist Sarnoff A. Mednick submitted a research proposal to the Office of Juvenile Justice and Delinquency Prevention to conduct a study of genetic influences on delinquency. Mednick proposed to identify 2,000 9- to 12-year-old boys for the experiment.[96] (He mused that though it would be better to pick six-year-olds, that was more likely to present political problems in applying the various tests.)

---

94 Allen, Scott, "Radiation Used on Retarded: Postwar Experiments Done at Fernald School," *The Boston Sunday Globe*, December 26, 1993, p. A1.

95 Schneider, Keith, "50 Memo Shows Radiation Test Doubts," *The New York Times,* December 28, 1993, p A8.

96 Mednick, Sarnoff, and Van Dusen, Katherine, op. cit.

    As Mednick put it, "If we were to begin with an early elementary school cohort and were successful in predicting at age six which boys would be chronic offenders, we would have a difficult moral, legal, and political problem in attempting to impose preventive treatment at this age. On the other hand, if we can identify a (9 to 12 year-old) delinquent as a future chronic offender, the authorities may find it appropriate to refer him to treatment."

Mednick's study was to include administering electroencephalograms
(to identify psychomotor epilepsy); measuring with skin galvanometers
of the electrical properties of skin response on the palms and soles of the
feet of boys exposed to artificially induced stress (to identify the unfeeling recidivist); measuring testosterone levels (though he admitted hockey
players might have the same levels); identifying laterality (left-handers
are more prone to delinquency); searching for physical anomalies such as
malformed ears, low-set ears, asymmetrical ears, soft pliable ears, high
palates, furrowed tongues, curved fingers, and a third toe longer than
the second, among other markers (the reference to third toes was reminiscent of Lombroso's view of the atavistic criminal with "prehensile"
feet); administering the ubiquitous IQ test; and a "30 minute interview"
covering such issues as family interaction, situational factors, attitudes
toward the law, and relationships with peers.

Although received positively by Alfred Regnery, the Reagan-appointed
administrator of the Office of Juvenile Justice and Delinquency Prevention, as a result of congressional pressure and concerns of some staff that
the proposal violated congressionally imposed bans to human experimentation, Mednick's project was not funded.

The studies to which Mednick and others referred were of mixed quality. The twin studies in which brothers raised apart had similar delinquency patterns were, to a degree, environmentally contaminated. Many
of the twins were raised together or similarly.

The adoptive studies were somewhat better. They showed that (primarily Scandinavian) boys placed for adoption whose natural fathers had
a criminal history were slightly more likely to break the law than those
whose natural fathers did not have a criminal history. This was particularly true if the natural father, in addition to breaking the law, was an
alcoholic. However, even among those whose natural fathers had engaged
in criminal behavior, 75 percent to 80 percent of the boys engaged in no
known criminal behavior.

Kamin discovered that a significant number of the adoptees who later
engaged in delinquency had been placed in adoptive homes wherein the
adoptive father had a criminal record – probably a result of social-class
matching by child adoption caseworkers.[97]

One fact emerged clearly and distinctly. It is impossible to predict that
anyone will engage in criminal behavior based on physiology, constitution, genetics, race, body type, or any other such measure. In most cases,

---

[97] Correspondence in *Science*, Vol. 225, March 1, 1985, pp. 983–89.

one might better toss a coin. One can, of course, do a bit better in predicting future criminal violence if the offender has already been imprisoned two or three times for violent crimes.

What if genetic and biological contributors to serious and violent offenses were to be well established? Harvard psychologist Jerome Kagan has suggested that a small number of individuals who engage in impulsive crimes of violence might have a "special biology" characterized by lower-than-average heart rates and blood pressure:

Most youth or adults who commit a violent crime will not commit a second.... The group we are concerned with are the recidivists – those who have been arrested many times. This is the group for whom there might be some biological contribution.[98]

Unlike Wilson and Herrnstein, Kagan was modest in his assessment of the potential impact biological and genetic factors might have on crime in general, and violent crime in particular. Kagan suggested that within 25 years, biological tests will be able to pick out about 15 children of every thousand (.015 percent) who may have violent tendencies. He admits, however, that probably *no more than one of those 15 children would actually become violent*. He then poses the most important question, "Do we tell the mothers of all 15 that their kids might be violent? How are the mothers then going to react to their children if we do that?"[99] Kagan's projections suggested that fewer than 10 of all the juveniles in all the state reform schools in the nation would be there for having committed a violent offense that could be seen as largely attributable to biology and genetics.[100]

Kagan made no claims of ethnic or racially skewed patterns of violence, preferring to concentrate on the individual. The impact on violent crime, even were his theories to prove correct, would be minimal. However, if history is any guide, the search would not likely hew to the boundaries set by Kagan, therefore hardly justifying the ethical and social risks inherent in the predictable spilling over of "preventive" strategies for those groups (that is, African-American) already perceived by much of the majority white population as prone to violent crime.

---

[98] Kagan, Jerome, quoted in "Seeking the Roots of Violence," *Time*, April 19, 1993, p. 53.
[99] Ibid. p. 53.
[100] Of the 53,000 juveniles detained in the reform schools of the nation on any given day, only about 18 percent (9,540) have been committed for crimes classified as violent.

It is true that a number of respected studies of offenders demonstrate that a small number of offenders commit a disproportionate amount of violent crime. This was the conclusion of University of Pennsylvania researchers Marvin Wolfgang and David Farrington, who followed a "birth cohort" of African-American males from 1945, and another from 1958 to the present. Similar cohort studies by Ohio State University researchers Simon Dinitz, Donna Hamparian, et. al. yielded similar results.

However, the implication of those in search of the genetics of violent crime has been that these high-rate street offenders are most likely to be the same persons whom genetic measures could identify. It is an unwarranted assumption. In fact, those studies most frequently cited as evidence of genetics at work in shaping criminal behavior (adoptive and twin studies) apply primarily to lesser property offenders – not to the so-called hard-core offender, violent or otherwise. The relevance of these findings to street crime would be minimal at best.[101]

Ironically, it is more likely that the Scandinavian studies upon which most current theories of genetic influences on criminal behavior rest would be more likely to apply to a rural or suburban white middle-class American adolescent than to the inner-city African-American juvenile subject to overwhelmingly debilitating environmental and social conditions. Though one could envision some limited medical diagnostic purpose in compiling Mednick's factors, history would have us follow a predictable script in this regard.

The more crucial question is why – given the meager returns and the limited relevance genetic influences are likely to have, even if found – there would be so much emphasis on the subject, particularly in light of the fact that there is so much already known but aggressively ignored regarding the social, familial, and environmental sources of violence and crime. I fear the answer resides in the fact that were we to acknowledge the obvious, we would also have to individualize, be understanding, thoughtful, and, God forgive me for saying it, "compassionate" toward too many criminals – all dirty words when one is at war with a dehumanized and demonized enemy, who, too often these days, turns out to have a black face.

---

[101] Wolfgang, for example, estimated that even were the Scandinavian adoptive studies regarding heritability to prove predictive of later violent behavior (which they haven't), they would have relevance to no more that 3 percent of the violent offenders in his cohort. Dinitz estimated the approximate same percentage (in private conversations with the authors).

Approaching Genes and Behavior

None of this is to say that racial, genetic, or "constitutional" issues are unimportant or to be ignored. For example, the recent work of researchers like University of North Carolina's sociologist/geneticist Guang Guo is geared less to confirm gut-cosseted conclusions that sell books than to identify the complex sources of those differences that exist within, between, and among races – including behavioral differences and cultural patterns that interact with genes in such fashion as to produce measurable "constitutional" outcomes. New approaches to these dicey issues have emerged that meld genetics, cultural anthropology, sociology, and neurology among others.

Science Daily reported Guo's research as among the first to link molecular genetic variants to adolescent delinquency – in the process identifying genetic predictors of serious and violent delinquency that gain salience when considered together with social influences (i.e., family, friends, and school). Guo identified three genetic polymorphisms that, when examined in the context of modulating social controls, were significant predictors of serious or violent delinquency.

As *Science Daily* summarized his ground-breaking study, "These findings about gene-environment interactions suggest certain genotypes and specific control influences (e.g. family characteristics and processes; popularity and friendship characteristics; and school attendance factors) are mutually dependent on delinquency."

While past behavioral studies of gene–environment interactions typically examined the relationship of a single factor (e.g., child abuse, stress) to genes, this research was unique in examining many layers of social context simultaneously (i.e., family dynamics, peer relations, and school-related variables). The study revealed "non-intuitive and complex relations among the researched variables."

Guo commented, "Our research confirms that genetic effects are not deterministic. Gene expression may depend heavily on the environment... Most delinquent and violent behaviors are considered complex. Understanding these behaviors requires understanding both their socioeconomic-cultural components and their genetic components."[102]

Indeed, recent approaches to genes and behavior call into question the racist-borne genetic conclusions of the Wilson-Herrnstein-Murray triumvirate of neoconservative propagandists. Consider for example, these

---

[102] *Science Daily*, August 9, 2010.

excerpts from an essay by two representatives of the newly emerging discipline of "neuroanthropology" concerned with human development "under conditions of inequality."

Inequality works through the brain and body, involving mechanisms like stress, learning environments, the loss of neuroplasticity, the impact of toxins, educational opportunities (or their absence) and other factors that negatively shape development. Neuroanthropology can play a fundamental role in documenting these effects and in linking them to the social, political and cultural factors that negatively impact on the brain. At the same time, technological and pharmacological interventions are playing an increasing role in managing behavioral disorders, often with great profit for companies, while cognitive enhancement drugs, brain-computer interfaces, and neuro-engineering will surely be used in ways that create new separations between haves and have-nots.

(S)ocietal appeals to "hard-wired" differences remain a standard approach by people in positions of power to maintain racial, gender, sexual and other inequalities; a deeper understanding of the complex origins and unfolding of key neural and physiological differences undermines accounts that assume these distinctions are inescapable. At the same time, neuroanthropology points to new ways to think about how people become talented and ways to understand intelligence, resiliency, social relations and other factors that shape success in life. Rather than assuming structural inequality is basic to all societies, neuroanthropologists ask how inequality differentiates people and what we might do about that.

(C)onscious reflection and experience-based accounts have a crucial relation to many of the phenomena we study. Experience-based ethnographic descriptions can offer valuable insights into brain functioning. At times these descriptions can help illuminate the influence of context and experience; at other times, neuroanthropological accounts may highlight the limits of conscious awareness and demonstrate the self-deceptions inherent in some kinds of neurological functioning. For this reason, neuroanthropology brings an ethnographic sensibility to brain research, including a willingness to take into consideration native theories of thought and individuals' accounts of their own experience. Thus, careful ethnographic research, in-depth interviews, and the analysis of indigenous worldviews will always be central to the neuroanthropological synthesis... For example, practices of child rearing and early formative experiences are clearly influenced by cultural ideologies about how children should be nurtured, but many of the organic mechanisms through which these ideologies take hold of individuals and affect their long-term development may be unknown, even invisible to the participants.

For this reason, subjects' eye-view accounts are critical to neuroanthropology in a way that they might not be to other cognitive theorists. First, we recognize that theories about how the mind works or what it needs are themselves part of the developmental environment in which the brain is formed. Even if these ideas don't accurately represent actual neural function, they do influence the brain-culture system, and can have an impact on the way the brain works even if that is in a way utterly unintended by those who hold the ideas. That is, whether indigenous theories of thought are accurate, they are part of the ecology of brain conditioning.

(M)ost of our cultural and neural functioning is submerged, only accessible to consciousness with extraordinary effort and special techniques, if it is accessible at all. Thus, research techniques should focus on capturing both our conscious awareness of why we do what we do and the inherent processes that shape the flow and outcome of that doing... and we lose a vital resource if we do not ask ourselves how ethnographic communities come to their own ideas about the mind and experience.[103]

It's ironic that we would first glimpse what we've become in a rambling old prison in Iraq – run basically by white people to contain brown people – and later, in euphemistically labeled "black sites" meant to shield our practices from the light of day lest our sense of basic decency be undermined and what has lain at the heart of our democracy from its inception, carrying the virus of its own undoing, be revealed – one spelled out in quite some detail by d'Tocqueville who, in a near-preternatural convergence of events, arrived on American shores to study its prisons.[104] We now see the abiding American dilemma once again undermining our democracy – this time, on a world-wide scale.

---

[103] Greg Downey is senior lecturer in anthropology at Macquarie University. Daniel Lende is assistant professor of anthropology at the University of Notre Dame.

[104] As he put it, "If there ever are great revolutions there, they will be caused by the presence of the blacks upon American soil. That is to say, it will not be the equality of social conditions but rather their inequality which may give rise thereto."

6

Banishing Indecision

When I finished the first draft of this book, I dutifully sent it off to my editor for his comments and suggestions. Most things passed muster relatively untouched. However, he took exception to the final chapter. It was too pessimistic, he said, and offered too few specific recommendations as to how the problems I had outlined might be redressed. If I didn't have any suggestions for future policy, he said, "Why write the book?"

It's not that I couldn't have proposed effective options. They have always been there for the taking. In my 40 years in the field of corrections, for example, I've watched alternative programs come and go with the wind – many "worked," some didn't, but it really didn't matter. That part of the justice system was apparently there to fulfill entirely different purposes, most of them symbolic, many of them venal. As the sociologist Robert Vinter found in his studies of juvenile correctional facilities and programs 35 years earlier, whether or not a model gained official sanction was virtually unrelated to its efficacy. Indeed, it appeared that the less successful the approach, the better its chances of becoming a fixture in the justice bureaucracy.[1]

The question is not whether we need to invent new techniques for crime control – or even whether we need new ways to approach rehabilitation. We have sufficient power and technology to control crime if we wish to use it. We know a good deal about rehabilitation. The more basic question is one of deciding at what point we are willing to sacrifice civility and

---

[1] Vinter, Robert, Theodore Newcomb, and Rhea Kish (eds.), *Time Out: A National Study of Juvenile Correctional Programs*. National Assessment of Juvenile Corrections, Ann Arbor, Michigan: The University of Michigan, June 1976.

decency in the service of crime control. Likewise, it is not whether we understand the roots of criminal behavior, but whether we can tolerate knowing such things. Such understanding potentially undermines a whole series of cultural traditions, most of them within the world of so-called jurisprudence.

The problem of reform is further complicated by the fact that those to whom we might have traditionally looked to devise progressive programs are now mostly absent from the scene. Contemporary liberals, having become so much a part of the "culture of contentment," while looking to credentialed law enforcement or "human service" experts for moral refuge, seem unable to offer much more than "me too" bleating to the arguments of the Right. Indeed, it is difficult not to conclude that humane alternatives were for a less complicated and more reasonable time.

University of Michigan Professor David Wineman's classic monograph on supervision of social work graduate students in correctional settings posed the damning question that now plagues most of the contemporary American justice system and those who work in it: How does one train professionals to work in a system that, at its core, hates people?[2]

The Sentimentalist versus the Ignoramus

It all hearkens back to George Herbert Mead's comment regarding those who would attempt to solve social problems through the criminal trial process: "The social worker in the court," Mead said, "is the sentimentalist, (but) the legalist in the social settlement in spite of his learned doctrine is the ignoramus."[3]

The rigid categories that the justice system produces in abundance are precious only to societies that have grown vicious on crime – offering refuge in a world of binaries and stereotypes that carry us ever farther from the human narrative. Knowing and acknowledging the vicissitudes out of which a particular offender might have arisen, at its core, would be far more threatening to our contemporary justice system than the criminal act itself. Knowing too much inevitably undermines the sense of certainty that feeds moral indignation – upon which the present system totally rests. It is much easier to gear the citizenry up to fight the devil

---

[2] Wineman, David, "Supervising Students in Settings which Hate People," unpublished monograph, Ann Arbor, Michigan: University of Michigan School of Social Work, 1968.
[3] Mead, G. H. "The Psychology of Punitive Justice," *The American Journal of Sociology,* Vol. 23, 1917, pp. 577–602.

they've been taught to recognize and hate than it is to ask that it consider how the demon came to be at their door. We would, as a nation, rather engage in a massive exercise in selective inattention.

At its best, the justice system affords a democratic society mostly short-term control of, and protection from, those whose lives are out of control and who represent a threat to others. Such control is obviously necessary in some cases. However, when the justice system becomes the definer of social problems or the ground for social policy, matters turn danger-ous for all concerned. Experience emanating from the justice system is dicey even in the best of circumstances. Its rituals and procedures distort social realities and feed stereotypes at virtually every step from arrest through trial, conviction, and sentencing. In its vain attempt to settle social concerns, the justice system has left the country with ineffective policies virtually devoid of humane impulse.

Jerome Bruner reminds us that research, when grounded in the nar-rative, tends to focus our attention on the *meaning* of human activity.[4] This observation carries profound implications that go well beyond that seemingly subjective world. Indeed, a well-cultivated sense of the narra-tive ensures that a pathway of communication will be kept open through which an informed citizenry can be kept at least minimally in touch with the grating, unpredictable, and frequently disorienting circumstances that inform the lives of those who live on the margins of society, and that sur-round most crime. In this sense, the personal narrative is an unwelcome intruder in the criminal justice arena in that it makes it impossible to artificially detach the individual from his or her familial and societal moorings.

---

[4] Bruner, Jerome, *Acts of Meaning,* Cambridge, Massachusetts: Harvard University Press, 1990, p. 2.

As Bruner put it, "Now let me tell you first what I and my friends thought the revolution was about back there in the late 1950s. It was, we thought, an all-out effort to establish meaning as the central concept of psychology – not stimuli and responses, not overtly observable behavior, not biological drives and their transformation, but meaning. It was *not* a revolution against behaviorism with the aim of transforming behaviorism into a better way of pursuing psychology by adding a little mentalism to it.... It was an altogether more profound revolution than that. Its aim was to discover and to describe formally the meanings that human beings created out of their encounters with the world, and then to propose hypotheses about what meaning-making processes were implicated. It focused upon the symbolic activities that human beings employed in constructing and in making sense not only of the world, but of themselves. Its aim was to prompt psychology to join forces with its sister interpretive disciplines in the humanities and in the social sciences... (p. 2)

Unfortunately, much contemporary criminological research avoids introducing such difficult-to-program realities into its models and machines. It demands that we deal with the offender in bits and pieces, thereby making a comfortable fit with a justice system that does the same. When it comes to a criminal defendant, if there is anything a contemporary criminal court (or criminological researcher) wishes *not* to hear, it is an honest story about a human being.

For this reason, the narrative presents a profound threat to the criminal justice system and those paid by its apologists to study it. It is why its major actors not only relish avoiding human considerations, but militantly flee from them. The symbol, *par excellence,* is the contemporary prosecutor who will shake heaven and hell to keep a jury from knowing a personal history of a defendant should it wander ever so slightly beyond a rap sheet or formal criminal history record. A sense for the authentic narrative undermines this.

To talk of "alternatives" in such a system is useless, if not silly. The system has grown so corrupt and its venal intents are now so buried in legalisms that it can no longer tolerate the most elementary human decency. As Bruner warned:

Our sense of the normative is nourished in narrative, but so is our sense of breach and of exception. Stories make "reality" a mitigated reality. Children, I think, are predisposed naturally and by circumstance to start their narrative careers in that spirit. And we equip them with models and procedural tool kits for perfecting those skills. Without those skills we could never endure the conflicts and contradictions that social life generates. We would become unfit for the life of culture.[5]

Absent such considerations, the justice system fashions worldviews, expounds theories and proposes solutions grounded in stereotypes carefully nurtured by the politics of the times. The threatening reality lurking behind the personal narrative is that it might mitigate individual personal responsibility and, indeed, suggest that all citizens in a democratic society might bear some responsibility and might even share some guilt, however far removed, for an individual's criminal act – a prospect totally out of step with the times. The narrative carries the implicit risk of draining the citizenry of its lust for the kinds of revenge that only a world of demons and avenging angels justifies.

---

[5] Ibid. p. 97.

If I were to propose a way out of our present moral *cul de sac*, it would probably be in rediscovering the personal narrative and finding some means of reintroducing it into the legal arena – something that I fear will continue to elude us. With the demise of individualized sentencing in favor of punishment by number and graph, the possibility of basic reform has pretty much vanished from the criminal justice system. The idea that a judge might expend some effort in understanding what may have transpired in a defendant's life that might bear on the crime allowed room for human judgment (albeit flawed) in fashioning a sentence. More important, it brought unsettling realities into the legal arena ultimately serving to inform the law – keeping it minimally in touch with human considerations.

Until relatively recently, there were always a few (exceptional judges lawyers, social workers, family members), who remained a thorn in the side of the criminal justice system, naively dragging into the courtroom (usually over strenuous objection) those stories and twisted strands of happenstance that didn't quite fit. Cantankerous realities that undid stereotypes and put a human face on threatening strangers.[6] But, no

---

[6] After *The New York Times* ran an unusually thoughtful series profiling 10 young people, most African-Americans from the inner city, the paper was deluged with offers of help and concern. The reporters had involved themselves in the lives of these youngsters, spending a number of weeks with each – young people who would otherwise be so easily ignored, or dismissed out of hand. The time with them on the street, with their friends, and in their homes, affected all concerned.

Here are the comments of the reporters regarding their experiences:

Don Terry writing about Marcus Tramble, 19 –

Marcus and I swapped war stories about being stopped by nasty police officers and being disrespected by waiters who seem to seat every white face first.

Then I say that if you think that is bad, listen to this, and I tell him about being dressed in a new Brooks Brothers suit trying to hail a cab when I lived on the Upper West Side of Manhattan, in the heart of yuppie New York City.

But the cabs passed me by the dozens. Then the rain started to fall. And my new suit had to go to the cleaners.

"I wish I could afford a cab ride," says Marcus, whose flight out of the Chicago projects is constantly frustrated by the demands of urban survival.

A few days later, he calls me to tell me about a job interview he is going on, and then he gets to the important subject: girls.

He is in love, but the girl broke up with him and now he thinks he might die. When I was 19 I was in love with a girl named Donna. When she broke up with me I thought I was going to die.

See, I'm still here, I tell him.

But you're losing your hair, he says.

Felicia R. Lee on Ladeeta Smith, 18 –

more. The means to present them no longer exist for criminal defendants in most courts across the country. Those few "sentimentalists" who, in the past, might have questioned where the courts were headed, have been

We had sobbed together one afternoon when Ladeeta told me that her mother no longer recognized her. For days, my heart jumped when the phone rang, expecting the call that would tell me that Mrs. Smith had died of AIDS. I sat with her and her family at the kitchen table in their Crown Heights apartment days after her mother's funeral, poring over photographs and listening to them relive memories.

Ladeeta and I talked about intimate, painful things – being lonely, wanting to leave the world a different place, what you do to keep going on those days when you want to bury your head under the pillow.

Yet, there was a gap. After all the questions, I could go home to my Upper West Side apartment, away from the chaos and the anger of the Brooklyn streets. Here we were, two black women, putting a lie to the idea that there is such a thing as one authentic "black experience" that creates an automatic solidarity and understanding.

Isabel Wilkerson on Nicholas Whitiker, 10 –

Nicholas rarely gets to leave his neighborhood on the South Side of Chicago. For a change of pace, I took him and his brother, Willie, to the Auto Show. They bounced from car to car, until a white salesman orders them out of a Range Rover.

"We've had some vandalism," the salesman said, hurrying the boys out. The children ran to a Jaguar where three whites were sitting inside. A salesman rolled down the window and said, "You are not getting in."

They hurried to the trucks, where a crowd watched a dance act. Blocked by adult shoulders, the boys climbed on a truck bed to see. Before they could straighten themselves, a white police officer ordered them down.

Undaunted, Willie saw some race cars and could not resist looking inside one. By now, Nicholas had got the message, even if Willie had not. At age 10, he is already his brother's protector. "You better get down before that policeman comes back, Nicholas said.

I recognized instantly the cavalier back of the hand, the instinctive prejudging and shutting of doors, the rush to see race and think criminal even in the faces of children.

John Tierney on Fernando Morales, 16 –

In hanging around with Fernando and his friends in Bridgeport, Conn., I did see flashes of appealing qualities; and occasional kindness, a display of wit or intelligence or charm, some genuine entrepreneurial skills as they were hustling drugs. But then their alienation and mistrust would surface, and I would have a hard time imagining how they could ever manage to hold a real job.

I suppose you can attribute some of their bad attitude to their being teen-agers, and I suppose some of them will change if they happen on the right job or the right woman. Some of Fernando's older friends and relatives have gone straight. But it's going to be very hard for Fernando to overcome his past. After being let down so many times by so many people, it's going to be hard for him to learn to trust anyone again.

Michael Marriott on Freddie Brown, 17 –

After more than three weeks of practically living in Freddie's world – following him with an open mind and notebook as he tried to steer clear of harm and the police in an impoverished corner of the Bronx – I could not help but wonder if I could have survived in circumstances like his. Could I have escaped? Succeeded?

pretty much driven from the halls of justice. The hope of educating the
courts and the citizenry about crime and its causes exited with them. It
confirms Bruner's prediction that, in losing the narrative, "we're going to
lose in many ways what we're all about."

Many would doubtless challenge this view – civil libertarians among
them. Nevertheless, the legal scholar Ronald Dworkin has suggested

In 16 years spent working as a journalist, writing from drug dens in East New York to
dusty townships in southern Africa, I've become well acquainted with the cruel grasp
of poverty. But it was something about the extent of Freddie's deprivation that haunted
me, that loomed large whenever I would leave him in the night to drive to my cozy
Manhattan apartment.

For Freddie, poverty was not only a dearth of material comforts and opportunities; even
more crippling, he wrestled with a poverty of hope.

Peter Kilborn on Derrick White, 19 –

I wanted to see Derrick's haunts around Memphis – the project where he grew up amid
the chronically jobless, the high school where he shone, the places where he spends his
time as he waits to get back on track after dropping out of college. I could not drive
and take notes, so I asked if he would mind driving. The car was a brand-new, bright
red Nissan Sentra from Avis. No one in his family has a car, but I did not ask if he had
a license or if he could drive. Boys his age just can. He rolled back the seat, adjusted the
mirrors, snapped on his seat belt, turned the radio on to rap music and drove faultlessly
all day.

He was easier to interview from then on, but it did not occur to me to wonder why.
Weeks later, Paul Hosefros, the Times photographer who went to Memphis to take
Derrick's picture, said that Derrick and his family commented on how the reporter had
trusted him with his car. Trusting him was not the point. I had to take notes.

Sara Rimer on Shawn Hunt, 17 –

Usually, people I interview don't ask me about myself, which is fine. But Shawn was full
of questions.

"What do you think of black people?" he asked me one day during a boring computer
class at Bishop Loughlin Memorial High School in Brooklyn, where he has become an
honor student, bound for college.

"What did your parents tell you about black people?"

"Would you marry a black man?"

"Why do white people wear their jeans so tight?"

"Don't white people get cold? I always see them ice-skating. And they run in those little
shorts in the middle of winter."

"What did you major in college?"

"How'd you get your job?"

None of this was meant to be unkind or to make me uncomfortable. I am a white woman
who grew up in a virtually all-white suburb. Shawn's world is just as segregated, and
he was simply asking the honest questions of an incessantly inquisitive young man for
whom people like me were almost total strangers.

Jane Gross on Jerina Gervais, 18 –

"Are all white people racists?"

that, indeed, the best road to legal interpretation lies with literary interpretation.[7] In 1989, *The Michigan Law Review* devoted an entire issue to the topic of "Legal Storytelling."[8] However, such approaches seem to have had minimal influence upon the contemporary criminal justice system, which increasingly demands a one-dimensional view of human beings and a reality of bits and binaries. It's why we cannot expect much but further harm to come of anticrime prescriptions devised by the contemporary criminal justice system – anticrime policies and procedures conceived by legalists who fit, only too well, Mead's definition of the "ignoramus" in the social settlement – unacquainted with, and uninterested in, the human complexities that infuse and attend criminal behavior.

Jerina and I are driving through Oakland, Calif., when she asks that question, early on in the process of learning about her struggle to put her old, wild life behind her, when everything she said or did felt like a racial-sensitivity test that I would no doubt fail. I steady the wheel and say, "No, all white people aren't racists, but sometimes they're scared and that may look a lot the same."

"Do you listen to rap music?"

We're in the car again, in a pounding January rain. I consider pretending but know I'll get caught. We wind up sitting on her driveway for a long time, listening to her rap tapes. But first she tells me that she hates it when outsiders – white people, rich people, middle-aged people – try to pass as cool. Maybe I've been trying too hard.

We are driving home from celebrating her birthday, near the end of our time together. I tell Jerina about my recent visit to a black doctor and my shame at discovering that I didn't trust him to take care of me. The experience made me rethink my answer about whether all white people are racist.

In the dark car, Jerina reaches out and pats my hand.

David Gonzales on Asenhat Gomez, 18 –

It was hard to be an observer and not participate, and as Asenhat's 18th birthday approached, her mother entrusted me with a half a week's pay and asked me to buy a typewriter as a present. I spent a Sunday afternoon visiting various stores searching for just the right one.

Peering into her life as a new immigrant in Brooklyn, I glimpsed what my own parents endured when they arrived in New York from Puerto Rico during the Depression, investing their meager working-class wages in the education of their three children, living in a crowded South Bronx neighborhood not dissimilar from the South Side of Williamsburg.

It was a world whose rhythms had a familiar cadence. Like a respectful Puerto Rican child, I would greet Dona Mercedes with a hug and ask for her blessing. "May God bless you and the Virgin Mary protect you," she would say, and in doing so fill me with a familiar comfort.

[7] Dworkin, Ronald, *Law's Empire,* Cambridge, Massachusetts: Harvard University Press, 1986.

[8] *Michigan Law Review,* Vol. 87, No. 8, August 1989.

Clifford Shaw, the respected sociologist of the "Chicago School" of the 1930s, defined the ground of this conflict:

.... The validity and value of the personal document are not dependent upon its objectivity or veracity. It is not expected that the delinquent will necessarily describe his life-situations objectively. On the contrary, it is desired that his story will reflect his own personal attitudes and interpretations, for it is just these personal factors that are so important in the study and treatment of the case. Thus, rationalizations, fabrications, prejudices, exaggerations are quite as valuable as objective descriptions, provided, of course, that these reactions be properly identified and classified. W. I. Thomas clearly made the point a near century ago.

There may be, and is, doubt as to the objectivity and veracity of the record, but even the highly subjective record has a value for behavior study. A document prepared by one compensating for a feeling of inferiority or elaborating a delusion of persecution is as far as possible from objective reality, but the subject's view of the situation, how he regards it, may be the most important element for interpretation. For his immediate behavior is closely related to his definition of the situation, which may be in terms of objective reality, or in terms of a subjective appreciation – 'as if' it were so. Very often it is the wide discrepancy between the situation as it seems to others and the situation as it seems to the individual that brings about the overt behavior difficulty.... If men define situations as real, they are real in their consequences.[9,10]

These perceptions come perilously close to undermining criminal procedure itself. That is as it should be, and it is probably why the great American legal scholar Roscoe Pound was moved to comment that establishing the juvenile court was as significant an event in the history of Western jurisprudence as the signing of the Magna Carta. It is also why the juvenile court could not be allowed to succeed. The question was never whether we had the means to understand what goes into the making of an individual delinquent or what influences a criminal act. Rather, it has been whether a given society could tolerate knowing such things. In a democratic society, such knowledge brings with it responsibilities that frequently are beyond our capacity to fulfill.

Some have suggested that both perpetrators and victims in the inner-city reveal the classic symptoms of post-traumatic stress as commonly seen among young survivors of war. This takes matters in another direction. Indeed, as the much heralded aggressive police techniques took root amid a surfeit of fawning press reports in the 1990s that proclaimed their

---

9 Thomas, W. I. and Thomas, Dorothy S., *The Child in America*, New York: Alfred A. Knopf, 1928, pp. 571–72.
10 Shaw, Clifford, *The Jack Roller*, Chicago, Illinois: University of Chicago Press, 1945, pp. 1–2.

success – (one of the more notorious con jobs in recent memory), it stood as a premier example of the emotional power of the "post hoc ergo propter hoc" fallacy still clung to by liberal and conservative observers alike and doggedly destined to carry the day. It's a fallacy that rests in the belief that it must be true, since "I feel it in my 'gut,'" subsequent research notwithstanding. And by God, it "works" – (albeit in convincing a public bent toward false belief) – a primary goal of neoconservatism all along.

In his narrative study of young black men and boys brought to shock trauma units and emergency rooms in Boston after suffering serious gunshot wounds, John Rich suggests that his experience as a physician did not support the stereotypical images. Rich notes for example, "The presumption that all injured black men deserve what they get is simple and powerful. It summons up images of black ghetto gangsters warring over turf and drug trade. It suggests that these young men are rarely innocent bystanders but rather willing soldiers in some vicious civil war in the urban jungle." He rejects this view, noting, "My own experience as a physician did not support this image, and most of the young black patients I saw in the Young Men's Health did not fit this stereotype."[11]

Rich writes compellingly about what he saw, "I recognized something in Kari that I had seen in other young patients who had suffered near fatal trauma. In the days and weeks after the injury, the transient light of hope and possibility burns remarkably bright. Even then, it can be hard to detect this hope in their numbed, expressionless faces. But it came through loud and clear in their words.

"But if this small fire lit by the near-death experience was not kindled, often it was smothered by the burdens that began to accumulate in their lives. Families and friends grew tired of caring for young men who should, in their estimation, have reverted to the vibrant teenagers they had been just months before. Regrets, disfigurement, pain, and fear rolled together and blurred their hopes for the future."

"'But you know I'm not giving up, Doc,' Kari said, interrupting my thoughts as if he had heard them. 'I know I'm gonna be all right. I gotta be all right.'"

Throughout Rich's notes, impressions, visits, and personal reactions, the narrative comes through clearly. In this, Rich is part of a very old and immensely valuable tradition, now largely lost to academic sociology

---

[11] John A. Rich, M.D., MPH, *Wrong Place, Wrong Time: Trauma and Violence in the Lives of Young Black Men*, Johns Hopkins University Press, 2009 Kindle location 123–125, p. 2515.

and virtually absent from the works of neoconservative ideologues masquerading in sociological mufti. One is reminded of the Chicago school that gave us giants like Ernest Burgess and Robert Park, Clifford Shaw, George Mead, W.I. Thomas and others who knew the stuff of their studies in an immediate sense and developed theories and practices accordingly – much of it totally beholden to the narrative.

In pondering Rich's work, I was reminded of the absence of narrative in the work of the neos when it came to addressing difficult issues concerned with crime and punishment. Take for example, the work of another apostle of punishment, John Dilulio on managing prisons. One came away with the impression that he seldom wandered much beyond the confines of the warden's office unless accompanied by one of his minions. The result was a "study" of Texas prison management that mouthed the official policies of the Texas Department of Corrections couching them in academic double-speak. It bore little resemblance to the entity I had come to know while under near constant federal suit for some of the more primitive practices in the nation. It perhaps explains why on one of my visits to Huntsville, the then-Director of the Texas prison system turned his head and refused to acknowledge my extended hand when we met in a corridor of that facility – again, largely constructed "by the inmates themselves."

Rich's approach is also in the tradition of social psychologists like Jerome Bruner – whose views on the narrative have virtually vanished from one of the dominant approaches (cognitive psychology) he championed in academia psychology Rendered devoid of meaning, it eventually came to define the problem and prescribe its solutions devolving into a soul-snatching exercise – disparaging history as irrelevant to the task at hand and concentrating solely on "what works." In the end, in its pretensions it's destructive to both the individual and the society, yielding the kind of professional that blessed Abu Ghraib, monitored water-boarding, and helped design Guantanamo – speaking the double-speak that characterizes so much of the contemporary psychological profession.

One comes away from Dr. Rich's narrative enriched and keenly versed in the complexities inherent in world of those he served. His comments on preventive interventions – particularly in the current national milieu – resonate strongly. He makes the kind of observation that would foredoom any contemporary request for a federal grant to address the problem of crime and violence among young black men and boys.

"As providers," Rich notes, "our job is not so much to fix the cycle as to understand it and to recognize it as an underlying cause of the seemingly bad decisions that our young patients make. Some of those decisions, while incomprehensible to us, make abundant sense on the streets, where any show of weakness can lead to victimization. Our job is not so much to judge their actions as good or bad, sensible or senseless, as to hear from them and understand how and why they arrive in these perilous places."

Rich leads us once again, to the dicey matter of "root causes." – that lingering bugaboo so inelegantly posed by James Q. Wilson in his defining work, *Thinking About Crime* and later, in a variety of troublesome venues, from the making of terrorists (in an essay for the "Manhattan Institute")[12] to the presumed genetic makeup of criminals (i.e. "black" criminals) in his and the late psychologist, Richard Herrnstein's *Crime and Human Nature.*

The uncomfortable fact remains that in the end, Rich is suggesting nothing new or radical. Since 1997, the Center for Disease Control has been studying the effects of childhood trauma among inner-city children on later development across a wide spectrum. Most of this has been available and well documented and the negative effects are legion. However, the country has opted for the quick fix or "what works." Now it's obvious that it doesn't work as well as we had presumed. But typically that no longer matters.

It has been a particularly curious turn of events that, when, for the first time in history, we have information systems capable of allowing us to individually tailor outcomes to the strengths and weaknesses of each defendant, we retreat to the meat ax of "mandatory sentencing" and the language of the convict: "If you can't do the time, don't do the crime."

This is because individualizing sentencing implies that one must know the defendant in ways that spill beyond the narrow limits set by the offense alone – for example, a burglar, a sex offender, a thief. We would rather use our technology to keep messy and confounding human matters at bay – spurred on by the clear reality that most of those we would place outside such consideration are black and brown – groups the white majority is predisposed to dehumanize, occasionally demonize, and near-universally hold to be of less value than themselves. Indeed, as our technology gets more sophisticated, our anticrime prescriptions grow more simple-minded.

---

[12] James Q. Wilson in *The City Journal*, Winter 2004.

Combating Crime

Most anticrime proposals polarize around two issues – whether to address so-called root causes, or whether to get tougher on criminals. The future, so the root cause advocates would have it, lies in prevention. The remedies are familiar – better prenatal care, family support systems, nutrition programs, improved education, employment opportunities, adequate housing, and minimum family income. Indeed, Janet Reno, the Attorney General in the Clinton administration, noted early in her tenure that 50 percent of the personality is formed by age three, and that once a child was past age five, we had probably lost the opportunity to effectively steer him away from a life of crime.[13]

Commonly, such root cause advocates present their case with the disclaimer, " . . . but, I fear we have lost a generation" – with its implicit call for the kind of social triage most now understand to mean the quiet disposal of African-American teenage boys and young men. Discussing root causes in this context doesn't really mean what it suggests. It simply provides a cover for guiltlessly walking away from immediate and difficult problems.

This is not to suggest that were we reasonable, we would not, as James Vorenberg recommended some 40 years earlier, once again wrestle with crime's root causes – particularly regarding the need for employment in the inner-cities – a matter that would be achingly self-evident were the subjects of the current national disdain mostly white. There is no gainsaying that prevention is basic to any hope of cutting crime in the long term.

Unfortunately, the root cause approach to stemming crime, whatever its intrinsic merits, has come to be seen as irrelevant, if not hackneyed. In an age seeking instant gratification (by those at the top as well as those at the bottom), few seem to have patience with models that seem removed from the realities of street crime or might appear to be soft on criminals. Authentic concern with root causes has no place in this scenario unless it can be totally removed from the realm of social causes.

The public is more sympathetic to unequivocal calls for toughness on crime than it is disposed to enter the hazy world of root causes. They presume that if law enforcement is quick, aggressive, and harsh enough, crime rates will be forced down. To a point, the premise is true, particularly insofar as it applies to those who have a stake in the society

---

[13] Interview on Public Broadcasting Television, *MacNeil Lehrer Report*, October 24, 1993.

(that is, so-called white collar offenders). However, when it comes to street crime committed by those with little stake in the society, such prescriptions lose their potency – particularly in a democratic society. The quality of deterrence differs dramatically as one goes up and down the socioeconomic ladder. For those at the top, it rests mainly on the possibility of losing one's status, privileges, and property. For those at the bottom, it demands a pound of flesh.

This is not to say that crimes cannot be deterred through a vigilant and harsh justice system. Were we willing to publicly execute all first-time burglars on the spot, the rate of thievery would probably subside. The issue has less to do with stemming crime than with the kind of society we wish to be. For criminal sanctions to have the kind of deterrent effect on street crime that is commonly credited to them, they would have to be so severe that the basic nature of our society would change. Such measures demand a society in which a significant percentage of law-abiding citizens and *most* of those who fit whatever the current profile of the potential criminal might be in vogue, would have to live in fear of the knock on the door by police.

Though few policymakers recommend such draconian measures openly – at least insofar as they might conceivably apply to young middle-class whites – the arrest data suggest there is less disposition to be equally chary when it comes to young African-American males, the majority of whom can now anticipate a policeman's knock at their door.

The fact that crime skyrocketed in Eastern Europe as former police-state countries emerged from dictatorship is an illustration of Durkheim's thesis that crime is to a society what temperature is to the body. Watch out if it's too high, but be equally concerned if it is too low.

However, if we are to deal with crime in our cities, we will have to return to the uncomfortable refocusing of anticrime efforts on problems now seen as peripheral to crime. The title of one study contains, within it, the range of problems that could define any so-called anticrime strategy: "Urban Desertification, Public Health and Public Order: 'Planned Shrink-age,' Violent Death, Substance Abuse and AIDS in the Bronx." Looking at crime in the Bronx in New York City, Rodrick Wallace suggested that

... the present overburdening of New York's criminal justice system arises from almost exactly the same causes as its accelerating inability to meet demands for acute medical service, so-called 'medical gridlock', in that both are expressions of the increasing social disorganization of poor communities initiated and continued in considerable part by government policy. . . . The critical role played by improper policy in triggering the syndrome suggests ecologically informed interventions, particularly essential service restoration, may hold the potential for great positive impact.[14]

Such an organic perspective is premised on factors mostly overlooked by those who study and plan anticrime strategies. As Wallace put it:

... [T]he origins of public health and public order are much the same and deeply embedded in the security and stability of personal, domestic and community social networks and other institutions.... Disruptions of such networks, from any cause, will express themselves in exacerbation of a nexus of behavior, including violence, sexuality, substance abuse and general criminality.[15]

The Likely Future

If we have learned anything over the recent decade, it's that anticrime policy in the United States is now highly unlikely to be derived either from humane impulse or from careful analysis. Rather, policy is judged for its potential to be distilled into succinct sound bites and applause-garnering throwaway lines. There is less interest in what is correct, or even what works, than in what sounds good for the times.

Major actors in the justice system – police, prosecutors, judges – can now be regularly counted upon to perform their roles in the manner of refugee thespians from the Victorian stage – unctuously giving the public a vision of the criminal as monster while enlisting a wide range of human service professionals and technocrats in validating that dishonest visage. Behind the hyperbole and hysteria stands a bureaucracy unparalleled in our history for the control and management of the underclass – having as its central task apprehending, labeling, sorting, and managing the absolute majority of young African-American males.

In contemporary America, public moralizing for its own sake has become more important than whatever putative effects such posturing might have in lowering crime. As the respected Norwegian criminologist Nils Christie commented, "American penal policy is really neither about punishing, nor rehabilitating: It is instead about identifying and managing unruly groups ... just what is needed in the control of the dangerous classes ... greatly helped by the distance created through the new penology; from individuals to categories, from morality to management and actuarial thinking.[16]

---

[14] Wallace, Roderick, "Urban Desertification, Public Health and Public Order: 'Planned Shrinkage,' Violent Death, Substance Abuse and AIDS in the Bronx," *Social Science and Medicine*, Vol. 31, No. 7, 1991, p. 801.

[15] Ibid. p. 811.

[16] Ibid. p. 165.

Several years ago, a blatant example of Christie's thesis caught my eye while reading the morning paper over breakfast. "California Prisons Turn on Electricity: Lethal Perimeter to Save Money on Tower Guards" was the headline, accompanied by a photo of Warden K. W. Prunty standing proudly alongside his new fence:[17]

Calipatria, Calif. – The signs show a man hit by a bolt of electricity, falling backward. "Danger. Peligro," they warn. "High Voltage, Keep Out. Alto Voltaje, No Entre." It's no idle threat. A new electrified fence at Calipatria State Prison means instant death for any inmate trying to escape. A prisoner advocate said she was horrified by what amounts to an automatic death sentence. . . . Guards threw the switch on the fence Nov. 8 (1993). It carries 4,000 volts and 650 milliamperes. About 70 milliamperes is enough to kill. . . . A special wire at the bottom prevents rats and other small animals from climbing up and dying.[18]

The warden characterized the lethal fence as a simple management decision. As he put it, "The fence doesn't get distracted, it doesn't look away for a moment and it doesn't get tired. This is simply a way to keep that same level of security while saving money." It was noted that as many as 20 other California maximum- and medium-security prisons would get electrified fences in the next few years as the state struggled to build more prisons on a tight budget.

The criminal and juvenile justice systems in the United States have grown so corrupt and venal that they can no longer tolerate the most elementary human decency. As Bruner warned:

Our sense of the normative is nourished in narrative, but so is our sense of breach and of exception. Stories make 'reality' a mitigated "reality." Children, I think, are predisposed naturally and by circumstance to start their narrative careers in that spirit. And we equip them with models and procedural tool kits for perfecting those skills. Without those skills we could never endure the conflicts and contradictions that social life generates. We would become unfit for the life of culture.[19]

Absent such considerations, the justice system fashions worldviews, expounds theories, and proposes solutions grounded in the stereotypes demanded by the politics of the time. The threatening reality lurking behind the personal narrative is the fact that it might mitigate individual personal responsibility and, indeed, suggest that all citizens in a democratic society might bear some responsibility and, indeed, might even share some guilt, however far removed, for an individual's criminal act – a

---

[17] Associated Press, "California Prisons Turn on Electrified Fence," *The Atlanta Journal/Constitution,* Sunday, November 21, 1993, p. E5.
[18] Ibid. p. E5.
[19] Bruner, Jerome, op. cit. p. 97.

prospect totally out of step with the times. The narrative carries the risk of draining the citizenry of its lust for the kinds of revenge that a world of demons and avenging angels justifies.

If I were to propose a way out of this moral *cul de sac,* it would probably be in rediscovering the personal narrative and finding some means to get it into the legal arena – something I fear will continue to elude us. With the demise of individualized sentencing in favor of punishment by number and graph, the possibility of basic reform has pretty much vanished. The idea that a judge might expend some effort in understanding what may have transpired in a defendant's life that might bear on the crime allowed room for human judgment (albeit flawed) in fashioning a sentence. More importantly, however, it brought unsettling realities into the legal arena and served, ultimately, to inform the law – keeping it minimally in touch with human considerations.

Until relatively recently, there were always a few (exceptional lawyers, social workers, family members) who remained a thorn in the side of the criminal justice system, naively dragging into the courtroom (usually over strenuous objection), those twisted strands of happenstance that never quite fit; vexing realities that undid stereotypes and put a human face on threatening strangers. But no more. The means for presenting them no longer exists in most courts across the country. Those few sentimentalists who, in the past, might have questioned where the courts were headed have been pretty much driven from the halls of justice. The hope of educating the courts and the citizenry about crime and its causes left with them. It confirms Bruner's prediction that, in losing the narrative, "we're going to lose in many ways what we're all about."

In this light, it has been a particularly curious turn of events that, when, for the first time in our history, we have technology capable of allowing us to individually tailor alternative criminal sentences to the strengths and weaknesses of each offender, it is precisely at this juncture that we retreat to the meat ax of mandatory sentencing and the language of the convict: "If you can't do the time, don't do the crime." This is because individualizing sentencing implies that one must know the defendant in ways that spill beyond narrow limits set by the offense alone – for example, a burglar, a sex offender, a thief. We would rather use our technology to keep confounding human matters at bay – spurred on by the fact that most of those we would place outside such consideration are black and brown, groups the white majority is predisposed to dehumanize, occasionally demonize, and regularly hold to be of less value than they. Indeed, as our technology gets more sophisticated, our anticrime prescriptions grow more simple-minded.

Of course, Christie is correct. The implications of the decisions like this go well beyond matters of management and efficiency. How far down this path are we willing to go? How harsh are we willing to get in the cause of control? Apparently, very harsh indeed. The past 50 years should have afforded sufficient examples of what emerges when law and order rhetoric is merged with efficient management techniques. Take, for example, the anticrime program to be undertaken in accordance with the principles of National Socialism, outlined in a memorandum published by the Prussian minister of justice in 1933:

...aggravated penalties are proposed for a majority of the acts already punishable... It is proposed to make a number of acts punishable which have not hitherto been treated as crime.... Mitigations are proposed only in very exceptional cases. It is urged that attempts should be punished with the same severity as accomplished crimes.... Drunkenness should be an aggravating and not an extenuating circumstance.... A liberal recourse to capital punishment is recommended. Dark cells and hard couches are mentioned as disciplinary measures to be applied at the discretion of the prison warden.

The criminal law, as administered by the (Weimar) Republic, is alleged to have been miserably inadequate because it permitted the products of such treasonable brains as that of Remarque to be published... and because it tolerated such insults to the religious feeling as the portrayal of Christ with a gas mask. But even that destructive law was not destructive enough to please the supporters of the regime then in power. Unscrupulous demagogues demanded the abolition of punishment for abortion.... It was even doubted that the state had a right to punish at all. It seemed that the welfare of the criminal, and not the welfare of the people, was the main purpose of the criminal law.[20]

These proposals, as well as the rhetoric outlined in this early anticrime "white paper" of National Socialism, would rest easily on the consciences of most Americans today – particularly if it were understood that by criminal we meant some dark-skinned other – preferably declared an enemy in this or that war.

The uncomfortable truth is that the aforementioned memorandum could have been written last week in Washington – down to the cheap political slogan parlayed about so freely today – "It seems that we care more for the rights of the criminal than the victim."

A 1992 U.S. Justice Department-sponsored "Attorney General's Summit on Corrections" provided an unsettling glimpse at the future of crime control in America. Characterizing the prison population in the hyperbole now routine in American politics, then-Attorney General Barr contended that 93 percent of state prisoners and 88 percent of federal prisoners were

---

[20] Ranulf, Svend, op. cit. pp. 10–11.

repeat or violent offenders. He called for more prisons and more inmates crowded into them. Significantly, race was not mentioned.

While acknowledging that prisons are expensive (with average building costs then amounting to $53,000 per bed plus $21,000 per inmate for each year of operation), the Attorney General nevertheless contended that failing to build more prisons would be even more expensive to society. Using opinion surveys that showed that the public would be willing to spend up to $2.6 million to avert one death through funding better highway safety or asbestos removal, Barr floated the proposition that given that about 6,500 homicides were committed each year by persons on bail, probation, or parole, the public might be willing to invest up to $17 billion to imprison more people. He did not address the issue of how one picks the 6,500 for incarceration – the 0.001 percent from among the roughly 5 million individuals on probation, parole, or out on bail on any given day nationally.[21]

The second speaker at the "summit" was the Republican Governor of Massachusetts, William F. Weld, who put these matters in philosophical context. He shared with the assembled guests his personal wish of eventually being able "to introduce inmates to the joys of rock-breaking," proposing his own vision for correctional reform. "I'm of the belief that prison should be like a tour through the circles of hell," he said. "In making it so, however, our task is a formidable one, since we have to undo many years in which (we) treated crime as a social services matter rather than a public safety problem."

Weld was apparently unaware of the proposals of Graeme Newman, the former head of the Department of Justice at the State University of New York – Albany, who, while proposing that prisoners be used for what he termed "risky medical research," softened matters somewhat by adding that obviously, prisoners couldn't "be subjected to the same terrible tortures in prison as Dante dreamed up for Hell or

[21] Maguire, Kathleen, Ann Pastore, and T. Flanagan, *Bureau of Justice Statistics Sourcebook of Criminal Justice Statistics – 1992*, Hindelang Criminal Justice Research Center, 1992. (See, in particular, sections 5.61, 6.2, and 6.112). Projecting from the 1990 figures published in this report, I estimated that there were approximately 3 million on probation and another half million on parole on an average day in 1993. In addition, approximately 70 percent of the approximately 12 million people arrested were released on some sort of money or recognizance bond. As many as one-fourth of these (mostly misdemeanor arrestees) repeated within the same year. On this basis, I estimated that about 3 million individuals are out on bond or being sought on warrants on any given day.

Purgatory."[22] As the combined percentage of African-American and His-panic inmates in our prisons nationally crept toward 70 percent, the country was psychologically prepared and economically poised to create less expensive camps – using closed military bases as so-called boot camps that would eventually provide the rationale for a national policy of even more massive, ultimately cheaper means of incarceration and exile. The initial plan was temporarily sidetracked by Operation Desert Storm. It was a curious proposal given the fact that there is virtually no credible research suggesting that boot camps either lowered recidivism or prison populations, which continued to grow side-by-side with the establishment of new camps.[23] In a field in which practice dictates theory rather than the reverse, one can anticipate the development of more florid justifica-tions and rationales for the national embarrassment of having most of the nation's young black men in prison or jail. That situation cries out for a rationale from the likes of a Wilson or a Murray. Taken to its logical con-clusion, the neoconservative agenda on crime has always defined those who break the law as either voluntarily wicked or damaged goods (with the implicit genetic [racial] implications). Deterring the wicked demanded more extreme punishments. Coping with the genetically flawed pointed us in the direction of quarantine and, ultimately, toward eugenics.[24]

---

[22] Newman, G., op. cit. p. 69.

[23] Parent, Dale G., "Boot Camps Failing to Achieve Goals," in *Overcrowded Times: Solving the Prison Problem,* New York: Castine Research Company, Edna McConnell Clark Foundation, August, 1993, pp. 1, 12–14. As Parent summarizes the available research, "Compared with similar offenders who do not go to boot camps, *participants' attitudes and behaviors are better while they are in boot camps; but, once released from boot camps, graduates' recidivism rates are not significantly different* (emphasis in original).

[24] When blacks use terms such as genocide, they are dismissed out of hand as radical, if not unbalanced. Perhaps, then, the reader will allow me, a white male, to utter the forbidden. As Lifton has so clearly pointed out, the word genocide was coined from the Greek *genos,* "race, tribe" and the Latin *cide* – "killing." It is defined by the Convention on Genocide passed by the UN General Assembly in 1946 and approved by the U.S. Congress in 1988, which "associated the concept with killing, seriously harming, or interfering with the life continuity of a 'national, ethnical, racial or religious group.'" (Lifton and Markusen, op. cit. p. 12.) The components of this definition come uncomfortably close to describing the present situation of too many African-Americans relative to the criminal justice system.

Too many of the themes outlined by Lifton as prerequisites for genocidal practices are firmly in place for one not to be wary. They include:

- The ideology of racism or the biomedical vision,
- Wide participation of professionals in the genocidal system, "e.g., physicians and biologists in the Nazi case, and physicists and strategists in the nuclear," and
- General societal involvement... "creating dangerous forms of bureaucratic momen-tum that can carry one across the threshold into genocide."

Christie set forth his disturbing vision of where he saw things headed in American justice as we approached the end of the century:

Hitler's idea was one of Volk, of purity of the stock, and of space – Lebensraum – for the purified product. He had the capacity to realize it. The extermination camp was a product of industrialization, one product among others of a combination of thought patterns, social organization and technical tools. My contention is that the prison system in the USA is rapidly moving in the same direction. It is also highly likely that this trend will spread into other industrialized countries, particularly in Eastern Europe. It will be more surprising if this does not take place, than if it takes place in this decade.[25]

Acknowledging that " . . . the very idea that criminal policy in industrial democratic societies could bear the slightest resemblance to Nazi times and extermination camps sounds absurd" because most contemporary highly industrialized societies are democratic and have "protection against crime as their goal, not extermination," Christie summarized his views in this way:

. . . I do not think prisons in modern industrial societies will end up as direct carbon copies of the camps. Gulags are, therefore, a more relevant term for what might come than concentration camps.

My gloomy suggestion is . . . that a large proportion of males from the lower classes may end up living their most active years in prisons and camps. . . . Industrial progress and civilization have no built-in guarantees against such a development.

On the contrary, we can see energetic first beginnings, in the changes in the legal apparatus, in the ideology of just desert, in the growth and efficiency of the controlling forces, in the increased numbers of prisoners, and also in the rationale for handling these prisoners.[26]

---

[25] Christie, Nils, *Crime Control as Industry*, London: Routledge, 1993, p. 163. As Christie puts it, "Even if the worst comes to the worst, most prisoners will not intentionally be killed in modern prison systems. A number of death sentences will be effectuated, but most prisoners will eventually be released or die by suicide, by violence during incarceration, or from natural causes." Christie notes that Human Rights Watch (1991) "reports (p. 38) that assassination by fellow inmates has been the second or third leading cause of death in state prisons over the past 10 years or so, with the first cause being illnesses and other natural causes, and suicides and inmate-to-inmate homicides alternating in second place." (*Crime Control as Industry*, p. 164).

[26] Ibid. p. 164. Christie cites the writings by the American criminologist Malcolm Feeley, who defines the "'new penology' . . . a penology that is not oriented toward individuals, and particularly not toward changing these individuals through rehabilitation or punishment, but instead focuses on management of aggregate populations. . . . The tools for this enterprise are 'indicators,' prediction tables, classification schemes in which individualized diagnosis and response is displaced by aggregate classification systems for purposes

The fact that Christie could detect no institutional constraints on the massive exiling of ever larger percentages of minority males to prisons and camps led him to conclude that the African-American male had become the most endangered species among the "captive consumers of the control industry."

The kind of reasoning that had come to dominate both criminal justice research and policy in the 1990s is laid out in ominous detail in a relatively obscure collection of papers prepared for discussion purposes at the jointly sponsored Bureau of Justice Statistics–Princeton Project. The discussants included, among others, University of Southern California's James Q. Wilson, Princeton's John Dilulio, the RAND Corporation's Joan Petersilia, and Harvard's John F. Kennedy School of Government's Mark H. Moore.

Their message confirmed Christie's perceptions of the American criminological scene. The crime and punishment industry should not saddle itself with problems of outcome, said the discussants. Lower crime rates or lower rates of recidivism are, in fact, not essential to the purposes of the industry. Rather, the central problem facing American penology is that of assuring *efficient management*. Calling for a "new paradigm" by which the justice system should measure its success, Dilulio summarizes the meeting by suggesting that "justice practitioners" must learn to be flexible and cope with changes in public sentiment (using, as an example, the shift from dealing with root causes to calls for punishment, deterrence, cost containment, and federalism). He bemoans the fact that a minority of practitioners were unable or unwilling to successfully make these shifts in the Reagan–Bush years. The idea that there might be other values at work here eludes Dilulio. Rather, he sees the problems facing the justice industry as resembling those that might afflict a fast-food franchise. As he put it,

For example, McDonald's Corporation has measured performance not simply by the conventional bottom line of profits, but by a dozen or so measures that roving teams of inspectors apply – Are the floors clean? Are the salt shakers full? Are the cashiers greeting customers and wearing their uniforms correctly? and so on. McDonald's recognized that the profits made by their stores were conditioned by

of surveillance, confinement, and control. . . . A central feature of the new penology is the replacement of moral or clinical description of the individual with an actuarial language of probabilistic calculations and statistical distributions applied to populations. (Feeley, Malcolm M., "The Privatization of Prisons in Historical Perspective," Huntsville, Texas: Sam Houston State University, *Criminal Justice Research Bulletin,* Vol. 6, No. 2, 1991, pp. 1–10).

economic and other factors over which their franchisees had little or no direct control. But the store owners, managers, and staff could be and are held strictly accountable for other factors that might affect business.[27]

At the same conference, Charles Logan outlined his view of the *mission* of the prison:

... a prison's mission ought to have intrinsic, and not just instrumental value. That is, it should identify activities that have value in themselves, when they meet certain standards and criteria of performance, not activities that have value only if, when, and because they are effective in achieving some further goal ... the mission of the prison is to keep prisoners – to keep them in, keep them safe, keep them in line, keep them healthy, and keep them busy – and to do it with fairness, without undue suffering, and as efficiently as possible.[28]

Logan then specified some of these criteria – for example, to "keep them healthy":

Convicts are entitled only to a very basic minimal level of personal care. ... At a minimum, prisons have the obligation to prevent suicide, malnutrition, exposure to the elements and the spread of contagious diseases.[29]

Or take the matter of conditions, "without undue suffering":

This broad term would include such things as population density, food, clothing, bedding, noise, light, air circulation and quality, temperature, sanitation, recreation, visitation, and communications with the outside. As with the dimension of "care," evaluation of living conditions and quality of life should not be completely linear. ... In principle, this dimension is curved, so that differences imply improvements at the lower end but have declining or even negative merit ("too good for them") above some higher point.[30]

In keeping with the franchise concept, the "performance measures" set forth by Logan could as easily be applied to an abattoir, a chicken farm, or a dog kennel. Outlined in the deathly language of the consummate bureaucrat, the tragic realities are robbed of virtually all sense or meaning. This is not to say, however, that the procedures and goals as set forth by the BJS–Princeton Project would not be supported by the majority of American citizens and by the neoconservative punditry that harbored fantasies of leading them.

---

[27] Dilulio, John J., G. Alpert, M. Moore, et al., *Performance Measures for the Criminal Justice System* (Discussion Papers from the BJS–Princeton Project, October 1993, NCJ-143505.

[28] Ibid. p. 29.

[29] Ibid. p 28.

[30] Ibid. p. 31.

Let me state here the uncomfortable truth as I see it. The white majority, now feeling quite able to recognize the quintessential criminal by skin color, is unlikely to muster sufficient moral honesty to shift directions. There is every indication that the country will escalate its reliance on long-term incapacitation as its major means of crime control. Precisely because we have so intertwined "help" with the "hostile procedure of law," we have, in effect, lost our reason and jettisoned our decency.

Indeed, as defendants and inmates of color have come to define the justice system, the white majority is positioned to bless the most extreme procedures in dealing with the monsters in their midst. Indeed, as early as 1993 (anticipating American correctional practices that would be put in place in the war on terror) Pennsylvania Democratic state representative Peter Daley found it politically safe to demand that the state's Commissioner of Corrections look into leasing prison space in South Korea, Mexico, or Turkey as a management decision. He noted that cell space could be rented in those countries for approximately $2,100 per year.[31]

As bizarre as Daley's proposal might have seemed, it was not that different from the suggestion of former New York Mayor Ed Koch that we send more young men to "isolatable" camps.[32] The matter of race was not mentioned by either. It needn't have been. The message was clear to the majority. It would doubtless be some consolation if all this were somehow "well-managed."

Dealing with the Disposable

The proposals of Charles Murray for eliminating welfare have now been largely accepted as national policy, with some objections.[33] Similarly, the

---

[31] "Lawmaker: Send State Prisoners to Turkey," *United Press International*, Harrisburg, Pennsylvania, Sept. 10, 1993.

[32] Buckley, William F., "Former Mayor of New York Analyzes Nation's Black/White Problems," Universal Press Syndicate, 1993.

[33] As Columbia University welfare experts Francis Fox Piven and Mimi Abramowitz summarized matters, "And rather than supporting families so generously as to encourage dependency, the grants are painfully low, averaging $370 per month in 1992. No state brings families up to the poverty line, even when food stamps are included."

But desperate poverty under governmental auspices is not the critics' main problem. Dependency is, and their solution is to force women to go to work. Not surprisingly, given high unemployment and plummeting wage levels for unskilled workers, the much-vaunted welfare-to-work reforms and experiments under way can claim only marginal gains.

Workfare is just one way in which "The Man" is trying to make women shape up. Wisconsin's "learnfare" reduces the checks of welfare mothers whose children are truant;

neoconservative doctrines of Wilson, Dilulio, and Murray have become the *de facto* anticrime policies of the nation. It is all there – objectification of offenders as another breed; policies that ensure that ever larger proportions of minority citizens fill ever larger prisons and camps; the destruction of hope through disparagement of rehabilitation; triage management of the disposable; shunting more African-American youths into adult prisons; and ultimately, the call to begin removing *nondelinquent* inner-city youngsters to state institutions, camps, or to what Murray uncharacteristically calls lavishly funded orphanages and Wilson calls boarding schools.[34]

Indeed, looking for the markers of the criminal personality in order to give preventive "help" was not entirely new to government. Advisers to President Nixon had introduced the idea of genetic screening for incipient criminality early in his first administration. Dr. Arnold Hutschnecker, a friend and former personal physician to Nixon, proposed chromosomal

Maryland's "healthfare" docks mothers when their children don't receive health check-ups or immunizations; New Jersey's "wedfare" offers a bonus to women who marry, while its "family cap" lowers the grant to women who have an additional child while on the rolls. And some politicians talk about making Norplant, the contraceptive implant, a condition for receiving AFDC money." (Piven, Francis Fox and Mimi Abramowitz, "Scapegoating Women on Welfare," *The New York Times*, Op-Ed, September 2, 1993.

34 Though at first blush, one might conclude that Wilson prescribes this approach as rehabilitative or therapeutic, his other pronouncements on the "underclass" suggest that he sees the institutionalization of children of the underclass in somewhat other terms. For example, writing in *The Public Interest* in 1992, he had this to say about the underclass: "The reason why it is called an underclass and why we worry about it is that its members have a bad character: They mug, do drugs, desert children, and scorn education." Though he notes that "the causes of bad character are complex and poorly understood," Wilson notes, "Individuals ought to have rights, but rights in what framework of common understandings and common undertakings? ... individual differences exist and are to a large extent *immutable*. Kaus may be the first neoliberal to take seriously the argument of Harvard professor Richard J. Herrnstein that, since people differ in their (largely genetic) intelligence and society tends to regard the most intelligent, hierarchy (that is, a ranking of people by pay and power) is inevitable, and it will reproduce itself no matter how open the opportunities for new entrants.... Immutable human differences limit dramatically the extent to which the distribution of status or power in society can be changed ... "

In this kind of philosophical context, one might legitimately question what kind of resocialization would await those "at risk" children Wilson and Murray propose removing from the homes of the "underclass." I would anticipate that the emphasis in these institutions would be upon accepting one's place in the genetically determined meritocracy while avoiding reaching too high for those opportunities that are clearly beyond one's racially determined genetic limitations – opportunities for the most part preordained for the children of the Wilsons, Murrays, Herrnsteins in our midst. (Wilson, James Q., "Redefining Equality: The Liberalism of Mickey Kaus," *The Public Interest*, No. 109, Fall 1992, p. 102).

screening of every six-year-old male in the country – looking for XYY chromosomes, which might be associated with violent offending in males. Dr. Hutschnecker had proposed sending what he called the hard-core six-year-olds to camps where they could be taught to be good social animals.

Nixon's views on these matters were revealed in previously unavailable tapes from the Watergate era. He casually remarked that although he remained opposed to abortion, he saw it as justifiable if the pregnancy was the result of a white–black sexual encounter.

In a slightly more benign version of the same search, in the early 1970s, Georgetown University psychologist Juan Cortes proposed a delinquency prevention project to the federal government based upon early and largely unsupported theories regarding the putative relationship between body type (for example, endomorph, ectomorph, etc.) and delinquency. Cortes proposed that a program be organized in Washington's "wickedest" (presumably majority black) precinct, aimed at identifying families who had children under the age of seven who might fit the physical profile of being potential delinquents. Both cooperative and uncooperative families, he concluded, should be "helped."[35]

Cortes' approach was based upon the Glueck "Delinquency Prediction Scale," which Lundman and Scarpitti subsequently found had a prediction error of 84 percent. They were sufficiently unimpressed with its merits to warn:

Generally, these subjects have not been found guilty of anything beyond possession of characteristics or behaviors which someone believes are predictive of delinquency. In our zeal to help, we must not lose sight of the fact that juveniles who have not been adjudicated delinquent have the right to refuse that help.

These kinds of proposals are inevitably camouflaged in the language of help and concern. For example, John Dilulio's *New York Times* Op-Ed piece on the need to put more black children in institutions was entitled, "Save the Children – make the cities safer. And get the kids out of them."[36] To those acquainted with the previous writings of this apostle of punishment, the newly discovered rhetoric rang hollow indeed. The emphasis of all these writers, of course, is upon putting in place the means to efficiently manage the "underclass." The contempt for minorities, particularly African-Americans, is palpable.

However, proposing real or fantasized exile will only serve current political needs for awhile. In this regard, Christie underestimates the

---

35 Cortes, Juan B., *Delinquency and Crime: A Biophysical Approach*, New York: Seminar Press, 1972.
36 Dilulio John, "Save the Children," *The New York Times*, Op-Ed, November 13, 1993.

average American politician's need for closure when it comes to untidy human problems. However, we have probably not yet reached the limits of the amount of pain we would be willing to inflict upon certain minorities were the populace sufficiently fired up. Indeed, given the rabid "moral indignation" that drives the nation on these matters, it seems entirely possible that we will eventually countenance ruminative and openly sadistic procedures in handling accused and convicted offenders, both adult and juvenile. Indeed, with the advent of the so-called supermax prisons in a number of states and in the Federal Bureau of Prisons, we have already passed that point.[37] I, of course, had not anticipated the "war" terror and all its pomps.

---

[37] Clarence Thomas, "Silent but Sure, Linda Greenhouse," *The New York Times*, March 11, 2010.

The subject is prison, specifically the meaning of the Eighth Amendment's prohibition against 'cruel and unusual punishment.' In February 1992, the Supreme Court ruled . . . that a prisoner need not have suffered a 'significant injury' in order to pursue a lawsuit against prison officials for the use of excessive force. Keith Hudson, the Louisiana inmate who brought that case, had been kicked and punched by three guards while he was handcuffed and shackled. He suffered bruises, swelling and loosened teeth, injuries that a federal appeals court, in dismissing his lawsuit, deemed so minor as to be beneath the notice of the Eighth Amendment. Mr. Hudson's appeal to the Supreme Court was supported by the George H. W. Bush administration, and John G. Roberts Jr., then a deputy solicitor general, argued on the inmate's behalf. In an opinion by Justice Sandra Day O'Connor, the court reinstated the lawsuit. What mattered in such a situation, the court held, was not the extent of the injury, but the nature of the force that was applied. "When prison officials maliciously and sadistically use force to cause harm, contemporary standards of decency always are violated," Justice O'Connor wrote. Justice Thomas dissented. He had been on the court for four months. During his Senate confirmation hearing, he had claimed a certain empathy for prisoners. He described looking out the windows at the Court of Appeals and watching prisoners being loaded into buses to be taken back to their cells. "I say to myself every day, but for the grace of God there go I," he told the members of the Senate Judiciary Committee. In his dissenting opinion in the Hudson case – which Justice Antonin Scalia joined, making the vote 7 to 2 – the new justice said that the Constitution's framers "simply did not conceive of the Eighth Amendment as protecting inmates from harsh treatment." The Eighth Amendment dealt with only the actual sentence, he maintained, and not with conditions inside a prison or deprivations that were not a formal aspect of the sentence. He said the Supreme Court had taken a wrong turn in the 1970s when it adopted a more expansive view, and he added, "The Eighth Amendment is not, and should not be turned into, a National Code of Prison Regulation."

Now let's move ahead almost exactly 18 years, to February 22 of 2010 – which happened to be the fourth anniversary of the Clarence Thomas Silence. The court had another excessive-force case, a prisoner's appeal that was so clearly meritorious that the justices ruled in the inmate's favor without bothering to call for briefs or hear argument. The prisoner, Jamey L. Wilkins, an inmate in a state prison in North Carolina, claimed that a guard had responded to his request for a grievance form by slamming him onto

It is taken for granted by the public that most inmates in supermax facilities are drawn from the most violent in the prison systems. This is seldom true. More commonly, inmates are placed in these kinds of facilities not because of egregious violence on the streets. Rather, they are defined by prison administrators as dangerous to others. In prison tradition, this means that the inmate has become a management problem and needs to be taught a lesson. Of the 288 inmates in Maryland's supermax

the concrete floor and then punching, kicking, and choking him until another guard pulled the attacker off.

The inmate's Eighth Amendment lawsuit had been dismissed by a federal district judge in Charlotte, and that decision was affirmed in an unpublished one-paragraph opinion by the United States Court of Appeals for the Fourth Circuit. Mr. Wilkins "has not established that the injuries he suffered were more than de minimis," the district judge, Graham C. Mullen, explained in dismissing the suit. (Sounding more like an insurance executive than a member of the judiciary, Judge Mullen added that "several of the injuries he lists were pre-existing conditions.") The lower courts' analysis obviously flew in the face of the *Hudson v. McMillian* precedent, which decisively rejected the same de minimis standard. "The Fourth Circuit has strayed from the clear holding of this court in Hudson," the Supreme Court said in its unsigned opinion, adding: "An inmate who is gratuitously beaten by guards does not lose his ability to pursue an excessive force claim merely because he has the good fortune to escape without serious injury." The vote was 9 to 0, but it was not a happy 9 to 0. Justice Thomas, joined by Justice Scalia, concurred only in the judgment, not the court's opinion. "I continue to believe that Hudson was wrongly decided," he said. But noting that "no party to this case asks us to overrule Hudson," he said that he was going along with the majority because as long as the precedent was on the books, it clearly required the result the Supreme Court had reached. Justices do not casually note that "no party has asked us to overrule" a particular precedent. It is an invitation to send the court just such an invitation, and it is a technique that Justice Thomas has used before to good effect. Concurring in a 1997 decision, *Printz v. United States*, which struck down a federal background check for gun purchasers on states'-rights grounds, Justice Thomas observed that no one has asked the court to look at the case through the lens of the Second Amendment's right to bear arms.... Justice Thomas is not likely to be able to replicate his Second Amendment success with the Eighth Amendment. Guns have a constituency that prison beatings do not, at least publicly, and evidently not on the Supreme Court. (It is quite likely that Chief Justice Roberts was the author of the unsigned opinion in the Wilkins case.) Justice Thomas has been trying and failing repeatedly to get someone to bring the court a vehicle for revisiting its prisoners'-rights jurisprudence. Dissenting from a 2002 decision, *Hope v. Pelzer*, he objected to the suit brought by an Alabama inmate who had been handcuffed to a hitching post and left to stand shirtless in the sun for seven hours without water or bathroom breaks. "I remain open to overruling our dubious expansion of the Eighth Amendment in an appropriate case," Justice Thomas wrote hopefully. No takers yet. Of course, as the Citizens United decision earlier in 2010 demonstrated in overturning two campaign-finance precedents that the parties had not directly challenged, the court always has the option of simply helping itself. However, when it comes to the Eighth Amendment, it could be a long wait. Nonetheless, it is comforting to know that in this uncertain world there is some certainty after all. Justice Thomas will be ready.

in mid-1993, 283 were African-American and that ratio has pretty much obtained for the past decade and a half.

In preparing this chapter in 1997, I wrote, "Though the country may be ready for widening the death penalty and making it applicable to juveniles and the retarded,[38] it is some consolation to hope that we are not yet ready for torture and public executions." I'm no longer sure this is true.

While a divided Supreme Court rejected juveniles for execution, the considerable ambivalence expressed by a substantial segment of the electorate toward the use of torture versus enhanced interrogations in pursuit of terrorists gives one pause. Such procedures would probably cause too much discomfort to a culture of contentment – peopled as it is by conservatives and liberals alike. How else then, to confront the problems of crime while avoiding the social realities that cause and sustain it? We will have to change the rules of the game. We will be left to devise a new paradigm that *redefines* the objects of our fear as damaged beyond repair – perhaps from birth. The unspoken premise that already sustains most national anticrime strategy will thus be hauled out of the closet – that is, that because most African-American males are ending up in our jails and prisons, they must, as a race, be genetically more crime-prone.

The door that Wilson and Herrnstein had worked so hard at cracking has, in effect, been thrown open widely to that alluring pursuit that has, at various times in our history, entranced liberal and neoconservative commentators alike – the quest for "criminal man." It risks setting the country on a new adventure that avoids the murkiness of root causes while offering the white majority a comforting analysis.[39]

---

[38] In 1993, the North Carolina Senate lowered the IQ benchmark to 60, making an offender eligible for execution.

[39] Indeed, we apparently need hardly depend upon dubious genetics to prove extraordinary things. For example, in 1992, a group of sociologists from the University of New Mexico concluded that advantages such as economic well-being, educational attainment, and family stability have precisely the opposite effect on African-Americans than they do on whites. The better off, more educated, and more stable the African-American family, the more prone are its members to murder, rob, and burglarize others. As the authors summarized their findings:

> ... for blacks, higher family income and educational attainment are generally associated with *higher* crime rates; conversely, increases in unemployment and percentage of female-headed families are associated with *declining* crime rates.

> ... White crime rates declined as family income and educational attainment increased, and increased as the consumer price index and criminal exposure increased ... black

We can then move on aggressively from incapacitation and deterrence to more sophisticated "preventative" social policies and strategies of what we now effectively have – permanent exile. The end-point will not change much – greater dehumanization, greater incapacitation and isolation – all in the service of research, science, and crime control. The researchers appropriate to this task are standing in line ready to guide us down the slippery slope toward eugenics.[40]

crime rates increased with higher family income and educational attainment, and decreased as the percentage of female-headed families increased." As the writers put it, "... it appears that common assumption(s) about legitimate opportunity and crime ... was largely justified for whites, but not for blacks." (La Free, Gary, Kriss Drass, and Patrick O'Day, "Race and Crime in Postwar America: Determinants of African American and White Rates, 1957–1988," *Criminology*, Vol. 30, No. 2, 1992, pp. 173–77.)

[40] Duster makes note of a number of pronouncements, surveys, and studies that suggest that eugenics has never been far from the mind of the majority, and is alive and well when it comes to ostensibly preventing crime. The tradition was established early in the twentieth century and continues today:

"It is better for all the world, if instead of waiting to execute degenerate offspring for crime, or to let them starve for their imbecility, society can prevent those who are manifestly unfit from continuing their kind." May 2, 1927, Oliver Wendell Holmes for the majority (8–1) in the Supreme Court decision, *Buck v. Bell*.

"Some people advocate compulsory sterilization of habitual criminals and mental defectives so that they will not have children to inherit their weaknesses. Would you approve of this?" From a 1937 survey of reader opinions, *Fortune* magazine learned that 63 percent of their readership responded "Yes" regarding the forced sterilization of criminals. (Reilly, P., *Genetics, Law and the Social Policy*, Cambridge, Massachusetts: Harvard University Press, 1977, p. 125.)

In a few score of reported cases, an XYY fetus has been unexpectedly diagnosed during prenatal genetic studies that were initiated because of advanced maternal age or other reasons. ... In the United States, an informal survey by one of the leading researchers on XYY males, Dr. Arthur Robinson of Denver, showed that about 50 percent of parents elected to terminate such pregnancies. (Milunsky, A., *Heredity and Your Family's Health*, Baltimore, Maryland: Johns Hopkins University Press, 1992, p. 58.)

As Duster put it:

There is already some evidence to suggest that to be ignorant of that history is to be doomed to repeat it, although not in the crass and unsophisticated way of the 1920s. It is true that Singapore today has a *genetic* policy of encouraging the wealthier to breed more and discouraging the poor from breeding (Gould 1985). Harvard Professor of Psychology, Richard Herrnstein, authored a paper in 1989 in which he suggested that *the genetic stock* of the United States would be improved if the wealthy had more children and the poor had fewer children. Even more striking as a reminder of our history, Herrnstein (1989) went on to suggest that unemployment rates might be explained by genetics. However, these are the fringes. It is not such unreconstructed twentieth-century versions of genetic "pollution at the bottom" that should be the main source of a new

Treating the predisposed criminal will probably play out as a slightly more benign form of the recommendations of E. A. Hooton, the American physical anthropologist of the 1930s, also resurrected by Wilson and Herrnstein.[41] Speaking his mind more honestly than his contemporary counterparts apparently dared, he called for the elimination of criminal stock through sterilization and breeding a better race. As he put it, matter of factly:

The elimination of crime can be effected only by the extirpation of the physically, mentally, and morally unfit, or by their complete segregation in a socially aseptic environment.[42]

It may be that the central task for crime control in a democratic society is to moderate, to whatever degree possible, the negative consequences that inevitably flow from an intrinsically "hostile procedure" – and that (particularly when it comes to the poor and minorities) carries as great a potential for destroying communities as it does for guaranteeing public safety. In this task, we could begin by:

- De-emphasizing our reliance on the positivistic research models that rule the day in criminal justice, the effect of which has been to reduce human experience to series of labels and simple-minded binaries drawn from even more questionable secondary sources that, as often as not, distort reality.
- Compile official crime statistics *not* on the basis of arrests, but on the basis of convictions. Current reporting procedures do not reflect the realities of crime in the United States and trivialize the very real violence and serious crime that must be addressed.

---

social concern. Far more seductive is the contemporary situation in which the banner of science, medicine, and forensic precision flaps over the new genetic technologies. (Duster, T., "Genetics, Race and Crime, Etc.," op. cit. p. 130.)

41 While criticizing Hooton for his "circularity" in hypothesizing that "physical correlates of crime reflect biological inferiority," Herrnstein and Wilson bemoaned the "rough treatment" Hooton "suffered (at the hands of) the criminological community, especially the sociologists who were bound to resent its skimpy treatment of sociological variables." In fact, Hooton did deal with some sociological variables, mentioning in particular the criminalizing effects of imprisonment on blacks. However, his anticrime prescriptions seemed somehow deserving of rough treatment.

42 Hooton, Earnest Albert, *Crime and the Man,* Cambridge, Massachusetts: Harvard University Press, 1939.

- Follow the example of nations such as Great Britain and Canada by making it illegal to print names and personal details regarding accused, but unconvicted, defendants.
- Divert as many young offenders from the justice system as possible – stressing individually tailored alternatives (involving reconciliation with, and restitution to the victim; unpaid community service; and graduated supervision), with particular attention paid to demanding accountability of publicly funded human service agencies – for example, mental health, drug treatment, family service, child welfare – to provide services to those who are now routinely dumped into the criminal justice system. In short, we would hold professionals accountable to work with those less glamorous individuals who present the more intractable social problems and who are now routinely shuffled off to the nation's jails, criminal courts, prisons, jails, detention centers, and reform schools.
- Unwind the overfunded, overblown, and counterproductive law enforcement and correctional industry, which now stands among the greatest threats to public safety and domestic tranquility.
- Mitigate the endemic opportunism that characterizes prosecutorial practice at federal, state, and county levels – an unanticipated consequence of misusing an office established for purposes of justice as a platform for seeking higher office by playing to people's worst impulses. We should consider appointing prosecutors for set terms, with bars on running for any public office after having served in the role of a prosecutor.
- Return probation officers to their original role as frank and open advocates for criminal defendants, not as agents of the court – or, as is now common, aggressive aides to the prosecutor. Probation officers should once again be required to find, construct, and recommend options to the courts and aggressively argue to mitigate the use of incarceration and divert clients from deeper penetration into the justice system. We would disarm that silly new breed of "attack" probation and parole officers who play at being policemen.
- Reject the triage philosophy that has overtaken the justice system – with its unspoken premise that certain individuals or generations (for example, African-American youths) are disposable. Though, clearly, there are dangerous, incorrigible individuals who are probably beyond our puny efforts at rehabilitation, we cannot allow that sad reality to become a pillar of social policy. Indeed, it is

more important that a society try its best with those who most threaten it.

- Place less confidence in criminal justice professionals of all stripes who, in their identification with the justice system, unashamedly leave ethics at the door, bless questionable practices, and dictate standards that are notable only for blessing justice ideology and protecting the bureaucracies they represent. The justice model has drained too many human service professionals of whatever moral impulse they may once have had.[43]

We should also reexamine the paths taken by the legal and helping professions in other societies as they go awry on crime and punishment.

- Focus law enforcement efforts upon bona fide violent and predatory crime. If we did this, we would be able to decrease, rather than increase, the law enforcement presence in the community at large. If we truly wished to return to the putative bucolic days of the 1930s and '40s, as longed for by Moynihan and others, we would have a system in which the police officer lived in, and knew most of the families, businesses, and individuals in his or her jurisdiction.
- Support a kind of community policing in which many of the "criminal" incidents that now occupy most of the average police officer's time would be dealt with informally through a visit with a family, an informal restitution arrangement with a store owner, a dressing down, or a referral to a schoolteacher, minister, or parish priest – much as was the case in many big city ethnic neighborhoods of the 1930s. In a sense, the personal narrative was forced into criminal justice decisions despite occasional lapses in procedure.
- In sentencing the guilty, we would once again face the possibility, in the words of one federal district judge, "that the basic premise of current sentencing 'guidelines' – that the human element should be wiped away

---

[43] An example emerged in the 1993 siege of the Branch Davidians in Waco, Texas, wherein a newly appointed and ostensibly well-motivated Attorney General publicly stated her reliance on the "expert" hostage negotiating teams on the scene of the siege. The result, of course, was a national scandal and tragedy culminating in the deaths by fire and gas of almost 100 individuals, including 38 children. The "experts" attempting to dislodge the cult members engaged in tactics such as playing, throughout the night, loud recordings of animals being slaughtered in an abattoir. One wonders where in the "professional" literature of these "experts" such strategies directed mainly to the ears of women and children are proven to calm an already unstable situation?

from the sentencing process and replaced by the clean, sharp edges of a sentencing slide rule – is itself highly questionable."[44]

• Scrap "just desserts" models along with the so-called minimum mandatory sentences so enthusiastically embraced by liberals and conservatives alike in the 1980s and 1990s. Predictably, they have fallen more disproportionately upon blacks and other minorities than did the so-called indeterminate system, which allowed judges flexibility in designing a sentence for an individual offender. Mandatory minimum sentences and sentencing guidelines have simply moved the bias from the bench to highly politicized prosecutors. The bias that emerged under this arrangement far outstrips any presumed disparities under former indeterminate sentencing models.

• Shift priorities and budgets away from law enforcement and corrections, which cripple and alienate ever larger segments of young male minority populations, to models that offer the hope of healing, inclusion, and productivity.

Finally, and most importantly, we must plumb the processes by which social problems are created in our society as assiduously as we study those problems themselves – outlining the part differentially endowed political and public corporate interest groups play in manufacturing particular social problems at given times – particularly where neither the incidence nor seriousness of a given phenomenon warrants a given public response.

None of this calls for new funding or a new set of alternative programs. It is a matter of changing focus for awhile – perhaps taking a rest from new wars on crime. Introducing more money or alternatives in the present milieu will only ensure fixing in further the present destruction while the alternatives will be distorted beyond recognition.

It was Graham Greene, speaking to a French conference three years after the fall of Nazism, who observed:

My conviction that the Christian conscience is the only satisfactory sign of a Christian civilization is reinforced by the fact that this trait was completely lacking in the pagan powers that so recently reigned over the world.... The totalitarian state contrives, by educating its citizens, to suppress all sense of guilt, all indecision of mind.[45]

Spurred on by the alienating procedures of a justice industry spun out of control, a media bereft of responsibility, and a dehumanized research

---

[44] Judge Jose Cabranes, quoted in *The New York Times*, April 12, 1992.
[45] *Reflections*, by Graham Greene, selected by Judith Adamson, Reinhardt Books, 1991.

and professional establishment, we now rest on the verge of relieving ourselves of whatever vestigial "sense of guilt" we might once have claimed.
One can only hope that when considering the African-American male and
crime, some "indecision of mind" will linger awhile longer. "Solutions"
proposed in our current state are likely to smack of finality.

Epilogue

Although a number of sociologists, criminologists, and historians have warned that the national approach to African-American men and boys in our criminal justice system is misinformed and have tried to bring these matters to public attention, there's scant evidence their warnings have either been heeded or will be attended to anytime soon.

After watching this problem metastasize for 30 years, with little hope of an end in sight, it may be time to recognize that the American correctional system is functioning in precisely the way a considerable part of the population wants. Simply admitting it, in the words of Charles Murray, might "make them feel better about things they already think but do not know how to say."

It's what the "neo" sociologists have devoted a substantial part of their lives to accomplish – permanently extruding as significant a number of African-American males from American society as possible. It's a hope attuned to a significant segment of the still-dominant American male population – in particular, the southern white male population.

Gunnar Myrdal, the Nobel Prize-winning Swedish economist of the mid-twentieth century, commonly hailed by progressives as having provided the rationale bolstering the U.S. Supreme Court's *Brown v. Board of Education* decision leading to the desegregation of public education, called attention to this not–too-subtle wish.

Although Myrdal held that the "Negro problem" was a "white man's problem" and that whites as a collective were responsible for the disadvantageous situation in which blacks were trapped, he also acknowledged other matters at work in the predominant culture.

Racial inferiority arguments repeatedly led white men to toy with what Rutherford would later come to term the eliminative ideal, should the nation ever free itself of slavery and, later, of Jim Crow laws. Myrdal summarized the problem this way:

[T]here is no doubt that the overwhelming majority of white Americans desire that there be as few Negroes as possible in America. If the Negroes could be eliminated from America or greatly decreased in numbers, this would meet the whites' approval – provided that it could be accomplished by means which are also approved. Correspondingly, an increase of the proportion of Negroes in the American population is commonly looked upon as undesirable.

Then, adding that these ideas were "shared even by enlightened white Americans who did not hold to the common belief that Negroes were inferior as a race," Myrdal commented that, nevertheless, virtually all white Americans agreed that *"if the Negro is to be eliminated, he must be eliminated slowly so as not to hurt any living individual Negroes. Therefore, the dominant American valuation is that the Negro should be eliminated from the American scene, but slowly."*

Myrdal then went on to muse about devising population policy, noting that "we ought start out from the desire of the politically dominant white population to get rid of the Negroes." Admitting that the goal was "difficult to reach by approved means, and the desire had never been translated into action directly, and probably never would be," because it would go strongly against the American creed, he wrote,

"The Negroes cannot be killed off. Compulsory deportation would infringe upon personal liberty in such a radical fashion that it is excluded.... Voluntary exportation of Negroes could not be carried on extensively because of unwillingness on the part of recipient nations as well as on the part of the American Negroes themselves, who usually do not want to leave the country but prefer to stay and fight it out here. Neither is it possible to effectuate the goal by keeping up the Negro death rate. A high death rate is an unhumanitarian and undemocratic way to restrict the Negro population and, in addition, expensive to society and dangerous to the white population."

Myrdal ended by recommending a massive program of birth control that involved a degree of deception by using "Negro doctors and nurses" to conceal the real goals of white society.

In many ways, this is what the American Criminal Justice System could be seen as being about for most of the past 30 years, with its concentration on African-American males in the criminal justice system's methodological "elimination" of them from the predominantly white society. The irony is that it continues apace even as the nation has elected an African-American president.

This reality suggests that those criminologists, sociologists, anthropologists, and social psychologists who have generally lived their lives in the honest pursuit of truth might take a bit of advice from one of their most respected early peers, the late University of Chicago "symbolic inter-actionist," Herbert Blumer.

For a brief while, they might turn their attention away from studying prepackaged social problems handed them by self-appointed claims makers and, instead, refocus on simultaneously plumbing the complicated means by which certain phenomena attain the status of a social problem, particularly when that designation appears unrelated to incidence or seriousness.

In his 1971 seminal paper, Blumer made the deceptively simple observation that "[s]ocial problems are fundamentally products of a process of collective definition instead of existing independently as a set of objective social arrangements with an intrinsic makeup."[1]

We decide what our social problems are to be in sometimes vague and wispy ways. As Blumer noted, "[T]he societal definition, and not the objective makeup of a given social condition, determines whether the condition exists as a social problem."[2] It's a paradox that the ways we define social problems depend neither upon their seriousness nor their incidence.[3] As Blumer summed up the process:

Poverty was a conspicuous social problem for sociologists a half-century ago, only to practically disappear from the sociological scene in the 1940's and early 1950's, and then to reappear in our current time. Racial injustice and exploitation in our society were far greater in the 1920's and the 1930's than they are today; yet the sociological concern they evoked was little until the chain of happening following the Supreme Court decision on school desegregation and the riot in Watts. Environmental pollution and ecological destruction are social problems of very late vintage for sociologists although their presence and manifestation date back over many decades. The problem of the inequality of women's status, emerging so vigorously on our current scene, was of peripheral sociological concern a few years back. I merely assert that in identifying social problems sociologists have consistently taken their cue from what happens to be in the focus of public concern.[4]

[1] Blumer, Herbert, "Social Problems as Collective Behavior," *Social Problems*, Vol. 18, Winter 1971, p. 298.
[2] Ibid. p. 300.
[3] Ibid. p. 298.
[4] Ibid. p. 299.

Blumer expressed some frustration with his professional peers for ignoring this in a democratic society. "I would think," he said, "that students of social problems would almost automatically see the need to study this process by which given social conditions or arrangements come to be recognized as social problems. But by and large, sociologists do not either see the need or detour around it." As a result, the field has "pitifully limited knowledge" of these highly relevant matters.[5]

Blumer called for studying the role of agitation and violence in getting recognition for a problem, along with the play particular interest groups might have in delaying or avoiding the recognition of a problem; he cited the possibility that some might see material gain in elevating a given condition to that of a social problem, giving as examples "the case of police with the current problem of crime and drugs" along with the part political figures might have in fomenting concern over certain problems, while putting the damper on others. He cited the need to examine the role powerful organizations and corporations might have in doing the same things, contrasting these concerns with the impotency of powerless groups to gain attention for what they might see as a social problem, and the role played by the mass media in selecting social problems according to "the influence of adventitious happenings that shock public sensitivities."

Blumer saw it all as a vast field needing study if we were ever to understand how social problems emerge in, and between, societies. "If they don't emerge, they don't even begin a life."[6]

Blumer's comments preceded the Internet, 24/7 cable television, the rise of the neoconservative movement, and the proliferation of privately funded think tanks with strong ideological and political agendas and massive funding from what Lewis Lapham would refer to as a "small sewing circle of rich philanthropists" who, in recent years, have demonstrated influence on setting national agendas on trade, defense, and environment. The same has happened relative to crime, violence, race, and justice.

Indeed, in recent years, we've witnessed the ability of privately run propaganda mills to exert great influence in ushering a nation into a "preventive" foreign war of choice while providing bogus rationales that ended in undermining basic American traditions, leading to the deaths of hundreds of thousands of innocent persons.

It's basically the same group of ideologues who now count crime control as one of their successes – while simultaneously continuing to build

<hr>

5 Ibid. p. 302.
6 Ibid. p. 302.

the case for the disastrous measures they originally prescribed, as explicated by one of their more influential prophets. Here's how Michael Ledeen characterized the neoconservative movement:

Creative destruction is our middle name, both within our own society and abroad. We tear down the old order every day, from business to science, literature, art, architecture, and cinema to politics and the law. Our enemies have always hated this whirlwind of energy and creativity, which menaces their traditions (whatever they may be) and shames them for their inability to keep pace. Seeing America undo traditional societies, they fear us, for they do not wish to be undone. They cannot feel secure so long as we are there, for our very existence – our existence, not our politics – threatens their legitimacy. They must attack us in order to survive, just as we must destroy them to advance our historic mission.[7]

Truly, "destruction" is what the "neo" sociologists have been about from the beginning, effectively banishing African-American men and boys from American society – albeit, "slowly."

As I attempted to demonstrate in the first edition of this book, there had always been relevant empirical studies that gave the lie to what was being touted on television or by one or another think tank and its political publicists. The problem has never been a dearth of countervailing criminological and sociological research. Rather, it resided in how that research came to be in practice and, eventually, in national policy.

In recent years, research was marginalized to the point of being largely banished from serious consideration. Research is valued primarily for its use in bolstering a very old ideological agenda – getting rid of "Negroes."

Despite occasional ebbs and tides in the trends, the abiding plight of African-American men in the criminal justice system has trundled on – the interests redoubling their efforts to drone on, undeterred and unabated.

This is unfortunate. Here are some countervailing opinions:

In 2006, Harvard sociologist Bruce Western published the results of an eight-year study investigating "the scope and consequences of growth in the American penal population."

Western's study demonstrated that fully 90 percent of the decrease in serious crime attributed to aggressive policing and heavy use of incarceration would have happened even without the run-up in incarceration rates and that "the gain in public safety was purchased at a cost to the economic well-being and family life of poor minority communities."[8]

---

[7] Ledeen, Michael, in *The American Conservative*, June 30, 2003.
[8] Western, Bruce, *Punishment and Inequality in America,* New York: Russell Sage Foundation, 2006, p. 5.

Western and his research staff took a panoply of factors into account –
including the effects of incarceration over the life cycle, the historical significance of the prison boom for that life course, lifetime risks of imprisonment, the politics and economics of punitive criminal justice, and the
effects of incarceration. Each yielded predictable results, suggesting we
were set on a path from which it would be difficult to withdraw.

Similarly, criminologist Todd Clear, now a Distinguished Professor at
the John Jay College of the City University of New York, recognized
where the country's turn to so-called incapacitation would lead. The idea
was originally introduced by Peter Greenwood at the RAND Corporation
and later painfully specified as policy by Edward Zedlewski, then heading
research projects in the Reagan administration's Justice Department.

Clear had written a short paper in the late 1980s questioning the
claimed benefits of this strategy. Clear's response was introduced largely
below the radar – published in the *Journal of the Oklahoma Justice
Research Consortium* under the title, "Backfire." In it, he suggested that
basing a national anticrime policy on massive long-term incarceration
would lead to a rash of problems that would outweigh whatever benefits
were claimed.

In 2007, Clear published his book, *Imprisoning Communities: How
Mass Incarceration Makes Disadvantaged Neighborhood Worse*, outlining in detail what had, in fact, resulted. He noted that:

1. The extraordinary growth in the U.S. prison system during the 30
   years had, at best, a small impact on crime.
2. Imprisonment had been largely aimed at minority males who lived
   in impoverished neighborhoods.
3. This strategy had broken families, weakened parental authority,
   eroded economic well-being, soured attitudes toward society, and
   distorted politics while increasing rather than decreasing crime.
4. The policies and practices needed to be undone – and this would
   happen only through a combination of sentencing reform and making a basic philosophical realignment.

Again, however, there is no evidence that Clear's call for basic change
in policies and practices in crime control has been heeded. Although
Clear's work should have been integral to the discussion of African-
American males in the criminal justice system, there is little evidence it
has affected local, state, or federal policies in any way. This is not the
fault of this respected researcher. His work, like that of so many others,
has been largely "deep-sixed" by those who now call the shots regarding

crime and punishment of African-American males in the United States. Clear's warnings were simply ignored by those who hold the power to ensure their recommendations have some effect – having organized the presentation to play to the public's lesser angels while covering it all with a gloss of pseudoscientific credibility. It gives further credence to the perception that discussions of violent crime among African-American men have little to do with violence.

Broken Windows – Post Hoc ergo Propter se Ipsum

In his detailed analysis of the anticrime goings-on in New York City during the late 1990s – strategies that set the agenda for most crime discussion for the next decade – Bernard E. Harcourt found no empirical evidence that the city's much-heralded "broken windows" approach to crime contributed in any substantive way, or indeed, had much of anything to do with the coincident drops in crime that occurred in New York and throughout the country. Crime fell virtually everywhere in the nation – including in many cities where police took diametrically opposed approaches to those being touted by the roster of outsized anticrime mavens and personalities that publicized the New York approach.

Harcourt noted that the broken windows model of policing went back to the 1950s, described by James Q. Wilson in his 1968 book, *Varieties of Police Behavior,* as "legalistic" policing whereby police "issue traffic tickets at a high rate, detain and arrest a high proportion of juvenile offenders, act vigorously against illicit enterprises, and make a large number of misdemeanor arrests." According to this model, the police act as if there were a standard of community conduct that the law prescribes – rather than allow, as Wilson put it, "different standards for juveniles, Negroes, drunks, and the like" (1968, p. 172).

As Harcourt noted, these order-maintenance disciplinary practices had been around "in this country and abroad dating back . . . to the early penitentiary model and beyond." He summed up the effect as simply piling on the punishment. Order-maintenance crackdowns weren't *alternatives* but, rather, *additions* to the severe penalties that already dominated American criminal justice – particularly as applied to African-American males. Aggressive misdemeanor arrests and intensive stops and frisks were implemented precisely to feed an already high number of detentions, arrests, and criminal records. "What we are left with," as Harcourt saw it, was "a system of severe punishments for major offenders and severe treatment for minor offenders and ordinary citizens, especially minorities, a double-barreled approach with significant effects on our citizenry. The problem, in a nutshell, is that order-maintenance crackdowns permeate our streets and police station houses while severe sentencing laws pack our prisons. We are left with the worst of both worlds."9 It's a measure of where the nation now stands that a significant segment would loudly hail what Harcourt sees as a social harm.

In a devastating analysis of the "unintended" effects on our society that neoconservative sloganeering (for example, zero tolerance, broken window, and declaring wars on various segments of our society) had had, legal scholar Jonathan Simon cited Nobel-laureate writer Doris Lessing's prediction in the 1960s that the United States would enter the millennium having built what Simon described as "a new civil and political order structured around the problem of violent crime."10

Lessing described the birthing process in this way: "For years," she wrote, "they had moved about by the grace of paternal or brutal police; or under the protection of some gang. *It was in the mid-seventies that it came out for how long the United States had been run by an only partly concealed conspiracy linking crime, the military machine, the industries to do with war, and government.*" Lessing referred to this concealed conspiracy as organized barbarism.

Simon acknowledged that, all along, the enterprise was based in a false premise, noting that "criminologists and sociologists had long sought to document that this fear of crime (was) irrational in its scope and priority." It was to no end. It was less a failure of documenting research – most of which lingers on government and university shelves – than a failure in marketing it.

It grits the conscience to mention that word – often synonymous with manipulation of the facts. However it has been accomplished with efficiency and alacrity – whether grounded in fact or fable – by neoconservatives. Their essential purpose has been to shill largely dishonest proposals to a public seen as prone to carry other agendas that lay just below the surface.

A cursory glance at the contemporary electronic media suggests that these dynamics are now essential to their purpose. As the director of a major conservative cable television news organization recently remarked,

---

9 Harcourt, Bernard E., *Illusion of Order: The False Promise of Broken Windows Policing*, Cambridge, Massachusetts: Harvard University Press, 2001, p. 6.

10 Simon, Jonathan, *Governing through Crime: How the War on Crime Transformed American Democracy and Created a Culture of Fear*, Oxford: Oxford University Press 2007, p. 3.

"I'm not in politics, I'm in ratings." In that kind of world, it is generally futile to pit academics or researchers with undetermined skills in projection or presentation opposite professional talk show hosts or news readers in perpetual pursuit of ratings – unrelated to whether they have to do with reality in virtual or "real-time." It's as much about celebrity and the art of entertainment as it is about facts.

In a culture in which global warming, even reiterated as climate change, can fall prey to the narcissistic bleating of a bloated talk show host or semi-glamorous news reader in search of a purloined e-mail, we are all at risk.

For example, a study of the effect of criminal records on the life course of those so labeled was published in 2007 by the University of Chicago Press in a marvelous book by Princeton sociologist Devah Pager under the title, *Marked: Race, Crime, and Finding Work in an Era of Mass Incarceration*. This highly detailed analysis of the effects of a criminal record upon life course is revealing and, in the end, devastating.

Her final comment speaks to the current dilemma: "At this point in history," she notes, "it is impossible to tell whether the massive presence of incarceration in today's stratification system is a unique anomaly of the late 20th century, or part of a larger movement toward a system of stratification based on the official certification of individual character and competence. In many people's eyes, the criminal justice system represents an effective tool for identifying and segregating the objectionable elements of society. Whether this process will continue to form the basis for emerging social cleavages remains to be seen."[11] Ms. Pager's comments suggest the corporate possibilities in using the criminal justice system – in particular, the criminal history records – as a way of ensuring profit while simultaneously confirming the exile of African-American males.

There are a number of other new and important books that touch upon the problem laid out in this book in particularly salient ways – among them, the compelling historical study by Douglas A. Blackmon, *Slavery by Another Name: The Re-Enslavement of Black Americans from the Civil War to World War* (Doubleday, 2008) and Robert Perkinson's *Texas Tough: The Rise of America's Prison Empire* (New York: Metropolitan Books, 2010).

However, most of the concerns regarding African-American males in the criminal justice system have been about something quite other than

---

[11] Pager, Devah, in *Marked: Race, Crime, and Finding Work in an Era of Mass Incarceration*, Chicago, Illinois: University of Chicago Press, 2007, p. 160.

research. They've been about the "practical" goal of getting a readily recognizable cohort of largely artificially created "violent" black and brown men and boys out of sight and mind through a series of stratagems that would rival the shell-game skills of a street corner con.

Empirical research and historical precedents are not germane to this purpose. It seems that when it comes to African-American males in our contemporary criminal justice system, we prefer to slog through a period of ascendant "know-nothingism" similar to that preceding the Civil War, wherein it has become a mark of honor in the United States to be militantly ignorant about certain things.

The fact that so many studies remain so absent from serious discussion of these issues – particularly in the electronic media – attests in a perverse sort of way to their importance.

Index